TILL BABYLON FALLS

Sleepily Robert opened the front door. He found himself facing an armed police officer. He slammed the door shut.

There were bright lights outside. Greta peered through the curtains. In the murky dawn the street was incandescent, a blinding, luminous, colourless glare, like floodlights. Everywhere she looked, silhouetted outlandishly in the burnished glow of headlamps from police cars and vans, were uniformed policemen – in the yard, on the road, on the rooftops. She noticed they were all armed.

'I walked slowly back to the couch, feeling that long hands were reaching out to grab me,' said Greta. 'My feet felt heavy. I felt numb.'

'*Maak oop*,' shouted a voice in Afrikaans, 'Open up. *Polisie!*'

Robert opened the front door. The police officer, a captain, had his rifle trained straight at him. '*Moenie beweeg nie*,' said the captain. 'Don't move.'

About the Author

Bryan Rostron, born in Johannesburg in 1948, was educated both in South Africa and England. He has worked as a journalist in South Africa, Italy, New York, and, for the past ten years, in Britain, where he now writes for the *Daily Mirror*. The author has written several plays, including *A Far Country*.

Till Babylon Falls

Bryan Rostron

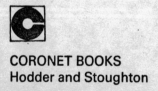

CORONET BOOKS
Hodder and Stoughton

The right of Bryan Rostron to be identified as the author of this work has been asserted by him in accordance with the Copyright, Designs and Patents Act 1988.

Printed and bound in Great Britain for Hodder and Stoughton Paperbacks, a division of Hodder and Stoughton Ltd, Mill Road, Dunton Green, Sevenoaks, Kent TN13 2YA (Editorial Office: 47 Bedford Square, London WC1B 3DP) by Clays Ltd, St Ives plc. Photoset by Rowland Phototypesetting Ltd., Bury St Edmunds, Suffolk.

British Library C.I.P.

Rostron, Brian
  Till Babylon falls.
  I. Title
  320.968

  ISBN 0-340-54061-3

For Sunny

Author's Note

Interviews in South Africa were conducted during March 1990, including visits to Robert McBride on Death Row and Gordon Webster on Robben Island; all dialogue is taken either from the accounts given by the protagonists to the author or from the three trial transcripts.

I am indebted to Professor John Milton and Professor Paul Maylam for their generous guidance, and I should like to thank Dr Gordon Isaacs, Bernard Bishop, and Jan Duncan-John for their help, Edward and Raymond Davies for their hospitality and wise suggestions, Paul Foot for his challenging enthusiasm, and my mother, Barbara Rostron, for her encouragement from the start. Finally, thanks to Tanja, Zolsa, Patrick and all those other families of political prisoners on Robben Island who courageously, and at risk to their own precious visits, went on 'strike' to enable me to carry off mine too.

Acknowledgments

The author and publishers are grateful to Bob Marley Music/ Blue Mountain Music Ltd for permission to reprint the lyrics from Bob Marley's *Babylon System*, *Zimbabwe*, and *Ride, Natty, Ride*; and they wish to acknowledge the following sources:

Tom Lodge's essay in *State, Resistance and Change in South Africa* (Croom Helm, 1988)

Like Lions They Fought by Robert B. Edgerton (Weidenfeld and Nicolson, 1988)

Mau Mau: An African Crucible by Robert B. Edgerton, (I. B. Tauris and Co. Ltd, 1990)

New Babylon: Studies in the Social and Economic History of the Witwatersand 1886–1914, Volume 1 by Charles van Onselen (Ravan Press, Johannesburg, 1982)

Contents

List of Illustrations

1. Doris and Derrick McBride on their wedding day.
2. Robert – 'Pepe' – on the left, with his sister, Bronwyn, and his cousin, in a freak snowfall.
3. Robert McBride: most family photographs were destroyed to prevent police identification. © *Daily News*
4. Paula McBride. © *Ellen Elmendorp*
5. Gordon Webster.
6. Wentworth storm drains: meeting place and playground. © *Daily News*
7. Magoo's Bar (right) and the Why Not Bar after the bombing. © *Daily News*
8. Robert McBride picked out on an identity parade.
9. 58a Hardy Place: the McBride family home. © *Daily News*
10. Doris McBride, in London campaigning for Robert. © *I.D.A.F.*
11. Greta Apelgren today.
12. Matthew Lecordier today.

And a mighty angel took up a stone like a great millstone, and cast it into the sea, saying, Thus with violence shall that great city Babylon be thrown down, and shall be found no more at all.
Revelations 18:21

Prologue

Invitation to a Wedding

'Attend my fable if your ears be clean
In fair Banana Land we lay our scene –
South Africa, renowned both far and wide
For politics and little else beside.'
Roy Campbell: The Wayzgoose

It was Paula's wedding day; a bright, crisply autumnal morning in May. Milky clouds hung in the pale turquoise sky. It was certainly the most unusual wedding in the history of this strange land: the ceremony would be held behind locked doors.

It was not a land renowned for Love; no one knew who they could trust.

The whites lived behind high walls, always with half an ear cocked to their electronic surveillance devices. They kept guns in their briefcases and handbags. Even the elderly slept with a firearm under the pillow.

They did business, played tennis, swam in their voluptuous swimming pools, and nervously waited. The longer they waited, the more nervous they became. Rumour, the worm of doubt, slithered through the affluent white suburbs. No one knew what to believe.

Murmured confidences circulated: terrifying accounts of maddened guerrillas on the rampage, of whites in outlying areas silently and horrifically slaughtered, and of unspeakable deeds visited upon the innocent. They also confided that the authorities were suppressing news of these abominations in order not to create panic.

They waited, listened, watched. What was out there, lurking, biding its time? They had no idea. The emergency regulations, midnight arrests and censorship – which they had been assured were indispensible to save them from the threat – prevented them from discovering exactly what it was. In this vacuum, the apprehensive whites manufactured a monster from their own worst imaginings. They created the very thing they feared.

Not, to be sure, the atmosphere for Love. In this land (*where lemons hang like yellow moons ashine, And grapes the size of apples load the vine*) there were strict laws regulating that too. After all, it was for the suppression of love, if little else beside, that South Africa was renowned both far and wide.

Paula came from a wealthy white family; her fiancé was a revolutionary. The date was set for May 10, 1989. She was to be driven to the ceremony by her mother.

Paula lived with her brother John, a disorganised pop musician, and three cats, Murphy, Lurgy, and Gormy, in a quiet, tree-lined suburb; a neighbourhood of pink, green, blue and white bungalows snug behind high walls, draped with extravagant cascades of pink, purple and violet bougainvillaea. Almost every other home posted prominent signs boasting their security system. Some had the emblem of a sword, others of a pistol. Opposite was a vivid yellow plaque: WARNING – PROTECTED BY 24 HOUR ARMED RESPONSE.

Paula occupied a small white cottage at the back of her brother's house. It had been converted from either a garage or servant's quarters and now had a large picture window with a jaunty yellow awning. There was a cramped study, scattered with papers and files relating to her fiancé. The narrow bedroom was disordered and there were no decorations, although among the rumpled folds of the unmade bed, along with the telephone directory and yesterday's newspapers, could usually be found a chunky romantic novel and a large fluffy, powder-blue toy elephant.

She was thirty, five years older than the man she was about to marry. She had light tawny hair, grey-blue eyes and spoke softly, hesitantly, picking her words carefully. When she'd completed what she had to say, she'd often smile apologetically and look away, which was deceptive; Paula was unshakeably determined.

Normally she wore jeans, pullovers and no make-up. But for her wedding day, Paula had borrowed a fawn linen suit from her sister. She collected all her documents and checked they were in order.

Her mother drove over at eight a.m. to pick her up. Annette was the only member of the family accompanying Paula. Her father, Peter, a director of the South African conglomerate Anglo-American, and of its powerful diamond-mining subsidiary De Beers, had gone to the office as usual; so far he had not met his daughter's fiancé.

From the capitalist frenzy of Johannesburg to the Calvinist primness of Pretoria is only thirty-six miles. The temperature rises two or three degrees. The terrain becomes rougher, there are scrubby patches of dry red soil, the waist-high camel-coloured grass is dotted with stunted bushes and sparsely shaded by pine and eucalyptus.

Approaching Pretoria, English gives way to Afrikaans. Grandiloquent names for modest suburbs evoke the old Afrikaner sense of destiny: to the east, Verwoerdburg, named after the fanatical Professor of Sociology, one of the icons of the volk and the guru of apartheid; to the west, Valhalla, in Norse mythology the place of immortality, inhabited by the souls of heroes slain in battle.

On both sides of the motorway is a vast militarised zone with barbed-wire fences, re-enforced concrete walls and watchtowers.

The road narrows and sweeps down, round a final curve. There, sedate and stolid in a hollow of the Magaliesburg Hills, is Pretoria. The first building, a mile or so before the outskirts, is a windowless fortress, squatting at the roadside like an infernal toll gate. It is Pretoria Central, the largest prison in South Africa.

The guards at the blockhouse were already raising the boom.

Pretoria Central is like a small walled city. Annette and Paula drove along the main street, Klawer, which is lined on one side by pretty red-roofed bungalows, whose uniform gardens are enclosed behind symmetrical white picket fences. These picturesque rows of well-disciplined suburbia are the white warders' homes. Opposite is the windowless brick mammoth which houses over two thousand prisoners.

Annette and Paula passed Oasis Road and the warders' trim club houses and sports fields. A chain of black convicts shuffled by. To the right was a dusty expanse of ground with patches of sun-scorched grass, skirted by a road named Wimbledon.

They turned left into Gedenk Street, following a glistening white wall up a slight incline. At the top was the splendid mansion of the Kommandant-General of South African Prisons, set well back in an undulating rich green lawn. Shaded and screened by trees and pink-flowering shrubs, the two storeyed villa was approached up an elegant white spiral stairway.

The two white women followed the curve round to the right, where at the summit of the small hill the road came to an end. The car drew to a halt outside the massive battlements of Maximum Security. Its thick walls were twenty feet high, and all around were lofty floodlights and closed-circuit TV monitors. At each corner was a glassed-in watch-tower.

This was as far as the bride's mother was going. Annette could see no hope – she couldn't understand why Paula wanted to get married. 'Why condemn yourself to certain unhappiness?' she had asked. But Paula was unwavering, and Annette knew she could never change her mind. She now accepted it, although the prospects looked bleak. She watched as Paula walked towards the huge electronically-controlled gates. That ominous black portcullis, however, was not the visitors' entrance. The usual black warder checked Paula's name and authorised number on his clipboard. To Paula's greeting, he half-smiled, before leading her through a small side-door, with a large sign in four languages: NO FLOWERS OR BOUQUETS TO BE LEFT FOR ANY PRISONER.

Death Row stood on the highest vantage point of the prison, overlooking the entire complex – this was the most secure citadel in the country. There were 294 men on Death Row and 280 of them were black. It was very quiet up there. The other prisoners called it Beverly Hills.

The steel side-door slid shut behind them. It was dark and cool in the small bare chamber. Paula was inside the first circle.

A skinny young white warder gazed sleepily from his chair. He had close-cropped blond hair and big ears. No one said a word. From behind a large, one-way mirrored panel they could hear voices crackling over an intercom, speaking Afrikaans. The black warder, clipboard in hand, led the white visitor back out into the harsh glare.

In the second circle, between the outer wall and the square block of Death Row, was a thirty-yard stretch of open ground. Sunlight reflected off the concrete. On the flat prison roof a guard with a rifle overlooked this bleak no man's land.

Set back to the left, by the side of a small pond, was a wide, thatched sunshade. In the centre of the grassy knoll stood a plump palm tree and a tall cluster of bamboo shoots. There were guinea fowl, chickens and ducks. Once there had been a couple of deer. Now a pair of baby rabbits nibbled at the succulent turf.

The gateway to the next circle, the Death Row building, was a massive teak door, with polished brass fittings. By its side stood an expansive hibiscus pouting with downy scarlet flowers. It was an impressive, baronial entrance.

The black warder rapped hard with the big brass knocker. The Judas Eye slid open: from inside, the visitor was scrutinised. Then the huge door swung back and Paula and her escort stepped into the third circle.

It was clean and quiet and well-lit by strips of fluorescent lighting. There was a faint whiff of detergent.

Pinned on the back of the door was a colourful day-glo poster advertising a barbecue party, with Castle beer, jumbo hamburgers and a beautiful baby competition. Nearby on the stark white wall was a green plaque, cautioning: TERRORIST WEAPONS, LOOK AND SAVE A LIFE. Life-size plastic reliefs showed SPM limpet mines, PMN anti-personnel mines and hand grenades.

The circles were narrowing. To proceed they had to wait for a warder to unlock the grilled gate. Beyond that was another foyer, and another grille; one gate had to be relocked before the other could be opened. Limbo succeeded limbo, scrubbed and deathly – the only sound was the constant jangling of keys.

Right at the centre of Death Row was a sunlit courtyard. On one side was the section for black inmates, on the other the section for whites. The courtyard was peaceful, like a cloister. On either side, like monks' cells, were the visiting rooms where families spoke to the condemned through thick, barred glass partitions with the aid of microphones. They were never allowed to meet face to face or touch, not even on the eve of execution.

In the middle of this secluded yard was a strip of grass, with flowers round the border: light gold cosmos, pink roses, the white canna lily, as well as dahlias, geraniums, snap-dragons and marigolds. At the far end was a chapel. This is where the coffin was placed after a hanging. It was a spruce, sparse room, illuminated by a lustreless brown and blue stained-glass window.

Immediately above the chapel were the gallows. Here, the hour come, the final circle: the noose.

Paula came to the prison every day. Normally she would have gone straight into the courtyard, but today Paula was taken down a side corridor, into the black cell section. A senior officer accompanied her down a bare white passage to a small room used by consulting lawyers. The wedding was to take place here – the first ever to be permitted on Death Row.

Her fiancé was waiting. He smiled at Paula. Robert McBride was not in the usual Death Row kit of dark green fatigues, he wore a white shirt and grey trousers. He was over six feet tall and slim. He'd lost a lot of weight in prison, but he kept himself fit. His face was soft and round, his complexion sallow.

He had been waiting 756 days for his execution.

For the first time the couple were allowed to embrace.

Paula and Robert were stepping into a potentially hysterical arena. The law forbidding marriage between people of different colour had only recently been repealed. Mixed-race marriages were still an exotic rarity, disapproved of by many whites and particularly repugnant to a large proportion of Afrikaners. Even if the McBrides would not consummate their marriage, it was the very thought of such a liaison which upset the khaki-clad white paramilitaries that Paula sometimes saw outside the prison. For them, it was against nature; contrary to the will of God. She was betraying the sacred commission of white women: it was an abomination. That is why they stared at her with such hatred.

To the authorities, the marriage was also bizarre. The young couple had been subjected to a challenging examination of their psychological states and motives. A Prison Major conducted the interview with Robert. A social welfare worker had visited his home. 'What do you feel about your child marrying a person of a different race?' she had asked.

Doris McBride, Robert's mother, had replied, 'Why should I have any objections? Paula's lovely. I couldn't have asked for a better girl for my Robert.'

'But how do you feel about your son marrying a white person?'

Doris was a stocky, proud woman, with a round, humorous face. She could be quite belligerent. 'Look, we don't hate all white people, just because white people have done such terrible things to us.' She was not going to be intimidated because all this would be read in Pretoria by some Boer. 'We have white friends in the movement. There are whites who are working just as hard as us for liberation. Some have died in the fight, you know.' The welfare worker had diligently written it all down. 'I did ask Robert if he thought it was fair for him to marry Paula,' said Doris. 'I mean, even if you get out, I said, you'd have nowhere to live, no job, no prospects. You know what he said? "I don't want to marry anybody else. I don't want any other woman." Well, there's nothing I could say to that.'

Most of the questions had concentrated on colour. 'I don't think there's any difference.' Doris was weary of this question, the mesmerising preoccupation of South Africa for over three hundred years. 'Robert can mix with anyone.' The interview had lasted forty-five minutes. 'Look,' said Doris, 'even if they allow Robert to live, even if one day – please God – he gets out, I'm going to be dead. It will not be my problem to see how they live. They must be allowed to live their own life, you know.'

The wedding was a very private ceremony. Robert and Paula had no guests.

Derrick McBride, Robert's father, was unable to attend. He was locked up on Robben Island, the bleak 'Alcatraz' for political prisoners, six miles off the coast at Cape Town. Robert's closest friend Gordon Webster might have been best man. But he too was on Robben Island, serving a twenty-five year sentence.

Doris McBride was unwell. Since her husband had been incarcerated and her son sentenced to death, Doris had suffered a mild stroke, and she was soon to endure two more which would leave her paralysed and imprisoned in a wheelchair.

It was a small, bare room. There was a table and two chairs. Robert and Paula sat together on a bench. Three warders stood to one side, coughing nervously and shuffling their feet, not sure where to look. One picked his nails.

The black priest, Father Mabena, did not have a permit to perform inter-racial marriages, so Father Ambrose, the white chaplain, had been assigned to conduct the ceremony. It lasted fifteen minutes.

Paula hardly heard a word. Then Father Ambrose was saying, 'I now pronounce you man and wife.' The warder who had been picking his nails smiled.

The honeymoon lasted forty minutes. The newly-weds stayed in the lawyer's consulting room, squashed together on the bench.

The Major stayed with them for the first twenty minutes; a Warrant Officer took over for the second shift. They each stood by the door and pretended not to look. Robert and Paula held each other for the very first time. Then the honeymoon was over.

'Time's up,' said the Warrant Officer. 'I'm sorry.'

He held the door open, and waited patiently. Robert had read about a man in England who put super-glue on his hand. It had become their private joke. He whispered, 'We should super-glue ourselves together, then they'd have to pull us apart.'

Part One

The Book of Life

1

To Robert it didn't seem odd when he was growing up that there weren't any white people where he lived.

He saw them sometimes when they were out in the car, and he noticed that his father used to get angry at them and curse them when they were on the motorway or at an intersection. He'd often say things like, 'Stupid bloody whites, look how they behave, they're so arrogant these people, they've no bloody consideration.' His father would denounce all white people, muttering harsh judgements that the young boy could not understand. But he didn't worry about it as that was the kind of thing his father did when they were out in the car and there were whites around.

The whites lived in Durban. It wasn't at all like where Robert and his family lived. The suburbs had a quiet, almost genteel English air about them; there were wide boulevards with names like Coronation Road and Chestnut Avenue, despite the subtropical abundance of the vegetation and the hot evening breeze that blew in off the Indian Ocean.

In town, alongside high-rise air-conditioned office blocks were the remnants of the colonial past, unlikely alien landmarks in the sticky heat. In the main square, a plump statue of Queen Victoria, erected by public subscription for those volunteers who fell in the Boer War, faced a Baroque Revival City Hall with field cannons standing ceremonial guard alongside tall palms on its trim lawns. Europe jostled uneasily with Africa, as if perpetually anxious that classical order and precision might be swamped by tropical excess.

Hidden among the palms were other stone memorials to frock-coated dignitaries in stiff collars. These exemplars of European civic rectitude stared sternly into the distance, searching far beyond the horizon for their inspiration, perhaps far away to the

Motherland or even ancient Greece, resolutely ignoring the immediate sultry reality of shrieking Indian Mynah birds which perched in the surrounding palms by night, or African workers from nearby offices and building sites who rested in their shade by day.

The city was full of Africans and Indians by day; at night they vanished, whisked away after sunset to their own racially exclusive locations.

Durban was a vigorous, modern city with the largest port in Africa, but its pride was the expansive beachfront of luxury hotels, the wide span of pure-grained sand and a shimmering aquamarine ocean warm enough to swim in all year round: a nirvana for sun-worshippers and surfers.

These beaches were reserved exclusively for whites, and in summer they were saturated with huddled droves of bronzed, oil-glistening bodies.

Along this stretch, bounded on one side by Addington Hospital where Robert McBride was born, and at the northern end by the snake park, were cafés, bars, restaurants and nightclubs: the playground of white South Africa on holiday, known as the Golden Mile.

Further south, on the other side of the busy docks and the landlocked Bay of Natal, was a promontory the shape of a finger. Here facing the ocean was a diminutive range of hills known as The Bluff, a luxurious white suburb with large gardens, swimming pools and double garages. Beyond that was a wide no man's land, comprising first a bird sanctuary, then a small swampy lake and finally a patch of scrubby bush. This acted as a buffer to Wentworth, a non-white residential area. Most of the racial arenas were divided by buffer zones.

The McBrides lived in Wentworth. Hemmed in on one side by an industrial estate and on the other by the Mobil Oil refinery, it sprawled over several lilliputian hills. Wentworth was eleven kilometres from Durban city centre, just off the freeway on the route to exotic South Coast holiday resorts like Amanzimtoti and Umtentweni. There was nothing exotic about Wentworth.

The main approach was up Quality Street, past the gloomy Girassol Café and at the crest of the hill the dour, decaying Palm

Springs Hotel. The sandy roads were rutted and uneven, often strewn with building rubble and household rubbish, and after a sudden tropical downpour the craters in the road would form small lakes. Packs of dogs roamed the dusty streets and children played in the open storm drains.

The houses were mostly cramped, identical redbrick units, or mean corrugated-iron shanties, with dusty backyards piled high with discarded tyres, rusty fridges and disused car parts.

And everywhere alongside this urban dereliction was a lush riot of tropical fecundity: mango trees, pawpaw, guava, banana, avocado and the brilliant flowering of the pink and purple tibouchina tree.

At night the Mobil Oil refinery glowed with a thousand pinpricks of light in the velvety dark, and its slender, fifty-foot chimneys belched out vivid flames like some vast starship from outer space. The refinery was heavily fortified with tall barbed-wire fences, concrete walls and commanding watchtowers with spyholes.

It had once been attacked, in one of the few military actions in that area, by an African National Congress unit armed with rocket launchers, but the police soon winkled the unit out of their strategic position on the hill and gave chase to the guerrillas right through Wentworth, finally pinning them down in a paint factory in Hime Street, where all four insurgents were shot dead.

By day the oil refinery emitted a constant plume of greyish-white smoke and sometimes by evening a sulphurous stench hung over Wentworth. It was a cloying, acrid smell that bit deep into the lungs, and if the weather was particularly humid (often before one of those sharp summer squalls) there would be a pall of pollution so palpable it was like a dust storm or a very fine drizzle. Sometimes on the darkest nights the chemical haze enveloped the whole ghetto like a light shroud of mist.

Wentworth was a 'Coloured' area, and white people never came near it. To young Robert, that seemed perfectly normal and he never gave it a thought. Most people in Wentworth didn't have any work and the main social activity was drinking. To Robert that was quite normal too. He didn't think there was anything odd about it for a long, long time.

That was the way things were.

Robert McBride was born on July 6, 1963. His parents Derrick and Doris were both teachers. Robert was a much wanted child, for the McBrides had been married five years and had previously lost a daughter at birth.

They had moved to Wentworth while Doris was heavily pregnant with Robert. This had not been a voluntary transfer: under the Group Areas Act, which stipulated in which area each racial group could live, all those whose classification was Coloured were forced out of the city centre and its immediate suburbs. As Derrick and Doris McBride were Coloured, they had to relocate.

For those being evicted, the municipality had set aside a zone which occupied approximately two square kilometres, officially called the Austerville Government Village, although everyone knew it as Wentworth.

It had been built as a Second World War military transit camp. There were drab rows of identical red-brick barracks, while most streets had no names or any form of lighting.

The camp was laid out on a grid system, divided into sections named after British naval heroes like Drake, Frobisher and Hardy, although this echo of imperial grandeur was not reflected in the bleak surroundings. There were no facilities such as schools or shops, so when the displaced new community first moved in they had to convert the existing military buildings. The old cinema became the Anglican Church of St Gabriel and the block houses in Drake which had been the kitchens were transformed into homes, often housing families of ten or more in one bedroom units.

The McBrides were assigned to Flat B, previously a First Aid clinic, in a road with no name in an area called Lower Assegai. It was not the home they had been promised, but it was clean and neat and there were burglar bars on the windows. It had a kitchen and lounge as well as a bedroom, so they had more room than many of their neighbours, and outside there was a small grass yard where Doris immediately began planting shrubs and herbs. Eleven months after Robert's arrival, their second child, Bronwyn, was born.

When Robert was a baby the family used to call him 'Pepe', after an animated cartoon Doris had seen with her younger sister, Girly, at the bioscope (as they called the cinema). The cartoon had a theme song that went, 'Face as funny as Pepe, smile as funny as Pepe,' and when Girly first saw Robert she shrieked, 'Pepe!'

Round-faced and smiling, with his large ears and puckish mouth, he had a deceptively mischievous appearance. Yet for a child in such turbulent surroundings, Robert was uncommonly tranquil and obedient. He was a skinny little boy and quite solitary, although he spent a remarkable amount of time with his father. He had an even, light brown complexion and close, curly dark hair. Doris was livid when a neighbour called him *Kroeskop* (woollyhead).

Doris was a big strong woman with a soft creamy tan complexion. Derrick on the other hand was dark; he had a long, animated face with strong, aquiline features, and he gesticulated energetically with his hands, constantly pushing back his thick-rimmed glasses. He was slim, and his wiry frame twitched with an anxious, edgy compulsion, the complete opposite to Doris's calm stoicism. Derrick was so zipped up that he was in constant motion, even finding it difficult to sit still for an entire meal. Words poured out of him in an assertive cascade and in conversation he ricocheted from subject to subject with demonic energy. The family nicknamed Derrick 'The Grader', though no one could remember why, and at school the pupils called him 'The Coke Bottle' – if you shook him up, he'd explode. His passion was politics.

Derrick and Doris were fearful about the prospects of bringing up their children in the harsh, unnatural conditions of Wentworth. Unemployment was high, with many families living below subsistence level. Over a third of all children were illegitimate and alcoholism was chronic. The despair among the young was endemic and most young men saw no point in finishing their schooling, attaching themselves instead to the wild youth gangs which could murder a rival from another area simply for stepping into their territory. Wentworth was regarded as one of the most violent communities in South Africa.

Derrick felt a particular sense of foreboding for his son's future. The government policy to separate the races in all spheres of life was being pushed ahead fast and all opposition to these policies was ruthlessly suppressed. In May 1963, two months before Robert was born, the government had introduced the General Law Amendment Act which gave the Minister of Justice the power to detain anybody in solitary confinement without trial for ninety days, and thereafter for further periods of ninety days – again and again, according to the Minister, 'until this side of eternity'.

This crack-down, and the increasing pace of apartheid legislation, was greeted by sporadic and sometimes amateur acts of sabotage, culminating in 1964 when a young white man placed a time bomb in the main concourse of Johannesburg railway station, severely injuring several people and killing one elderly woman. White opinion was outraged and by 1965 the Minister of Justice had extended the period of detention without trial to 180 days.

It fell to Doris to teach her son the practical ins and outs of where he could legally go or not go. 'It all depends,' she explained to Robert, 'on the colour of your skin.' The world was divided into two simple categories. On park benches, playgrounds, buses, in post office queues, or on the beach, the sign SLEGS BLANKES meant that he was not allowed. It meant 'Whites Only'. The sign Robert had to look for was NIE BLANKES. That meant 'Non-Whites'.

Robert was a quiet, reflective boy, and at an early age he kept asking why he couldn't do certain things. Doris found herself having to explain the situation again and again.

'It's very sad,' she says. 'You don't know how to explain it to your children. You have to find a way to say, "You're different." It was usually left to me to explain. Robert was always wanting to know. Derrick would give me a look. So you'd try to find a way to answer that didn't make him feel inferior. It was painful. Sometimes I'd lie.

'Once we were walking along the beach and we came to a paddling pool with white kids playing in it. Robert wanted to jump in. I said, "You can't – you'll drown." Robert couldn't understand

28

why he wasn't allowed to join in. "But I can swim better than them," he said. "I won't drown." In the end it always came down to simply saying, "You're not white."'

The first racial incident that Robert can remember occurred when he was nine years old. He and two of his friends from Wentworth went down to a floodwater channel which ran out to sea, where they would trawl for small fish with old sacks employed as makeshift fishing nets. White children played down at the floodwater channel too, and they always got along well with the Wentworth boys until one day a white man came along and, without any warning whatsoever, kicked Robert and began shouting at him in Afrikaans that he should not be there.

Robert was holding an old jam jar, full of water, in which they had put some of the guppies they had caught, and the red-faced white man snatched the jar out of his hands and smashed it on the concrete causeway. Robert burst into tears and the three Wentworth boys fled home as fast as they could.

After that, whenever they returned to the same floodwater channel to fish, the white children jeered at them and tried to chase them away.

The second racial incident took place a year later when Robert was ten years old. His family had gone on a trip up to Johannesburg and one afternoon they visited the zoo lake. Robert and his sister Bronwyn wandered off and came across a gang of small children all roughly his age who were crowded round some buckets. In these buckets were goldfish and the other children were looking at them and twirling their fingers in the water. Robert joined this little knot of children, and after a while he too began to dangle his fingers in a bucket.

Suddenly a large Afrikaner youth raced over and kicked Robert from behind, right between the legs. The youth shouted furiously, 'You can't do that you little bastard!'

Robert stood there stunned and in pain. Unable to speak, he pointed to the other children, then burst into tears. The young Afrikaner was shaking with rage: '*Voertsek*,' he yelled. 'You are not allowed here. You're not white.'

It was Robert's first experience of real hatred, and ever afterward this episode remained his own private symbol of injustice. Racial prejudice, arbitrary and inexplicable, seemed like a savage kick from behind.

The racial divide for Robert McBride, however, was not that simple; he was not white, yet neither was he black. In 'The Book of Life', the popular term for the forty-nine page identity document the South African government was attempting to issue to everyone, he was classified as Coloured.

This referred to a person of mixed race. Originally the term Coloured lumped together anyone who was not European or African, with several sub-divisions, which in Proclamation 46 of 1959 were defined as Cape Coloured, Cape Malay, Griqua, Indian, Chinese, 'other Asiatic' and 'other Coloured'. The Japanese, after much soul searching, were exempted and granted honorary white status as their country had so much trade with South Africa, and subsequently Indians were hived off and officially designated as a separate group. These distinctions were very important for they determined almost everything in life, from where a person could live, to what job they were allowed to do, and whom they could legally marry.

The rigidity of this racial classification, however, was made extremely tricky by families like the McBrides. Doris McBride's father was a white municipal worker of Scottish extraction, while her mother had been the daughter of an Irish father and an African mother. Derrick McBride, on the other hand, had Irish and Malay ancestry.

This sort of elaborate mosaic led to numerous subsequent amendments to the Population Registration Act. Proclamation number 46 was declared void in 1967 by a judge of the Cape Town Supreme Court on the grounds of vagueness, and later that same year the Population Registration Act, number 64, was introduced in an attempt to plug those gaps. It made a determined effort to clear up the exact criteria to be used for racial classification, declaring a white person to be someone who: *(1) In appearance obviously is a white person and who is not generally accepted as a Coloured person; or (2) Is generally accepted as a white person and is not in appearance obviously not a white person.*

To keep these lines clearly demarcated, and to mop up the

truants and anomalies, the adjudication was done by the Race Classification Board. This was the final arbitrator. Where the question of a person's skin colour was not clear the Board investigated, evaluated and passed definitive judgement. Fingernails were examined, the shape of a nose scrutinized, or a comb pulled through the hair. A man's barber could be summoned to give evidence, or a strand of hair examined by the police laboratories.

It was the Race Classification Board's prerogative to re-classify a person's colour. Every year an average of over a thousand people officially changed colour: Coloureds became white, some whites became Coloured. There were Coloureds that became black, Indian or Malay, Griquas or Chinese. There were Malays that became Indian and Indians that became Malay and Malays that became African and Africans that became Indian.

Blacks, however, did not become whites.

If this confused anyone as to where all that left the Coloured group, the wife of South Africa's future State President, Marike de Klerk, spelt it out in 1983, 'You know, the Coloureds are a negative group. The definition of a Coloured in the population register is someone that is not black, and is not white and not an Indian. In other words, a non-person. They are the leftovers.'

2

As a child, Robert idolised his father. Derrick spent hours playing with his young son and would take him everywhere. Derrick had given up drinking when Robert was born, but disappointment and frustration had driven him back to the bottle. At one point his closest drinking companion was a policeman and sometimes the two of them would patrol the ghetto looking for drinking dens and gambling parlours to raid. Derrick took his little boy along on some of these mischievous sorties, much to the fury of his wife, and Robert would come home beside himself with excitement, babbling incoherent tales of police chases and people fleeing.

Derrick was a maverick, and it was uncharacteristic for him to consort with a policeman. He was an adversary of all authority and particularly disliked the police, whom the McBrides called 'The Weedkillers'. The local community knew Derrick as an uncompromising political firebrand; the police kept a close watch on him and caused Derrick McBride as much aggravation as they possibly could.

Derrick was well educated and widely read. The McBride's small living room was stacked with books on history and politics. Derrick was deeply embittered about the mean and restricted life that being a Coloured forced upon him. He found it particularly difficult to stomach the task of training a new generation of young Coloureds for a life of menial tasks, where they could never hope to be more than the underlings of white men.

He hated whites. He used to say, 'There's never been an honest white man in history.'

Derrick saw absolutely no point in continuing as a teacher in these grubby conditions. His outspoken views had blighted his teaching career. Branded as a trouble-maker, he was moved from school to school in Wentworth. He had become disillusioned at seeing even his brightest pupils going out into the world with very little prospect of employment, and with absolutely nothing for them to do in the ghetto where they were legally obliged to live. Most took up a life of petty crime and drunkenness, smoked a lot of dope and joined gangs like the Hime Street Flat Cats, the Drain Rats, F-Section and the Young Destroyers.

For long periods his bitterness, resentment and disillusion found expression in drinking; it anaesthetised his disgust at the hopelessly inadequate, racially-segregated schools. In 1975 Derrick finally resigned his teaching post and became a welder.

Derrick McBride looked to his son Robert to redeem all his unfulfilled hopes and ambitions.

Doris also had strong aspirations for her son, so in 1976, when he was thirteen, the McBrides decided to send Robert to a high school five hundred miles away in Kimberley in the northern Cape, where Derrick himself had gone to school. This was partly to remove him from the gangland atmosphere of Wentworth, and to instill a sense of independence in this quiet, self-effacing boy. Robert was enrolled at the Florianville High School and it was arranged that he stay with friends of the family in the Coloured quarter outside town.

This was a dramatic year for all black school children in South Africa. The compulsory use of Afrikaans in schools, a language which was seen by black pupils as an instrument of oppression, had sparked rioting initially in Soweto, outside Johannesburg. The police responded by opening fire on the children; this triggered a wave of anger which swept through African townships across the country. The protest swelled into a general outburst of fury against apartheid. By the end of the year over a thousand blacks had been killed, more than five hundred of them children.

In Kimberley the pupils of Florianville High decided to boycott their classes in solidarity with the students of Soweto. Robert joined in, not because he had thought about it much, but because everyone else was doing it. Their demonstration consisted of walking around the courtyard during their lunch-break, with placards demanding equal education. After they had been marching round aimlessly for a while, a troop of riot police appeared. Through a loud hailer the students were ordered to go back into their classrooms. The students responded by chanting slogans.

Suddenly the police fired tear gas at them and charged. The children screamed and ran. Robert found himself choking and blinded by the gas, and a policeman was laying into him with a *sjambok*, a long, snake-like rhino-hide whip. Then it was all over, but for the first time Robert had experienced the brutal response to peaceful protest that his father had always insisted was the white man's way.

His second encounter came only a few months later when the New Zealand All-Black rugby team, touring South Africa, visited Kimberley. Robert and a group of friends from school went to the hotel where the team were staying in the hope of catching a glimpse of them and perhaps getting some autographs. There was quite a crush of fans outside the hotel, and when they pressed forward the police beat the young Coloured boys back with their batons, allowing the white school children through.

Derrick told him, 'These Afrikaners only understand the language of the gun.'

He gave Robert, aged thirteen, a book called *Coloured: a Profile of Two Million South Africans*, by Al. J. Venter, which made a powerful impression on him. Venter, although a conservative white writer, claimed history had been rewritten to embellish an Afrikaner mythology. He maintained that many of the cardinal landmarks in this tradition, celebrated as quasi-religious rituals, were in fact as Coloured as they were white. For example, when the Zulu king Dingane killed the Boer leader Piet Retief – central to the Akrikaner sense of outrage and martyrdom – thirty of the seventy men who died with him were Coloured; while at the Boer victory over the Zulus at Blood River – the Day of the Covenant, venerated by Afrikaners as confirmation of their anointment as a chosen people – half of the 'whites' were in fact Coloured.

But what most affected Robert was the treatment by the early white settlers of the indigenous Khoikhoi and San peoples. The first commander of the Cape, Van Riebeeck, referred to the Khoi as 'black stinking dogs', while a few years later another settler wrote, 'Although descended from our father Adam, they yet show so little humanity that truly they more resemble the unreasonable beasts than reasonable man.' The settlers formed commandos to hunt them as if they were wild animals and they waged a war of extermination against the San.

Robert vividly remembers watching the then future President P. W. Botha giving a crudely belligerent display on television, stabbing his finger at the camera and denouncing his opponents in ferocious hyperbole, and Derrick saying, 'You see, that is why we have to have the armed struggle – it's the only language they understand.'

At the end of one year in Kimberley, Robert passed his Standard Six exam and returned to Wentworth to go to the Fairvale High School. His Aunt Girly noticed a considerable change. He had lost weight and was pimply from a bad diet. Although he was very withdrawn for the first few days, she also felt Robby, as she called him, had matured remarkably.

Fairvale High was an old pre-fab school with up to thirty-five or more in a class. There was no playground, just a patch of open ground with a little grass and scattered bushes round the edge. For assembly, the thousand or so pupils would gather in the open on a concrete quad while the principal would stand on a makeshift wooden dais. Some of the classroom walls were so flimsy that chunks could simply be broken off and there were holes big enough for smaller pupils to crawl through. If it rained the walls would be damp for days and there were occasions when bits of ceiling caved in during the middle of a class. The school was infested with rats and cockroaches.

Robert was an excellent student, particularly at maths and science. He also began to shine at rugby, the South African national game, although the Wentworth teams had to play on makeshift and dusty grounds very dissimilar to the carefully tended green pitches available to their white counterparts. This discrepancy in sporting facilities incensed Robert, even if during his teenage years – despite his father's influence – he was generally regarded as being fairly passive and apolitical.

Meanwhile, Wentworth had became a tougher, more unruly place. A whole generation had now grown up in the converted military barracks. Many of Robert's contemporaries soon dropped out of school, having no hopes or expectations, and they joined the street packs. Some of the gang members were as young as ten years old. The gangs themselves had also become more vicious; territorial wars were fought with guns, knives, stones and broken bottles.

Every weekend there were murders. Funerals were held on Mondays and Tuesdays, when the solemn line of hearses would make its way to the cemetery on the other side of Quality Street. The cemetery is the largest expanse of green in Wentworth and it is littered with the graves of young men. Occasionally a knifing would take place in broad daylight; some had their stomachs slit open or organs sliced off, and late one afternoon in front of a large crowd the Woodstock Vultures burned a rival alive.

The Trucks and the Vultures were the biggest gangs and the most hostile rivals, the dividing line between them being Austerville Drive, the main road through Wentworth, and at the height of their feud it was known as the Cassandra Crossing. The Trucks controlled the Drake and Frobisher districts, the Heartbreakers ruled in Ogle Road, while between Alabama and Dromedaris Road – known as Dooms Island because of the drinking problems – the F-Section held sway. Nearby, on the other side of Fairvale High School and just along from the Mobil Oil Refinery, the 88s lorded it over the most dismal area in Wentworth – long squat rows of concrete coops with flat asbestos roofs, bluntly designated as blocks A, B, C and D, but known by everyone as Rainbow Chicken, after a well-known Natal battery farm.

Sometimes alliances were formed, as when the Young Destroyers teamed up with the Weekend Spoilers against the Drain Rats and F-Section. But generally each gang held to its own turf, expecting all young men within it to join up and if necessary defend their domain to the death.

No one gang controlled Collingwood, where the McBrides lived, so there was lively competition among the gangs to recruit the youngsters in that area. There was tremendous pressure on all teenagers to join an 'outfit', and every day on his way home from school Robert faced a torrent of abuse and sarcasm from groups of loitering youths. Most of the time they just hung around in the street, bored, frustrated and angry, looking for something – anything – to happen. Robert was an easy target. He was different: light-skinned, soft-spoken, a quiet boy, known as a good student. Most of all, though, he was considered to be different because he refused to join a gang.

Robert knew he was regarded as an alien. To defend himself, Derrick taught Robert jujitsu and sent him to karate lessons. Under his father's guidance, Robert began to see this violence as a political fact: Derrick argued that these young men were victims of a political system that denied them any room for hope or improvement. Instead, trapped in their own ghetto, they turned their hopelessness and anger upon themselves and their own people.

Derrick gave his teenage son books on politics and history. He tried to give Robert a perspective which would save him from the cycle of self-destruction that condemned most of the inhabitants of Wentworth. Derrick talked about politics endlessly. Robert's friends used to relish these discussions with the quixotic Mr McBride, but Robert often got bored with his obsessions. Derrick's theme was always the same, 'Don't trust whites. There's never been an honest white man in history.'

Elsewhere in South Africa, others were beginning to strike back. In 1978 the chief of the Security Police, Brigadier Zietsman, estimated that four thousand black South Africans had gone abroad to Angola, Zambia and Tanzania for guerrilla training. Many of these had been the young Soweto schoolboys who had fled into exile after the mass uprising of 1976. Brigadier Zietsman warned the public they could be expected to return soon – equipped with arms and explosives.

In March 1978, two bombs went off in the coastal city of Port Elizabeth, leaving two dead and three injured. In October, two guerrillas were shot dead by a police patrol near the Botswana border. In November, a guerrilla band entered the northern Transvaal from Botswana, and in an ambush on a remote farm in the Louis Trichardt district a policeman was wounded.

But underground resistance was sporadic and often haphazard. The security police, with its huge network of paid informers in the townships, always appeared to be one step ahead. Hundreds of activists were arrested and held without trial. Nevertheless there continued to be isolated outbreaks of urban violence. In November 1979 a bomb exploded in the Cape Town Supreme Court without any casualties. These incidents were beginning to mount up and the whites were having to take notice; some on the extreme right were getting so rattled they decided to take the law into their own hands, and vigilante attacks on blacks began to increase. The whites were becoming uneasy.

The standard of living among white South Africans, which had always been among the highest in the world, flourished and prospered. The earnings from gold rose enormously, investment poured into the country and there was an unprecedented property boom. Consumer spending had never been so high.

By now the McBrides' home was too small. In 1979, they'd had another daughter, Gwyneth, and at sixteen Robert felt he was too big to share a room with his two sisters, and was unable to get much school work done at home. Doris applied for a larger house and was told to walk around Wentworth in search of a vacancy. Eventually she found a family who were moving out of Hardy Place.

This was another area with no street names or lighting. The McBrides' new home, 29a, was a small, square brick block with a tin roof, surrounded by a ten-foot wide grass yard and cordoned off from the uneven dirt road by a slatted wooden fence, an exact replica of all the other houses in the vicinity except for the lordly avocado tree outside the front door. In the days of the military camp, 29a had been a laundry.

It had three cramped bedrooms, a tiny bathroom and kitchen. The gloomy living room had dark cream, pitted walls and a threadbare brown matting carpet curling at the edges. The McBrides regarded 29a as a temporary address; they always hoped they might be allowed to own their own home.

For the next seven years, Derrick wrote constantly to the Department of Community Development and Doris badgered them with visits. In their aspirations to better themselves, the McBrides were essentially middle-class people trapped in a slum. Doris was never happy with Hardy Place, and some of the neighbours used to say to her, 'Who do you think you are?' The McBrides were forced to remain as tenants in 29a (a consequence, they believed, of Derrick's belligerent opinions) yet they did not relinquish their efforts to escape to a better neighbourhood. As a result, they never bothered much with decorating. The furnishings remained sparse and there were few embellishments. In the shadowy living room there was a calendar with a picture of an angelically blond Jesus and a copper clock in the shape of hands at prayer, while on a dark brown sideboard was a six-inch plastic replica of Michelangelo's David with the head missing.

Robert's bedroom was painted a pale lilac colour in an unsuccessful attempt to gloss over the uneven red-brick walls, and the smudgy outcome was cruelly highlighted by the single bare light hanging from the middle of the white hardboard ceiling, decorated with limply dangling remnants of brown fly paper. Through a hole in the corner a naked electric cable ran down to the floor, which was covered in a mahogany brown linoleum. There were no curtains at the window, only flimsy white netting. Robert's sense of a lack of privacy resonated from the graffiti he'd scrawled over the wall opposite his narrow bed: THE LOVABLE QUALITY OF A NOSE IS NOT ITS LENGTH, BUT ITS ABILITY TO KEEP OUT OF OTHER PEOPLE'S BUSINESS.

At 29a, Robert had even more trouble from the local adolescent mob; at first simply because he was a new face, and then because he wouldn't join their troupe. The faction that controlled Hardy were the Drain Rats. They took their names from the open storm drains by the side of the road where they had played as children, and as young men often simply sat with their friends, feet in the drains, because they had nowhere else to go.

The Rats used to kick him or throw things, and he was hurt badly when a brick hit him on the head. At one time the pressure on Robert was so intense that he was sent away for a while to stay with his godmother. Mostly, however, he kept his eyes down and hurried past, trying not to respond to the taunts, but sometimes a confrontation was unavoidable. Robert had many fights with these street corner gangsters. He was stabbed twice.

In 1980 there was once again a formidable boycott campaign in 'non-white' schools throughout South Africa. These protests were milder than those of four years previously; they were peaceful and concentrated on demanding a better standard of education and an end to the massive discrepancy between what the government spent on white and 'non-white' pupils.

Robert helped organise the demonstrations at Fairvale High. He hated his inferior schooling, and was particularly angered by the history syllabus which he felt glorified white victories over Africans. He could not respect his teachers either, for he believed they were academically inadequate, some of them knowing even less than himself, and – unlike his own father – prepared to co-operate with a system which was expressly designed to perpetuate their subordinate status. Most school principals were no better than government stooges, Robert argued, bribed by the whites to control their own people to the extent that not only did many co-operate with the police, but some were actually police reservists.

The Fairvale High students boycotted their classes and went on a number of protest marches. They carried banners proclaiming ALL STUDENTS ARE EQUAL and EQUAL EDUCATION FOR ALL. One day they arranged to have a joint meeting with Wentworth High, the only other senior school in Wentworth. Both groups were due to meet at Fairvale, but as they were marching towards the school grounds the police ordered them to stop and turn back.

Before anyone could react the police fired tear gas. The students immediately took cover where they could. One group, including Robert, ran into a nearby clinic. The police chased after them and fired tear gas into the clinic, killing a three week old baby.

Robert was appalled. He was deeply upset and angered about the police response and the death of the baby, but still he did not know where to channel his fury.

His father's anger, on the other hand, had always maintained a precisely articulated focus. Derrick despised whites. He made this quite clear to his son, and repeated over and over as if it were a litany, 'Never trust a white man. I have never come across an honest white man in my life.'

By this time Derrick had opened his own welding business and he expected Robert to devote all his spare time after school to helping him in the workshop. Derrick was obsessive as always, and now that he devoted his manic energy to his work he required Robert to show the same dedication. Prevented from exercising authority in the wider world, Derrick imposed himself dogmatically at home.

At first, Robert adored being involved in all his father's projects. They were often seen as they drove around the pot-holed streets of Wentworth to make deliveries. Robert's Aunt Girly remembers, 'Even when Robby was a boy his father used to discuss work with him like an adult.'

Father and son had always spent a lot of time together. On Sundays they invariably rose at five a.m. and drove down to the nearby Treasure Beach to run with the family's three dogs, Fonzie, Striker and Chunky, before going to collect the Sunday newspapers. They also enjoyed playing chess.

Robert admired his father's intransigence. He remembers going with his father to cost a job for a British immigrant called Campbell, who called Derrick 'boy'. Derrick told the man that he must not call him that as he was old enough to be his father.

'What do you expect me to call you?' asked Campbell. 'Sir?'

'Just call me Mister,' said Derrick, knowing he would inevitably lose the contract.

He impressed upon the quiet boy his own stark philosophy, 'You have enemies and friends, nothing in between. Most are friends, but those that aren't are enemies. If you can't avoid them, then hit back at them hard. Go right in and . . . *whap!*'

Robert had always been considered a fairly passive character but gradually he became more confident and assertive. At school he took up boxing. Aged seventeen he was tall, quite bulky, and extremely fit. As a boxer he was a junior heavyweight, but among his contemporaries they couldn't find anyone big or strong enough for him to fight, so instead he trained on a punchbag, pounding the inanimate adversary for hours with a solitary intensity.

His incoherent anger made him increasingly aggressive. He stopped avoiding confrontations, and sometimes even deliberately picked routes where he knew he would have to deal with a hostile group.

One afternoon he accompanied his sister Bronwyn, who ran for her school, to a track meeting. 'As we went down,' he said, 'there was a big group of guys. I was walking behind Bonny, one guy grabbed her and began pawing her. He was big, and much older, about twenty-eight. They were laughing at me because I was so much younger, but they let us pass to the Ogle Road Sports ground.

'There, I took one of the stakes out of the ground to go back with. Instead of picking another path home, I deliberately went back the same way and that guy was still there with his friends. He came straight for me and threw a punch. I ducked away and struck him with the stake – it broke and I began stabbing him. I yelled at Bonny to run, and when she was clear I ran after her and we got clean away. But it paid off, hitting back. Later, that gangleader came and apologised to me. It made me lots more self-assured.'

Robert increasingly resented Derrick's demands on his time. There was considerable tension between them and frequent rows, but Robert still did not dare to defy his father openly. Derrick expected him to put in a spell at the workshop every day although Robert was studying for his final school exams. Robert was exhausted, and when swotting he often stood on a chair to keep himself awake. It particularly riled him that he often had to sacrifice playing in rugby matches on Saturdays because Derrick insisted he help out at the workshop.

When Robert finally tried to confront his father with these feelings, Derrick immediately offered to pay him for his work. This only exacerbated Robert's indignation. He regarded this as a bribe, and privately he began to blame his father for robbing him of his childhood.

'The difficulties between us were mostly about me not having enough time for myself,' said Robert. 'Father was obsessed with making money and becoming a successful businessman. His rationale was that he wanted us all to succeed. But he was not successful – he tried too many things and didn't concentrate his energies. And he'd battled so hard to get those premises and set himself up.'

Robert's youthful rivalry with his father was agitated by the fact that they both recognised a singular affinity in character and outlook. Robert admired his father intensely, and although this respect was reciprocated, he was not yet sufficiently mature to break away and assert his independence.

Even so, they could act in complete harmony. Once, standing in the yard at home they witnessed two policemen, Swarts and Tiflin, arrest a well-known gangster, but the next moment the gangster had wrested the guns from both policemen. Without a word, Derrick and Robert vaulted over their fence and disarmed him.

Another time, just after midnight, there was a fire at the Manuel's house at the end of the road. Quite a crowd had collected outside by the time Derrick and Robert arrived, and rafters were already collapsing. Somebody shouted, 'There are people in there.'

All the doors were locked and windows securely bolted. Derrick kicked in the burglar guard and Robert slithered through to open the front door from inside. They couldn't see much for the smoke and the heat was ferocious. Eventually Robert came across the unconscious bodies of Mr Manuel and his two year old son, while in another room Derrick located the asphyxiated Mrs Manuel, and together they carried the three of them out.

Father and son were also regularly forced to defend themselves against Wentworth's marauding street gangs. Then Derrick was especially pugnacious and sometimes even delighted in hitting back. One evening when Robert was a teenager, he came home flustered and told his father that a large local gang had been hassling him.

Derrick jumped up and said, 'Right, let's go and get them.' They picked up sticks and went out. At the end of the lampless street they saw a large group coming towards them. As the gang emerged from the shadows, Derrick saw there were at least a dozen hoodlums.

He whispered, 'Don't run, that will be the end of us.' As the gang approached, Derrick said loudly, 'We are looking for some sailors who insulted our sister.' As the group parted, and before they could resist, Derrick and Robert laid about them with their sticks and then ran off as fast as they could.

Robert, however, was left in no doubt as to who was the real enemy. Derrick drummed it home again and again: it was the white man.

There were many similarities between the two male McBrides, but Derrick was an unforgiving task master. He was determined that his son should succeed where he had been foiled.

As Robert grew older, Doris saw how strongly he resented his father's obsessive demands upon him, and she frequently wondered if Robert would ever stand up to his father and assert himself.

Then, when the son finally rebelled it seemed like the most insidiously contrived rejection. Robert put aside all his father's edicts about never trusting a white man.

The world of the whites, so different from the ghetto life of Wentworth, not smelling of the oil refinery, beckoned over the horizon, like the Golden Mile seafront.

Robert decided to try the other side.

3

Gordon Webster was born the same year as Robert McBride, on November 29, 1963, on an isolated smallholding lost in the lonely rolling grasslands of Natal's high interior plateau, set right at the edge of the silent gum and wattle forests of the district of New Hanover. His family were very poor and far from any medical amenities. Gordon was the last of ten children; he was born at home, without the help of a midwife. Eighteen months later his father died.

The family homestead consisted of two plain mud and cement whitewashed shacks with grey corrugated iron roofs, and a smaller stone outhouse. Across the rough dirt courtyard was a *rondavel*, the circular mud hut with a conical thatched roof in tribal African style. Chickens scavenged in the yard, roosted on the rusted van in the corner and stalked beneath the lines of washing hung out on the dilapidated verandah of the larger, three-roomed building. There was no electricity or running water and their meagre settlement was enclosed by a thorny hedge.

It was a small agricultural holding and the family chiefly subsisted off the two-acre patch at the back, planted with mealies, sweet potatoes and vegetables. They had tried to grow other crops, including nuts, but the monkeys had plundered them: the forest loomed over their precarious homestead, only twenty yards away on the other side of the furrowed dirt track that led up to their rickety wire gate.

Gordon's mother Agnes was a Zulu, and her maiden name had been Xuma, while Gordon's father Artie Webster had been half Irish, half Zulu. Gordon's grandfather John Webster arrived as a child from Ireland in the 1870s. By the turn of the century John Webster was running a transport business with three or four wagons hauling goods up from the port of Durban to the newly discovered gold-rush town of Johannesburg. This was a gruelling trek that could take weeks, even months, over the steep passes of the Drakensberg mountains. John courted a Zulu woman, Nohlela Ndlela, who, after marriage, took the Christian name Jane. They settled in New Hanover in the hamlet of York, twenty miles from the town of Pietermaritzburg, where John established the modest family homestead.

There are only two decorations on the bare walls of the candle-lit rooms in the Webster home. They are oval, sepia-tinted photographs behind glass. In one, Gordon's grandmother, Jane, a striking African woman dressed completely in black, stands alone in a field; in the other, a handsome European gentleman poses stiff and erect in sombre suit and tie – her husband.

Their son Artie inherited the smallholding and continued the transport business, eventually swapping the wagons for a truck, with which he transported timber from the forests around New Hanover. Artie met Agnes, a domestic worker, in 1941 and their seven sons and three daughters were all classified Coloured. Artie had been registered at birth as White, though later he was demoted to Coloured, while Agnes was of course classified African.

Gordon, their youngest child, had a gentle, moon-round face, a satiny, light brown complexion, and large, luminously dark, almost feminine eyes, as well as his mother's handsome African features.

At home the family spoke Zulu. It was a struggle to get by after Artie's death, and Agnes supplemented their meagre resources by selling any extra produce, as well as eggs, milk and cheese, to neighbouring timber plantations. The Websters were better off than the few African families working on these plantations who were paid pitiful wages; if the husband died the entire family was usually expelled from their home immediately. The Websters also had a dozen or so cattle which the children were expected to herd in the nearby pastures.

Agnes was over-protective of her youngest and even when he had grown up she persisted in referring to him as 'my child'.

Gordon was breast-fed till he was five years old and he was known as *Gugwane*, the favourite.

His mother was a devout Methodist. She was also a ferociously strict disciplinarian. She beat her children for the smallest misdemeanour, taking a rough sprig from the hedge, making the miscreants lie down on a wooden bench and thrashing them, often till they cried.

There were two churches in the district, but both were for whites. A few miles down the rutted path which cut a ribbon through the forest there was St John's, a low grey slate church with a neat graveyard, built by the first English and Irish settlers to arrive in New Hanover in the 1870s. Then there was the Methodist Church, which Agnes used to clean. Even though she kept the keys of this church in her home, she was not allowed to attend services there. Instead, a minister visited the Websters once a fortnight to conduct a makeshift private ceremony in the sparse, dark stone outhouse.

There were three other families in that area: one white, one Indian, another African, and in this rural backwater the children used to play together, unaffected by the racial obsessions that gripped the rest of the country. They fished and swam in the small stream a hundred yards down the valley, hunted birds and played 'cowboys and crooks' in the forest, or soccer with an old tennis ball in the surrounding meadows.

The Webster children were never invited to their white friends' home, but they continued their companionship till they were about ten, when suddenly the white boys didn't come over any more. They stayed away, without a word. After that, the white teenagers went off to boarding schools, and in later years they would be embarrassed if they met the Websters. They didn't have anything to say to them. They'd wave and pass by quickly.

The African family, the Ngubanes, worked on a nearby farm and Bheki Ngubane was Gordon's best friend. When Bheki's parents separated, the mother was anxious her two sons would not grow up to become virtual serfs as farm labourers, so she asked Agnes if she would look after them. The Websters had always taken in or helped anyone less fortunate than themselves, despite their own poverty, so Bheki and his older brother Ndaba became part of the extended Webster household.

Bheki, or 'Beh' as they called him, was seven at the time, exactly the same age as Gordon, and the two were inseparable. Ndaba was three years older and an extrovert, whereas Bheki was as reserved and shy as Gordon. They were like brothers, except that Bheki, as a Zulu, was able to attend the tiny farm school for Africans only a mile away, while the Websters were barred because they were Coloured. There was no school for Coloureds in the district, so at an early age the children attended an Indian Primary School in New Hanover. Gordon and his sister Margaret walked the ten mile round trip barefoot every day in all weathers.

It took them an hour, setting out at six forty-five a.m., on the narrow strip of gravel that disappeared into the blue distance towards New Hanover, winding among the mealie fields and undulating fertile pastures that stretched away to the hazy wooded hills on the empty horizon. There were clumps of dense woodland on one side of the track and sometimes they would surprise a buck, which would crash away into the bush through the long grass. Otherwise there were just lonesome vistas and silence.

Each child had three sets of clothes; one for home, one for school and one for Sundays when the minister came. The financial position eased a bit as the older children departed to find work and began sending home a portion of their wages. By this time, some of Agnes' grandchildren were also living at the crowded smallholding, and they used to walk miles to raid white farmers' orchards for apples and peaches, or sugar cane from their vast plantations.

Gordon and Bheki were expected to herd the family's cattle to a meadow three miles distant, before and after school. Sometimes Gordon would tell his young nephew, Godfred, 'Tell Ma I'm going to fetch the cows,' and he'd run off with Bheki to play. If he had any money he liked to go to the Indian store and buy bread and tinned spaghetti, then he and Bheki would go into the forest and have a feast. Sometimes he stole an egg from the chicken run, though if his mother discovered it she'd thrash him.

His sister Margaret remembers coming home from school on a

number of occasions and encountering a bunch of white children by the side of the road. They'd shout, 'You black *kaffir*!' Another time, Gordon was profoundly unnerved when some white children shot at him with a pellet gun.

But in this rural backwater they had little idea of any wider meaning to these unpleasant experiences. Their mother had no formulated political views. She was semi-literate, having spent only a couple of years at a Methodist mission school, and her strict religious observance, which emphasised obedience, led to a submissive conservatism in all things. Agnes bowed to authority and the accepted way of the world as being the will of God. If asked, she simply said, 'It is our fate.'

They were all, however, afraid of Hillerman. He was a local plantation owner of German extraction, an irascible, rough man, whom all the black children regarded as a cruel and unpredictable tyrant. Hillerman was fair and Aryan-looking, with a red face. He always wore shorts and braces over his khaki shirts. He was said to whip African children, though he didn't dare with the Websters as they'd had a 'white' father, though he'd cuff them over the ears. It was Hillerman who gave Gordon his first, savage taste of white intolerance.

Hillerman owned many cattle and he was in charge of the local government cattle dip. Margaret Webster says, 'One day, as usual, Gordon and his friends took our cattle to the dipping tank, and when Hillerman counted the cows and found there were only fourteen instead of fifteen he became very angry, even though they were not his cattle. Gordon explained that one of the calves had been struck by lightning the night before.

'Well, Hillerman didn't believe him, and said he was a liar. He whipped Gordon across the chest with a sjambok. Hillerman was cruel and particularly nasty to Africans. He whipped him hard, and told Gordon that he wouldn't believe him till he brought the dead animal to him as proof.

'Gordon was crying and terrified, but he and his friends dragged the dead calf all the way there to show Hillerman. Gordon came home frightened and still weeping to tell me what had happened. I think it is perhaps the incident in his life that he feels most bitter about.'

By the early 1970s the effects of the Group Areas Act had reached New Hanover. It was declared a white area. Black families not required to work on white farms were evicted, as were the majority of Indians; the New Hanover Indian primary school was closed down. Children Gordon knew were summarily uprooted and removed elsewhere.

The Websters were also issued with expropriation orders, but due to the fact they owned their own small parcel of land, they successfully resisted this attempt to dislodge them. Nevertheless the blueprint of discrimination from Pretoria, which had previously seemed so remote, now hung over them as a perpetual threat.

As the world closed in on his secluded childhood, Gordon soon discovered that lurking beyond the protecting Blinkwater range were further, more insidious, indignities.

4

The more Robert McBride ventured into the wider world beyond Wentworth the more he came up against white intolerance. At Ansty beach with his nephews he was chased off by an angry crowd of whites; going shopping with his mother to a supermarket in a white area on a Saturday he got into a fight with local white youths who jeered, 'Get out – this isn't your area!' Even so, he was fascinated by his white ancestry and wanted to know everything about his European background. Robert began to pester his parents, particularly Doris, with questions about the white strands in their families.

Doris answered him with amused tolerance . . . her father was an Afrikaner called Van Niekerk who drove buses in the rural area of southern Natal, and he fell in love with one of his passengers, a Coloured nurse named Grace. They had to elope to Pieter-maritzburg in order to marry, as Van Niekerk had been engaged to marry the daughter of the local magistrate. This was 1928, twenty-one years prior to the Prohibition of Mixed Marriages Act.

After having five children, the Van Niekerks came to Durban in search of better work, and Doris's father got a job with the Corporation. Doris met Derrick when they were both teaching at Clarewood, a primary school for Coloureds. At first, she says, old man Van Niekerk didn't like Derrick at all. 'My father was a peculiar bird. He had his funny habits, and he was very old-fashioned, from the country, and he thought Derrick was this terrible city slicker from Johannesburg and he thought that Johannesburg was . . . you know . . . Sodom and Gomorrah.

'Derrick was loud and quite argumentative and drank a lot. People in the country areas are inclined to keep quiet and accept things and Derrick was the absolute opposite of that! He was always rowdy and if he'd been playing rugby he'd come back with a swollen eye or something and my father would say, "This animal has been fighting". He also didn't trust him because he drank. Derrick drank a lot in those days.

'My father watched me closely. It wasn't because Derrick was dark. My mother's mother was black and he adored her. A black person was fine with him. He didn't really like Derrick because he had different ways and ideas. Derrick was hot-headed, always ready for a fight – the devil from Jo'burg!

'We had a secret wedding. My mother knew but kept quiet. Actually, after the wedding we had the cheek to go back to my parents' house. My cousins had been making little snacks while my father was asleep and I said to my mother, "You must tell father we are married." But he just walked away. He sat on the back porch and got drunk with some other old men.

'For some time my parents had been living in a white area, number 55 Berriedale Road, near Ridge Road. Nobody said anything to us, in fact the neighbours on both sides were quite friendly with my mother. They would see her going off in her nurse's uniform and they would be pleasant and talk. It was a nice house, spacious and pretty, especially compared to what we had been living in before. It was white outside, my father painted all the doors black, and there was a lovely big brass letter box on the front door. There was a comfortable, enclosed verandah and about half an acre of garden, with big shady trees, avocado and peach.

'It was in 1963–64 when they really started dividing and moving people. They put them in trucks and moved them out. They were saying, "This is an Indian area or a white area and you cannot stay here anymore." They appropriated the houses, just took everybody out and people simply lost their homes. That's when Derrick and I were moved to Wentworth.

'My parents continued to live in Berriedale Road till 1964, when my father died – as my father had been white, they'd been all right, but after that they just wanted my mother out of there. She went back to Harding.'

When Robert tried asking his father about his white antecedents, however, he met with an intemperate response. Derrick's great-grandfather had been white, either Irish or Scottish. But he detested his white blood. He loathed the whites for what they had done in South Africa. He particularly hated the psychological distortions racial discrimination had visited upon its victims: indoctrinating some (who didn't quite make the grade as white) to hate themselves and pathetically aspire to be accepted as white. Derrick himself was a victim of this perverse psychology.

Derrick McBride had hated his own mother. He was too black for her, and she never forgave him for it. He told Robert, 'Anyone who practises discrimination in their own family is deserving of contempt. My mother discriminated against me. God, how I despised her! When I was born, someone told her she had a son, and someone else said, "But Alice, he's black." She never let me forget that.'

Derrick McBride's father was dark, but Alice's mother had been white and Alice was inordinately proud of her own fair complexion and straight brown hair. Her first two children inherited this colouring, but Derrick was born with a dark complexion – a constant reproof to her white aspirations. She punished him by withholding her affections and making him work harder than the other children.

They lived in Johannesburg, and Alice used to send the young Derrick into the neighbouring white suburb to hawk her home-baked cakes from door to door. He was often set upon by bigger white boys and robbed of his wares, and when he returned home empty-handed, Alice would beat him. He had three brothers and a sister, but Derrick was the only one Alice selected for these unpleasant errands.

Although she was discriminated against herself for not being white, it was Alice's dearest wish to be part of the world that rejected her. She would even refuse to take tea with people darker than herself, whom she would refer to as 'the bushman type'. When people came to visit she would explain Derrick away by saying, 'I have five children and this is my dark one.'

Alice made Derrick do much of the housework, including scrubbing the floors, and in a desperate attempt to earn his mother's affection the little boy worked frantically hard. One day

Derrick overheard a relative remark, in Afrikaans, '*Hy werk homself wit.*' ('He's working himself white.') Derrick says, 'I grew up with a deep hatred of whites. I made up my mind to get even, no matter how long it took.'

Religion, he felt, had also been appropriated by the whites. He believed the church encouraged whites to feel superior and taught blacks subservience. As a child, Derrick had been a devout altar boy, but had resented the fact that Coloureds had to sit in a separate section from whites, while blacks were barred altogether. When being prepared for his confirmation he was asked if there was anything he disliked about the church, and Derrick replied, 'The colour bar.' Only when he recanted this heresy was he confirmed, but thereafter he lost his confidence in the church.

In the years immediately after the Second World War, when he was at school in Kimberley, Derrick associated with a group of young communists, but he wasn't really anti-capitalist, he was anti-white. In 1948, following the formation of the Afrikaner Nationalist Government, he and some teenage friends made homemade bombs which they placed on minedumps around Johannesburg.

With a group of other young Coloured intellectuals, Derrick formed an association called the Inner Circle. They debated the options of joining other organizations dedicated to the overthrow of apartheid. The regulations implementing racial segregation had been stepped up considerably since the Nationalist Party had come to power, and every single aspect of their lives was fenced in by rigid race laws. In 1955 Derrick attended the historic meeting of the Congress of the People in Kliptown that drew up the Freedom Charter. But by then Derrick and the rest of the Inner Circle had come to the conclusion that talking and passive resistance campaigns had got the opponents of apartheid absolutely nowhere. They believed only armed insurrection would bring about change.

Totally isolated and unwilling to join other more widely based movements, the Inner Circle collapsed as its disillusioned members retreated into passivity. They withdrew from politics and devoted themselves to individual pursuits. One became a doctor, another went into exile in Zambia, becoming a wealthy business-man. Derrick became an alcoholic.

He had been drinking heavily for several years. Doris says it was his mother who really drove him to it. 'He applied to the medical school at Wits University in Johannesburg to study as a doctor. In those years it was almost unheard of for a Coloured to go there, and Derrick was one of the two Coloured students accepted. He had a really good pass and was so happy. His father was also thrilled, but Derrick had to pay for the entrance fee . . . his father, Bobo, had actually put some money aside for Derrick to go to university.

'Derrick completed all the forms and asked his father for the money. Alice asked, "What does he need the money for?" His father replied, "To go to university".

'Well, Alice said, "What does he want to be a doctor for? I need the money for Spuddy's wedding!" At the same time, in December, his eldest brother was getting married, you see. His nick-name was Spuddy, like in potatoes. It was a toss-up between Spuddy's wedding and Derrick's education. Spuddy won – Spuddy being the favourite with fair hair, green eyes, all those sorts of things.

'That incident did a lot to influence Derrick's way of thinking in later life. Oh, Derrick talked about that a lot. He left home because of it and was very angry. He cut himself off from all his family and never wanted to go back again. I think that was the point that made him drink, you know.

'He was frustrated and disillusioned, but above all he wanted his mother's affection. Yet there was nothing he could do to change the colour he was.'

Not being white, Derrick could see no point in getting a regular job; he would only have to travel long distances every day for very low pay. Instead, he became a street-corner hawker. He sold anything, particularly spare auto parts, but gradually he found it more profitable to deal in stolen property, and this degenerated into running a gambling school and then a shebeen, one of the thousands of illicit drinking dens that flourished in the vigorous underworld of Johannesburg's dispossessed and rootless black population.

Eventually he enrolled in a teacher's training course, but the facilities for Coloureds were so inferior that Derrick made himself highly unpopular with the authorities for constantly denouncing the system as unjust, comparing it with the excellent facilities provided for white student teachers. Having completed the course, Derrick gave up teaching almost immediately.

He took a job as a clerk in the Labour Department. By now he was drinking brandy heavily: 'I felt I had nothing to live for – life seemed worthless. I felt excluded, so I drank.'

After finishing work one afternoon, Derrick went for a few drinks with a colleague, Desmond Stoltenkamp, who was also a qualified teacher and, like Derrick, a prodigious drinker. Desmond told Derrick he'd heard there were so many vacancies for teachers in Durban that agents would actually be waiting on the railway platform to offer qualified people jobs on the spot. They decided to leave for Natal that evening. They did not even go home for a change of clothes but simply headed straight to the station and caught the first train to Durban.

There were no eager recruiting agents to greet them on the platform, in fact there were no teaching jobs at all. Desmond, having sobered up, renounced drinking the very next day and thereafter never touched a drop, though he has remained in Durban ever since. Derrick continued drinking, and the pair of them sustained a succession of jobs, on a motor assembly line, as carpenters and chimney sweeps, before they finally found teaching posts and Derrick met Doris Van Niekerk.

Meanwhile Spuddy had prospered. He had performed the South African miracle, the apartheid equivalent of passing through the eye of a needle. He now passed for white.

All over South Africa there were people who lived in a twilight zone of racial identity, always terrified the police would catch them out. In slum areas of Cape Town, not yet embraced by the Group Areas Act, there were wives and daughters who went in through the front door because they looked white, and husbands and sons who entered furtively by the back because they didn't. There were Coloured prostitutes who had freckle-faced blond children; they would hire white prostitutes to play 'mother' for the white school sports day.

For others, who had always assumed they were white, re-classification could come like a celestial revelation. Men came home after work to find officials waiting on their doorstep with papers that proved they were not white after all. People were summoned daily to be questioned and scrutinised. In Cape Town those under suspicion reported to Room 320, where sittings were held in camera.

Among those deliberately 'trying for white', the lucky ones managed to procure documentation to back up their assumed white status. Spuddy not only passed for white, he now had papers to prove it.

Spuddy had acquired his nickname when his mother worked in a Fish and Chip Shop and he had gorged himself on potatoes. He was tall and sallow and people assumed he was white. As a teenager he'd got a job as a scaffolder because the foreman thought he was white. It was not a job open to Coloureds, and after Spuddy had completed some official forms the foreman called him into his office and closed the door. The foreman tore up the forms, handed him a new set and told him to fill them in again. In the section marked 'race' Spuddy had put Coloured. The foreman told him to put down that he was white and never, ever mention that he was Coloured again. Spuddy did as he was told. He got his first set of papers. He was officially white.

Derrick made his contempt for Spuddy extravagantly plain. He maintained his brother had reneged on his background and associates in return for privileges from people who were persecuting his own family. Derrick used to say to Robert, 'My brother is an idiot, but he's got the vote and I haven't!'

Derrick vented all his pent-up resentment in denunciations of Spuddy. 'He's selfish and stupid. We've never been to visit him in his white area. He told another brother that he didn't want him to visit – he'd done all right and he didn't want to be compromised.'

Spuddy had accrued all the trappings of a white man. He lived in a white area of Johannesburg. He had worked himself into a better job as a French polisher and spray painter. He was a respected member of the community. Spuddy had always been a devout church-goer and now he was a lay Minister in the New Apostolic Church. He was married with three children and the children went to private white schools. His son was even conscripted into the South African Defence Force.

Robert was fascinated: 'Once my uncle Leslie saw Spuddy's daughters in the street with their white friends, in their school dresses and straw boaters. They walked away, pretending not to know him. They didn't want to be seen with a Coloured relative.

'At first, listening to my father, I felt quite condescending towards my cousins. But later I was jealous of them, because they were going to a white school and all our relations talked a lot about them.'

It was an enticement: 'I felt they were different. You know, in another world.'

No one could tell Robert where the McBrides had actually acquired their surname. There were two family legends locating the origin with Derrick's unknown great-grandfather, but details of this European inheritance remained an exotic rumour. Doris had once heard talk of two drunken Scots brothers jumping ship in Durban at the turn of the century, but that was as much as she knew, and the story fizzled out.

The other version traced the lineage, via a misspelling, to an Irishman named John MacBride who had fought in the Boer War on the side of the Boers. MacBride, from Westport in County Mayo, was a Fennian, a member of the Irish Republican Brotherhood, dedicated to the expulsion of the English from Ireland. Forced to leave Ireland for political reasons, he arrived in 1896 in Johannesburg, where he worked on the mines.

In the summer of 1899, as the British were trying to provoke a war against the Boers, MacBride issued an appeal 'to Irishmen to remember England's manifold infamies against their own country, and on this account to volunteer the more readily to fight against a common enemy for the defence of Boer freedom.'

MacBride helped form and lead the Irish Brigade and was given the rank of Major. They fought at Colenso, Spion Kop and Ladysmith, and Major MacBride was wounded at the battle of Tugela River. After the British occupied Johannesburg the Irish Brigade fought a ferocious rearguard action to keep the road to Pretoria open. Finally as the Boers resorted to a desperate guerrilla war, suitable only for those who knew the veld, the Irish Brigade disbanded and MacBride left South Africa via Delagoa Bay in 1900. But according to McBride family lore, during his stay the Major had a liaison with a Malay woman, who bore him an illegitimate child, thus abandoning in South Africa both progeny and a bastardised version of his name.

MacBride was a small, wiry, unattractive man with red hair and skin burnt brick-red by the South African sun. He continued to style himself 'Major' for the rest of his life. Unable to return to Ireland, he settled in Paris where he married the Irish actress and revolutionary Maude Gonne. The poet W. B. Yeats had unsuccessfully proposed to Maude Gonne and Yeats wrote that from the moment he met this beautiful woman, 'the troubling of my life began'.

The troubling of Maude and Major John's lives began shortly after they married in 1903. He drank, beat her, and following the birth of a son, Sean, they parted. He was later allowed to return to Ireland, where he became a water bailiff for the Dublin municipality.

The end came when MacBride took part in the uprising of Easter 1916. For five days a small band of Republicans held key points in Dublin and the 'Major', returning from a wedding, joined up with a group that took over Jacobs Biscuit factory. After the surrender, MacBride was among those executed, refusing the customary blindfold.

In his elegy, *Easter 1916*, Yeats refers to MacBride as, *A drunken, vainglorious lout, He had done most bitter wrong / To some who are near my heart*, but concludes,

> *Yet I number him in the song . . .*
> *He, too, has been changed in his turn,*
> *Transformed utterly:*
> *A terrible beauty is born.*

Whiteness, in the theology of apartheid, was the Holy Grail: venerated, sought after, source of myths and tribal longings for purity and salvation. To some, whose genealogy gave them a tenuous link to this elusive Grail, it became a state of mind. Robert was proud of his European ancestry, and says, 'I spoke

61

about it openly and proudly whenever I got the chance.' The symbol of all those aspirations, the Open Sesame to a decent life, was just visible on clear days from Wentworth. To the north on a distant hill like a shadowy obelisk, he could just make out the tall central tower of the university.

Robert did so well in his final school exams that he was accepted into the University of Natal, Durban campus, in the faculty of Engineering. This was the different world – a largely white world.

The campus stood high on a ridge above Durban: spacious, tranquil, landscaped, privileged. Approached by steep, tree-lined avenues with names like King George V, Bowes-Lyon, Princess Anne and Queen Elizabeth, it had an expansive colonial graciousness. At the top, looking down at the remote docks, a statue of King George in his Garter robes was surrounded by flowering shrubs, palms, cacti and green shaded trees with tropical birds. Behind the university were lush rolling foothills, the beginning of the Valley of a Thousand Hills which stretched away to the Drakensberg Mountains.

White youths wandered between classrooms in multi-coloured shorts and T-shirts as if they had just come in from surfing. There were some Indian and African students, but Robert preferred to keep the company of white students. 'I was leading a false life,' he said later, 'forcing my company on white people.'

There was no transport from Wentworth so Robert had to walk, getting up at four in the morning if he had an eight a.m. lecture. Doris would see him sometimes standing at the bottom of the hill at the shabby intersection of Quality Street, hoping for a lift. 'It was so discouraging because there was nothing you could do to help. He'd have a big bag with all his books, and if it was raining he'd get soaking wet.'

Although he was trying to ingratiate himself with the white students, Robert was aware of odd looks and comments behind his back and overheard remarks such as, 'He looks like he's just come out of the trees.' He compensated by trying to act and dress more white than the white students. He had his curly hair cropped very short. No white student ever said anything to his face. Instead, those who resented the presence of 'non-whites' on their campus expressed their unambiguous feelings in graffiti on the toilet walls: BLACK IS BEAUTIFUL BUT IT LOOKS LIKE SHIT ON A *KAFFIR*.

Doris remembers Robert describing this disparaging closet dialectic. 'One would start on top of the wall as high as he could and say something about black people, then there would be a reply from a black student under that about white people. Robert said he could stand reading for hours in the toilet. I thought it was funny, because when I was a teacher you would catch little guys scribbling – they'd take a chance and write dirty things on the wall and run away. But university students?'

Robert, like his father, had actually wanted to study medicine, but Derrick had insisted that he enrol in engineering. It was not a subject Robert enjoyed. After five months, the exhaustion brought on by walking to the campus and back, as well as having to work in his father's workshop when he returned home, meant that Robert dropped out.

By now Robert had a girlfriend, Claudette, who was very fair, with a pretty, freckled face and red hair. She worked in town as a secretary for an insurance company, and although she was classified as Coloured and lived in Wentworth, white people in Durban simply assumed she was white. Her little brother called her 'White Spook'. Claudette was a simple, uncomplicated girl, with no interest in politics, and the family nicknamed her 'The Cat'. Doris thought she was a sweet girl but a bit silly; and quite clearly she was besotted with Robert.

He says, 'Claudette was an extrovert. We never had a serious conversation. She was happy. She wasn't ambitious. She wanted to be a housewife and have lots of children. She liked dressing up and looking smart. She liked going to the movies, the drive-in. She loved dancing – I don't, and sometimes we'd have an argument over that. She wanted to know why I wouldn't take her out dancing and I said that dancing was for younger people, when they are looking for someone, and I used the argument that our dancing days should be over. She liked to go out and be sociable and the centre of attention. She liked to gossip. She liked food – I used to cook from a book, and her favourite was custard trifle. Mostly Claudette liked simple pleasures . . . like going down to a particular ice-cream parlour near the beach-front where they had exotic fruity ice-creams – banana, pineapple, mango, pawpaw.'

It was when they went into Durban that there was trouble: 'It was hurtful. I used to be stunned. It was like a blow to you. I just felt as if I'd been hit with something hard.

'Old ladies in an arcade would stare at us, for example. One would draw the other's attention. You could see her expression change – shock, as if something nasty had dropped out of the sky. Then they'd stare after us till we disappeared.

'Claudette ignored it. She didn't seem to worry. I never said anything but it worried me a lot. It irritated me, made me angry.

'Maybe I developed a complex. I became self-conscious. Walking in town with her became an ordeal. I realise maybe I was going out with Claudette because she looks white, and now this was drawing attention to, you know . . . because next to her I wasn't white, and seeing us together in Durban, the whites didn't like it.

'Men would deliberately go out of their way to bump into me. I never retaliated. Only afterwards I'd think – I should have hit that guy. At first, though, I'd be shocked and hurt, then angry.

'Claudette noticed, but she knew it was best to be quiet. She was a peace-maker. After five minutes it would blow over, but I'd feel disappointed that I hadn't retaliated. They were only jostling and bumping me because of my colour. Sometimes there'd be sniggers. I used to worry – am I doing the right thing in walking away?'

Despite these indignities, Robert pressed ahead with his quest for acceptance in the white world. The next step was to join a sports club. One of the top white rugby clubs in Natal was Northlands, now re-named Durban Crusaders, and they had opened their doors to a couple of non-white players without asking too many questions. Robert signed up.

The club was situated along the coast a couple of miles to the north of the city, past the Durban Country Club, the Windsor Park Golf Course and over the Blue Lagoon, in the comfortable white suburb of Broadway. An imposing, white-pillared entrance led down the curving, palm-lined driveway to a spacious modern club house.

It was effortlessly poised and unruffled: the gentle whirr of a lawn mower, the trilling of birds and from behind a tall hedge entwined with pink hibiscus, a faint clack of bowls. Elderly white folk, with leathery faces and impeccably dressed in white, crouched intently at their leisurely game, with muted cries of, 'Well done, sir,' and, 'Nice one, Reg!' In front of the clubhouse, surveyed from its wide terrace, were two immaculately maintained rugby pitches with floodlights.

The idyll did not last long. For a while Robert managed to keep the fact he had joined a white rugby club from his father. But when Derrick found out, he was angry and contemptuous. He wanted him to resign, and when Robert tried to convince his father that he merely wished to see the way whites lived and understand the way they thought, Derrick warned his son that he would regret it, and kept repeating his mocking nostrum: 'Never trust a white man.'

Doris felt differently about these escapist ambitions, says Robert: 'Mother was happy I was playing for white. My father was not. My mother is also a little mixed up about what she is because she has got a white skin and a black brain.'

Because of his chunky build and strength, Robert played in the lock forward position, and at first he was selected for the B squad. He suspected he was good enough for the first team and he wondered if he was being kept down on account of being different. After training or a match, instead of socialising with the other white players, Robert would pack up his kit and head straight back for Wentworth, where his father would be expecting him to give a hand in the workshop. Derrick's disgust for his son's social goal was quite open. 'It'll come to no good,' he warned. 'Those whites will turn on you.'

There were occasional snide remarks from opposition teams. During one match against the police, an opposition player – a lieutenant – got into an argument with Robert and ended it loudly, for all to hear, by dismissing him as a Hottentot.

Then Robert became aware of some of his own team-mates casting sly aspersions behind his back. He ignored them. But the strain between the two worlds – the gaunt reality of Wentworth and the white figment of his hopes – could not be reconciled.

While he had been unable to cope with the university, and the anxiety generated by accompanying Claudette into white areas was intense, it was the hypocrisy encountered at the rugby club which ultimately forced the break. This compelled Robert to acknowledge he was striving for an illusion.

He might be a member, but that didn't mean acceptance. Robert had hoped to find a certain image of himself in the response of these white sportsmen – and all he saw in the mirror of their attitudes was that he was not white.

So he became the opposite.

There was a decisive moment for this conversion. It came when he was finally picked for the A team. In the changing room Robert overheard another player commiserating with the dejected lock forward who had been dropped to make way for him. 'Garry, don't worry about it,' said one white sportsman to the other, 'Robert is just a bushie.'

5

Pietermaritzburg lies in a wooded hollow of the green hills of the Natal midlands. It is a compact, sedate, rather Victorian town, which prides itself on its azaleas and its Englishness. In the suburbs are expansive avenues, and orderly sports fields where white schoolboys in immaculate white flannels play cricket, watched by others in purple blazers and straw boaters. In the city centre, lawyers maintain cramped offices in the warren of narrow alleyways round Chancery Lane and Gray's Inn, alongside the boutiques selling chintzy floral dresses and colourful African trinkets.

Pietermaritzburg was founded by the Voortrekkers, dreaming of an independent Boer state. They declared the short-lived Republic of Natalia (which resolved to 'drive all blacks not working for the whites beyond the Umtamvuna River'). In 1842 it was occupied by the British and became a garrison town. Today it remains the provincial capital and is still dominated by the tall red-brick tower of the ornate Victorian City Hall. There is a cult of preservation and restoration which occasionally strays into caricature, like the Victoria Club, a glum imitation of a London gentleman's club, crankily flying the Union Jack. On the whole Pietermaritzburg slyly plays up to this old world affectation and settler nostalgia. It is trim, quiet and composed: a contented echo of British colonial sensibility.

Gordon Webster became aware of the true consequences of his colour when, at fourteen, he left the protective wilderness of New Hanover and was sent as a boarder to the Haythorne High School for Coloureds in Pietermaritzburg. It was a severe shock. As his elder brother George had found: 'You left home and you realised there was apartheid. You were suddenly "Coloured". At

67

the small Indian school you were just one of the pupils, but now you were something to be kept separate, like a special, second class caste.

'On the bus to Pietermaritzburg, the front was reserved for whites only. We hadn't been prepared for this total segregation of facilities. We hadn't really been exposed to whites. Then suddenly we were exposed to apartheid, and you realised you didn't belong here. There were so many divisions, a hierarchy of prejudice, from different shop entrances for Europeans and non-Europeans, to things like Coloureds being able to drink in their own pubs or buy alcohol, whereas Africans couldn't even buy a drink unless they got an exemption from a magistrate . . . .

'Coloureds also had their own segregations, and you soon learnt that at school. A lot of Coloureds, because of their sense of inferiority, take pride in their white ancestry. They are very aware of the colour of skin and the texture of hair. Even some of the teachers discriminated, being softer on lighter-skinned kids and giving the worst punishment to the darker students. The children can also be quite cruel about these colour differences, like calling the darkest *sneeu*, snow. This colour fixation marks everyone, though some are more affected than others. Gordon was very distressed by it.'

His teachers remember him as a conscientious and able pupil, but shy, lonely and withdrawn. He was darker than most pupils and his features were distinctly African, for which he was teased. Some pupils also mocked him for the faint trace of an Indian accent he had acquired at his primary school.

Gordon hid from the school that his mother was an African and he did not let on to his class mates that his mother tongue was Zulu. One day when Agnes came to the school, the Principal said in front of Gordon, 'What does this girl want?'

There was something feline, almost demure, about Gordon. With his fresh, round babyish face and slim body, he was sensitive and inordinately timid. In addition, he had begun to wear thick-rimmed glasses for his near-sightedness.

There was one boy who was particularly picked on. He, too, was from a rural area and looked and sounded African. Gordon got dragged into several fights for objecting to other pupils calling his friend '*kaffir*'.

In Pietermaritzburg, Gordon was at last able to make some comparisons concerning the conditions of his own life: it was immediately apparent that the white schools were incomparably better off. They had swimming pools, tennis courts, sporting facilities, good buildings and smaller classes. At Haythorne there was no school hall, no library, one soccer pitch and up to forty-five pupils in a class.

Gordon played soccer, took up boxing and weight-lifting. But gradually he retreated into contemplation and passivity. The shy reserve which had been apparent at home became an unsettling solitude at school. He confided his thoughts only to his diary, a black hardbacked school notebook, which he completed diligently everyday, attempting to make sense of his adolescent confusion.

A recurring theme of this diary was his mother's severity. She still continued to beat him, even for trifling misdemeanours. Agnes' one aim was to ensure that her son should follow her other children and rise well above the subsistence level of a rural peasant. Gordon's nephew Godfred remembers how Agnes began to have to chase after Gordon to beat him.

But there were also happy times at home. His friendship with Bheki Ngubane was as strong as ever. Bheki and his brother Ndaba continued going to the African farm school. Bheki and Gordon shared a passion for soccer and supported the Kaiser Chiefs, a black Soweto team. At night they would play reggae records on the *gumba-gumba*, an old-fashioned gramaphone. Gordon spent much of his holidays reading, particularly Westerns.

One vacation, the boys had a secret drinking party, and Gordon got drunk for the first time. 'He was so unruly,' says Godfred. 'He became noisy and happy. He announced he was going to be a doctor.'

Gordon had always told his mother that when he grew up he wanted to be a doctor; she had never had the heart to tell him what an improbable ambition that was. Agnes was concerned that he should escape from their rural poverty, but that he should also understand his station and 'learn the ways of the Lord'. But if Gorden ever introduced the subject of politics at home Agnes would dismiss it by saying, 'White is white and black is black. It is our fate. It is retribution and there is nothing we can do about it.'

Gordon was eventually appointed as a prefect. This was not because he showed any distinctive leadership abilities. The school authorities, on the contrary, seem to have perceived him as compliant and submissive, and therefore a malleable agent. Certainly he did not appear to threaten authority in any way.

In 1980 came the school boycotts. Although a prefect, Gordon did not organise or lead these protests at Haythorne. He merely followed, swept along with the strike action against their inadequate facilities and emasculated education. His mother was appalled. Agnes came to the school and insisted Gordon return to his classes.

She pleaded with the principal to let her son back in. Agnes and the school principal came to an agreement: Gordon would be permitted to rejoin on condition that the principal should administer a sound thrashing. Gordon was dismayed that his mother should have been party to such a deal, yet he was not sufficiently sure of himself to either repudiate her authority or stick with his political protest. He bowed to the humiliation.

Behind that veneer of obedience, however, Gordon was beginning to resolve his personal confusion. He had a clear idea of his own sense of justice. He now felt his school reflected the misrepresentations of apartheid. He did not make an outright challenge, but as a prefect he avoided administering punishments for traditional misdemeanours. Unobtrusively Gordon attempted to ameliorate the effects of discrimination, both by teachers against their own pupils, and among the pupils themselves. He understood how insidiously prejudice can undermine those it is practised against. Gordon wished to find a way in life that would help counter such distorted experience. By the time he was due to leave Pietermaritzburg, he had decided to become a teacher.

Robert McBride was working as a welder. He joined a Durban firm and after a year's apprenticeship as an instrument fitter, he went to work for SASOL, the state oil-from-coal corporation.

Here he experienced the full effects of job discrimination, with incompetent immigrants often lording it over more experienced African workers.

Robert McBride's outlook was now transformed: rejected by the white world, he had retreated badly hurt. He put away his 'white' suit, and cut off his white friends. 'After the incident at rugby,' he said, 'I suppose I changed to the other side.' The white way of life, which he had previously so desired to embrace, was now reviled. He dressed in what he considered to be a more African fashion, with bright, bold colours and chequered tops. He allowed his hair to grow long again and combed it out into an Afro. He spent as much time as he could in the sun. He wanted to be darker. 'I became,' he says, 'more African than the Africans – a radical black.'

Robert started making enquiries about his black ancestry. Derrick was delighted that his son had renounced the white world as it had been a source of considerable antagonism between them. 'Derrick just didn't like Robert trying to be on the white side,' says Doris. 'He didn't care who they were or what they were doing, he just didn't like Robert mixing with them.

'Of course it was a feather in Derrick's cap, this change. He said, "I told you so, I told you about associating with them." '

Robert and Derrick were now completely reconciled; in May 1982 Robert agreed to work full-time with his father and returned to live with his parents at Hardy Place. While working, particularly when away from Durban at the Secunda SASOL plant, Robert had given most of his earnings to his mother. That same year Doris finally resigned her job as a remedial teacher and opened up a take-away. The family were still desperately trying to improve their financial position.

The Day 'n' Nite Take-Away was right opposite Derrick's workshop, twenty yards across a concrete forecourt, in a small enclosed area of a dozen or so other workshops. This unit was called Factorama, situated on the edge of the Jacobs Industrial estate, near the Police Training College for Indians and opposite the Wentworth youth community centre, whose premises had previously been prison cells for the old military camp. Like all the workshops in Factorama, the take-away was a red-brick block with corrugated iron roofing.

The shop was open from six a.m. till eleven p.m., and the licence required them to stay open even later if any of the workshops at Factorama were working late. All the family were involved, including cousins. Doris did the cooking and operated the till, while Bronwyn and Gwyneth helped serve the customers. They provided cool drinks, fish and chips, pies and bunny chows – a Wentworth speciality consisting of half a loaf of white bread stuffed with curry.

It was exhausting, but the family enjoyed being in such close proximity; Derrick and Robert were able to pop over for their meals, or to give a hand if necessary. From across the courtyard they kept a wary eye on the shop in case of trouble. 'There were a lot of incidents at the shop, people who were drunk or trying to steal,' says Robert. 'My father and I were often there, and at night we used to serve through the hatch because it was so dangerous.

'There'd be things like this drunk pissing in the front of the shop. My father stopped him, so he brought out a knife. His friends came in to back him up. I hit one of them with a coke bottle – he caught me on the side of my cheek with a knife. My mother opened the hatch and passed through a long pole used for opening a high window, and I chased them away with it.

'Another time a guy sent my father to make a bunny chow and when Derrick went out the back, he came through the window to get at the till. It set off the alarm. I was outside and I blocked his way out of the window. He took out a knife – father grabbed his hand and burnt it on the oven. The guy dropped his knife and Derrick knocked him unconscious.

'One afternoon three men came to the shop, causing trouble, and two of them attacked my father. My mother started shouting, so I ran up. One guy kicked me – I'd been eating bread and began to choke. Another ran for the car to get a gun and my father hit him with a bin. There was a five-minute fight and then we overpowered them. We called the cops, and that's when we found out these guys were themselves cops.

'The police charged us, but the magistrate threw it out. One of them came back later, with another cop and pulled out a gun. He threatened us but then backed down. The cops always gave us a lot of trouble. The fact is they didn't like my father.'

Father and son had re-established that striking rapport which people had noticed between them when Robert was a boy. Robert recognised this affinity: 'The way we think about things is very similar. Politics was our hobby together. Both of us knew, without debating, that we stood in the same position.

'Something I particularly admired was that he never backed down from what he believed, even when the odds were totally against him. I mean, in business you should not be politically inclined because you can't be too fussy about getting contracts, there's all sorts of grafting involved – and Derrick would never get caught up in that. He's very proud and I've inherited a lot of that. Our experiences, in many ways, are very similar.'

One predicament both endured was the hostility of whites when they saw them with what they assumed to be white women. According to Doris, 'It happened quite a lot to Derrick and me. They'd say *sies* as they passed, or crude things in Afrikaans. You know, "She prefers a black man . . . or a whatnot." That's what they call Coloured people, whatnots and Hottentots. If they didn't say anything to you they'd look, stare in such a way that would make you feel like a heap of dirt. Once the police came to my home. My father opened the door and they told him, "Do you know your daughter is going out with a black man?" My father said, "What black man?" The policeman said, "Kaffirs and Hottentots." I was married at that time. My father said, "She's a Hottentot herself, so what must she do?" The policeman felt so small, he just turned red.'

Robert began to see the absurd, pitiable side of all his attempts to align himself with whites. One evening he went into Durban to collect Claudette after work and was sitting on a marble flower pot on the pavement, right next to a lorry with a squad of black labourers on the back. When Claudette crossed the street to join him, he became aware of the black labourers' approving attention: 'They were talking loudly, commending me. They were happy I had a "white" woman.'

He found it impossible to accept himself as a Coloured, he thought the term itself to be derogatory, a dirty word. At this point his friend André Koopman introduced him to the philosophy of Black Consciousness. André was older than Robert, and had been detained by the police for six months in 1977, at a time when all Black Consciousness organisations were being banned. He also exposed Robert to a whole range of radical black writers and black musicians.

Robert seized upon this black literature and music: 'Mentally, I suppose, I commenced resisting. I began taking an interest in the struggle, and I paid a lot of attention to what had happened in Zimbabwe. I felt very anti-white. I was angry. I'd say things like, if a black child gets killed, a white child should be killed. I was very bitter.'

Robert's greatest passion, however, was reggae music, particularly that of Bob Marley. It gave voice to his sense of a universal racial iniquity, as well as his search for personal identity. He particularly liked 'Zimbabwe':

> *So arm in arms, with arms*
> *We will fight this little struggle*
> *'Cos that's the only way*
> *We can overcome our little trouble.*

It was purely rhetorical for Robert, for his involvement in politics was still no more than discussion and denunciation. He listened obsessively to the music, as if the words and the sound alone would bring the walls of Jericho tumbling down. It did not propel Robert to take any action, but it drew him out of his insecure sense of isolation. *It's you, it's you, it's you I'm talking to* . . . It gave him a renewed confidence in himself and the possibility of change. *Slave driver, the table is turned / Catch a fire . . . you gonna get burned.* There was an optimism in reggae, a driving, infectious faith that there was indeed a Kingdom of Justice, and it was at hand:

> *Now the fire is burning* . . .
> *Ride, natty, ride*
> *Go deh dready, go deh*

Robert responded to this yearning expressed by Bob Marley, an apocalyptic desire for an end to exploitation, the millenial dream that the meek may inherit the earth:

> *Let righteousness cover the earth*
> *Like water cover the sea . . .*

Marley was a devout Rastafarian, venerating Haile Selassie, Emperor of Ethiopia, as the Messiah, the King of Kings, the Lord of Lords, the Conquering Lion of the Tribe of Judah. He believed that his people had been taken into captivity, like the Jews to Babylon, and that Ethiopia was the Promised Land:

> *We're leaving Babylon*
> *Into our Father's land . . .*

Robert was not influenced by the Rastafarian belief that there was a Promised Land somewhere else on earth – just as some black Christian sects promised their followers a kingdom in the here-after for their suffering here below. But for Robert, Babylon came to be the symbol for all evil, a powerful image of everything that weighed people down and oppressed them, as in his favourite Bob Marley record 'Babylon System':

> *Babylon System is the vampire*
> *Sucking the blood of the sufferers . . .*

For all his talk about how he wanted to 'destroy the sickness' in his society, Robert had done nothing at all. He extended his excitable interest in politics, which he discussed avidly with his father, but he had still taken no active steps to oppose apartheid, other than to continue to dress 'black' and listen to reggae.

However, he was bored as a welder. He was restless, inquisitive, frustrated, hemmed in by all the restrictions which cramped his life. In 1983 Robert finally elected to follow in his parents' footsteps. He decided, like Gordon Webster, to become a teacher: he would go to a Coloured training college where he would be taught by Coloured staff to become a Coloured teacher for Coloured pupils. It seemed, after all, that Robert was not going to demolish Babylon; he was going to try and make the best of a bad world.

Part Two

Spear of the Nation

6

Robert McBride and Gordon Webster met on their first day at the Bechet College of Education. Robert soon established that Gordon was the younger brother of Trevor Webster, who also lived in Wentworth. Robert went straight up to Gordon and said, 'Your brother saved my life.'

Robert explained that three years previously, during his last year at school, he had been playing soccer in the school grounds when some local gangsters bust up the game and took the ball. Robert had challenged the leader who pulled a knife on him. Unknown to Robert, Trevor Webster had been watching. He came up softly behind the gangster, clouted him over the head and disarmed him.

Robert and Gordon were both cautious and highly suspicious by nature, but they established an almost instantaneous rapport. At first, Gordon told his brother Victor, Robert came across in such a challenging macho fashion that he thought jokingly to himself, 'I'll have to hit this guy to test my strength.' Victor Webster recalls: 'They shared many interests, including a dedication to physical fitness. Gordon was a keep-fit fanatic. He loved running, boxing and soccer, though he couldn't do too much of those because of his eyesight. But the main thing was that he could talk to Robert in a way that he couldn't talk to anyone else.

'Gordon was so shy and quiet, and Robert seemed to bring him out. Gordon used to hide his feelings, he was a one-word man, though not with Robert, who also made him laugh. Gordon had a shy, captivating smile, quite mischievous really, and when he laughed it was quite explosive. They were very close. In our family we discussed a lot of things, but not politics, not a word. I never showed my hurt to anyone, except my older brother Trevor.

I think Gordon took the same view – and the person he could show his hurt to was Robert. Gordon was extremely mild-mannered. But if you wanted to make him mad, you only had to say something bad about Robert and he would get really angry. They had a very profound friendship.'

The Bechet College of Education which they attended was the only teacher training college for Coloureds in Natal. In its fifty year history it had never had permanent premises and the college was housed temporarily in a former white girls' high school, which had abandoned the building for more suitable accommodation. For a while the site had been used as a store-house by the Durban Corporation and then turned over to Bechet in 1979. The building was a faded, worn out colonial dream.

Bechet College (motto: 'Through Toil to Victory') was immediately opposite the Greyville Race Course, home of the exclusive Durban Turf Club with its plush modern covered stand and circular lush green racetrack, which adjoined the Royal Durban Golf Course. The racecourse was the venue for South Africa's most socially competitive and fashion-conscious event, the Durban July Handicap. Many of the surrounding streets mimicked a polished, thoroughbred pedigree: Ascot, Epsom, Newmarket and Derby. On the other side of the race course were the luxuriant Botanical Gardens, on the ridge beyond that snuggled the red roofs and trim gardens of the white suburbs of Musgrave and Essenwood, and in the distance loomed the grey obelisk-like tower of the University of Natal.

The college was a frayed, two-storeyed, turn-of-the-century colonial building, with a red-tiled roof and shabby, creamy white facade; along the entire front of the rundown building, under a red tin overhang propped up by slender wooden columns, was a long, gloomily-shaded verandah. The college was screened from the road by a row of densely-leaved wild fig trees and the worn entrance gate was flanked by drooping palms with dying, flaccid fronds. Inside, the shadowy corridors and sombre classrooms were permeated with an unmistakable aura of transience and decay. The college was dilapidated and overcrowded with few facilities – no sports ground, no laboratories, a cramped library and paint peeling off the walls in the stark classrooms.

There had always been dissatisfaction among students about the conditions, and when Robert and Gordon arrived it was simmering again. Bechet was exceptionally over-crowded, with between three and four hundred students at a time. There was considerable anger that, by contrast, the two white teacher training colleges in Natal were dramatically below their enrolment quotas; at the Edgewood Teacher Training College, with superb facilities and sports grounds, there was only one third of the possible intake, while the Afrikaans *Durbanse Onderwyskollege* was under threat of closure due to the lack of students.

Teachers at the college remember Robert well, but Gordon was so shy and self-effacing that few can even recall what he looked like. In contrast to the casual, colourful 'African' style Robert had adopted, Gordon's dress sense was as neutral as possible: neatly-pressed beige slacks and freshly ironed white shirts. He never did anything to draw attention to himself.

The college deputy said, 'Gordon was very quiet and unnoticeable. On a couple of mornings I gave him a lift in and you just couldn't draw him out at all. Robert was much more forceful. He was outspoken, like his father. I remember he came to me once and said, "You teachers are frightened – go and tell the Department what our conditions are like."'

Other teachers remember Gordon as 'pleasant, nice, gentle, shy', but recall nothing else apart from the fact that he wore glasses. They used to ask each other, 'Which one is Gordon Webster?' One teacher said, 'Gordon was the absolute opposite of Robert, who would never sit back and accept what you told him. Gordon wouldn't speak unless spoken to, and then he would be as brief as possible. You never expected him to air any views.' Another said, 'Gordon was particularly reticent, he just didn't participate. He used to sit in the corner, silent. Robert on the other hand was quite outspoken and opinionated. One felt one had to be tactful, or he might be irritated. He was quite volatile, not the ordinary, run-of-the-mill student. He was articulate and had a big mouth, always challenging. In class, he seemed to have quite strong views about everything, speech training, poetry . . . I remember he always used to say, "Isn't that a contradiction?" He was bright, and obviously thought a lot. Robert was original.'

Gordon proved to be hopeless at maths and Robert spent a lot of time helping him as it was one of his strong subjects. Gordon was also sensitive about his rural accent, for which he still got teased. When asked where he was from, Gordon would say, 'Pietermaritzburg'. Robert remembers how angry Gordon got when another student said in front of a group, 'Come off it, man, you're from the *bundu* – you're a *plaasjaapie*!'

They spent a great deal of time together, and Robert found Gordon a thoughtful, calming influence. 'At college they used to tease me a lot about fighting gangsters and he talked me out of getting angry with them,' says Robert. 'Gordon was always someone who was moderate, though he was not scared of anything. He was a very gentle person. I was not at all calm and he had a steadying influence on me. He gave me a sense of direction.'

Once when Robert had fallen out with his father over working after college, Gordon had actually taken Robert home and pressed him into apologising to Derrick and making up.

'Gordon was quite formal, and sometimes it would seem like he was pulling your leg,' says Robert. 'He would always say, "Hello, how are you?" and "Really?" in that heavy rural accent. The moment you spoke to him, you liked him. He was impressive. We became friends quickly. We're like brothers, really.'

Gordon is more emphatic. 'Brothers?' he says. 'More like twins!'

They shared the same taste in music, both of them having a passion for reggae; particular favourites were Toots and the Maytles, Jimmy Cliff, and above all Bob Marley. His redemptionist lyrics gave them pride and confidence in black culture. But most of all it was politics that they discussed.

After the brutal repression of the township uprisings there had been several years of relative calm. Suddenly in 1983 that changed dramatically with a powerful upsurge of black organisation and resistance. The catalyst was the whites-only referendum pushed through by the Prime Minister, P. W. Botha, making him an executive President.

Botha was implementing a doctrine known as the Total Strategy, formulated by the Department of Defence, which observed, 'We are today involved in a war, whether we wish to accept it or not.'

Part of the strategy was to try and drive a wedge between Coloureds and Indians on the one hand, and Africans on the other. In the 1983 referendum, the whites voted for the establishment of a separate House of Representatives for Coloureds and a House of Delegates for Indians; Coloureds and Indians, while still denied the vote in general elections, were being allowed to vote for these bodies which had puny legislative powers and could be easily overridden by a white veto. This device was greeted with derision by the majority of Coloureds and Indians. Blacks, as ever, were excluded. Resistance to this divide-and-rule strategy revitalised black organisations and trade unions, leading to the formation of the United Democratic Front, an alliance of over a thousand organisations representing over two million people.

That year the number of acts of sabotage rose noticeably. One ANC action stunned the white population, for it brought this intermittent guerrilla war right into the heart of their capital with a huge explosion in the centre of Pretoria, close to the South African Air Force headquarters, killing nineteen people and injuring two hundred. The South African government retaliated with an attack on the Mozambique capital of Maputo, where ANC personnel lived; an air raid destroyed fifteen houses and a nearby jam factory, killing five and wounding twenty-six. The following month Pretoria extended the call-up period for all white males between the ages of seventeen and sixty-five.

Robert and Gordon spent much of their time together discussing these developments. 'We agreed on a lot,' says Robert. 'We realised singing and symbolism was not enough. We were not people who could go to a meeting and feel easy about putting our fist in the air, or *toyi-toying*. We did not just want to talk.'

Robert was still strongly influenced by Black Consciousness, which held that blacks needed to free themselves psychologically and shed their slave mentality, that blacks could only be liberated by themselves and therefore whites should be excluded from their struggle. Gordon, on the other hand, was profoundly influenced by reading the Freedom Charter, the declaration drawn up by the Congress of the People at Kliptown in 1955, which had been adopted by the African National Congress. This called for a multi-racial front against racial oppression and declared in its preamble, 'That South Africa belongs to all who live in it, black and white, and that no government can justly claim authority unless it is based on the will of the people.'

Unlike Derrick McBride, Gordon did not hate whites, yet when discussing violence he used a phrase reminiscent of Robert's father: 'The only way to speak to them is to use their own language.'

The question he constantly put to himself, and repeatedly asked Robert, was, 'Can I live with myself and do nothing, when every day I am insulted by my life?'

While at college Gordon lived with his eldest brother George and his family in the Coloured district of Sydenham, which was divided from the white area of Sherwood by a buffer zone of tall grass and bush. Sydenham was more respectable and middle-class than Wentworth, where Trevor Webster lived. Gordon definitely did not want to live in Wentworth. After they had left home, his older brothers had all been forcibly removed to Wentworth and settled in a rough former barracks known as Ack-ack Camp. Gordon had visited Ack-ack as a boy and been shocked by the squalor and violence.

George Webster had finally qualified as an attorney after a long, arduous struggle – or as he says, by 'sheer lunacy'. He owned a small, neat villa in Sydenham facing the buffer zone. Gordon was almost as much of an enigma to his own brothers and their families as he was to everyone else. He would seldom join in and voice an opinion; usually he retreated to his room and kept to himself. Gordon was so elusive that his image is even absent from photographs. When the Websters search among their family snaps, they are astonished to find that Gordon fails to appear in family groupings, even when they remember him being present on those occasions. He had almost succeeded in making himself invisible.

George's wife Lucy used to worry, 'How will this timid boy ever be a teacher?' Her sister Moira, says Lucy, used to get furious with Gordon. 'What sort of teacher are you going to be?'

she wanted to know. 'You don't express an opinion, you're not interested in politics, you never go to any meetings.'

When people came to visit, Gordon usually hid in his room, but during his first year at college Moira and her friends came round for a party and insisted on dancing with Gordon. He was thrilled, so they took him with them into Durban to an 'open', racially mixed disco; it was the first time Gordon had seen blacks and whites mix freely or seen whites dance. When he returned Lucy wanted to know what he thought. Gordon smiled and said, 'Whites have no sense of rhythm.'

Gordon was painfully shy with girls; his mother had imparted a strict sexual code to him, insisting on no physical relationship outside marriage. Once at school when he was fourteen he had been caught petting with a girl and had been severely punished. For a while he'd also had a girl pen friend in Zimbabwe, but that, as far as George and Lucy could make out, was as far as his shyness would allow him to go.

After a while, however, they discovered that when Gordon was not out with Robert he was seeing a girl. He never brought her home or talked about her, so all they knew was that her name was Anne and that she worked as a nurse for the local dentist, Dr Adams. Anne was African, a Xhosa from the Transkei, whose mother was a domestic servant in Durban. Anne herself, they discovered, lived nearby in the white area of Sherwood in servants' quarters; but, as with everything else, Gordon kept that side of his life to himself.

Whenever he could Gordon returned to visit his mother in New Hanover. He was much more relaxed about his relationship with her, for he now understood her severity and rigid discipline as a mother's desire for her children to escape her rural poverty. But he was also increasingly anti-religious. Agnes had become a Presbyterian and Gordon believed that his mother used religion as a shield against reality and as a way of denying the political enormity that surrounded them. He said, 'I was impressed when the minister spoke about us humans being made in the image of God, and that all human beings are the same in His eyes. But I was quite baffled by this because in reality this was not so.'

He maintained that religion, soccer and music were the opium of his people. His childhood friend Bheki Ngubane had no interest in politics at all; he was soccer mad. By now Bheki was working as a driver for an electrical firm in Pietermaritzburg, though he too came back to New Hanover to visit Agnes at every opportunity. Bheki's elder brother Ndaba had become a police-man, and at first Gordon avoided him and told Bheki the reason was that Ndaba was a *gattes* (urban African slang for cop). However by the end of his year at Bechet, Gordon felt this was unfair, accepting that Ndaba was not as bright as Bheki, and that with high unemployment he simply needed a job.

Under Gordon's steadying influence Robert was developing a more coherent political outlook. At the end of their first year at college Robert was elected to the Students' Representative Council, and at the beginning of the following year he opted for the full four-year course of a Higher Educational Diploma. Robert's optimism and long-term confidence was not reflected by Gordon; he was increasingly pessimistic and weighed down by political events. In 1984 black youths and students were once again in the forefront of protest marches and demonstrations, but violence was on the increase and Gordon felt they were engaged in a fruitless venture.

'There's no point in protests and demonstrations,' he con-cluded. 'They are futile. The real patriot must act.'

Robert was aware of his friend's gathering sense of desper-ation. The crisis came that August. It was the first election for the new tri-cameral parliament, where Coloureds were to have their own House of Representatives. Gordon felt this was not only a sham for Coloureds, but an insult to Africans who were not even given this palliative. He would have a token vote, denied to both his mother and to Bheki Ngubane. A week before the elections he asked Robert, 'What kind of law is it that makes my mother less human than me?'

Together with George and Lucy, he attended a protest meet-ing at St Anne's, the local Catholic Church. It was packed with Coloureds and Indians; the crowd was so large that people had to stand outside. 'On the way back in the car Gordon was very quiet,' said Lucy. 'He asked, how could anyone vote on a colour basis – and when our black brothers have no vote?' Gordon felt that all talk of reform was utterly empty. The government had responded to the new wave of civil unrest by sending in the military to help the police. All he was being offered was a vote in a token election which excluded even his own mother: that decided him. He told Robert of his decision first, and then he told his girlfriend Anne: he was going into exile to join the African National Congress.

'He wanted to talk to someone,' said Robert. 'He was very hurt. It was not an intellectual thing, but something he felt – we both felt – very deeply. Activists were having to run away, not people who preached violence or anything, just people who demonstrated and organised, and we felt that was no good. They couldn't even sleep at home. We didn't want to run. We wanted to do something, get involved. I started thinking, we must hit back! I understood how Gordon felt. I put myself in the victim's shoes. I understood his pain, I began to feel the pain with him.

'He wanted me to go with him, but I felt I couldn't. He knew I had responsibilities at home. Also, I didn't want to sit in a refugee camp, so he was going to send a message to me. He was sad, but his mind was made up. He was disappointed I was not going with him, but he was going to go anyway.'

The day Gordon left South Africa, he and Robert went into Durban to see a film, *Purple Hearts*, about Vietnam. 'It was like a last drink, only Gordon doesn't drink,' said Robert. 'He joked, "You mustn't sell me out!" Then he said, "I know you won't." That element of trust was there between us right from the beginning. It didn't need to be discussed.'

They parted in Grey Street.

With Gordon gone, Robert felt more confused. He missed his friend's clear sense of direction and his quiet advice. Although troubled by the yearning to take some dramatic action, and strongly tempted by his friend's example of going into exile, Robert was still contemplating a more conventional future in South Africa. He and Claudette planned to get married a year after he finished college. They discussed having children, and Robert told her that he wanted to move away from the city. He proposed applying for a post in a rural area, and they dreamed about a happy family life with Robert teaching in a country village school.

He continued working after college, both at Derrick's workshop and at the take-away. It was so dangerous working nights at the take-away now that the McBride family had applied for a firearm licence and nick-named their 9mm Beretta Parabella 'Betsy'.

At the beginning of the following year Robert had to take even more responsibility as Derrick went into hospital with diabetes. One evening he closed up the take-away at eight p.m. and was walking home because the car had broken down; he was carrying all the day's till takings and he also had the Beretta. In Craton Road a group of five men appeared out of the shadows, blocking his path. One of them asked Robert for a cigarette and he explained that he didn't smoke. 'OK,' said the gangster, 'if you haven't got the cigarettes, just give us the money – and don't tell us you haven't got the money, because we know you've just come from the shop.'

Robert turned and ran, but he hadn't got far before another group appeared in front to cut him off. He was cornered, and as they moved in, Robert saw they were armed with *pangas*. He took out the Beretta and fired a couple of warning shots in the air. The leader of the group laughed. 'Those are just blanks,' he said. Desperately Robert made a break, and sprinted towards a grassy bank; if he could make it to the top he would be clear away. But he was wearing rubber-soled sneakers and the grass was damp. Close to the top, he slipped and tumbled back; rolling over, he saw one of the gang members was right above him with his knife raised. Robert reached inside his jacket and fired: the gangster fell dead.

The others fled and Robert went straight to the police station. An enquiry found that he had acted in self-defence and the matter was taken no further. But Robert was upset and appalled; he was stunned that life just went on the next day as if nothing at all had happened and nobody seemed to be asking why the victim had become a petty gangster in the first place or what circumstances had led to Robert pulling the trigger. He concluded that this death was the effect of a cause: the philosophy which trapped both him and the gangsters in cages like Wentworth.

It was Doris who saw how the incident haunted him and she remembers Robert waking night after night, shouting. The gangster had been shot clean through the head and he had recurrent nightmares about the huge, gaping hole.

Robert began spending more time with his friend Jimmy, a slim, nervous intellectual who lived nearby. They talked rather wildly and unrealistically about what actions they might undertake against apartheid, but mostly they listened to reggae music and Jimmy showed Robert his poetry. He also introduced him to more black music and writers like Malcolm X and the Black Panthers. Jimmy gave him a book, *Soledad Brothers: The Prison Letters of George Jackson.* It had a tremendous impact on Robert. Later he told the sociologist Fatima Meer, 'It had an overpowering effect on me. I identified strongly with George Jackson and was moved in a way which I can't explain, by his younger brother Jonathan, who rescued his brother George and two other comrades from the court house where they were being tried. Jonathan was shot dead. His action was so powerful – he gave his life for his brothers. George had been unjustly imprisoned and he was brutalised, and his brother was right to rescue him. George was later killed while attempting to escape from prison. They had taken military-style action and the world respected them for it. They had showed audacity and contempt. I believed that the whites would respect us when we too showed audacity and contempt.'

Jimmy says, 'The more we read, the more we burned.' Afterwards, when the enormity of what they were contemplating hit him, Jimmy had a nervous breakdown: he would sit up night after night, with a bottle of tranquillisers at his side, watching the dark road that led up to his house, waiting for the Special Branch to come and pick him up. They never came, but his hands still shake.

Robert used to get angry at what he felt was the empty posturing of some prominent anti-apartheid leaders; he and Jimmy agreed there was too much talking, too little action. One day on a spur of the moment decision they decided to leave the country. They planned to go to Lesotho, but on arriving at Durban station they discovered there were no trains, so they changed their minds and caught one instead for Johannesburg, thinking to leave from there for Botswana. In Johannesburg, however, an Afrikaans ticket collector informed them there were no more trains that night for Botswana either. Thwarted, Jimmy and Robert retreated to Durban.

Throughout 1985 violence erupted in the townships as blacks vented their anger against apartheid. On March 21st, the anniversary of the Sharpeville massacre, police in armoured vehicles fired into a funeral procession of unarmed Africans at Langa township near Uitenhage, killing twenty people. The uprising spread and soon two or three people were dying every day. In July the government declared a State of Emergency in thirty-six districts.

At Bechet College the demands were mild by comparison; the students were still pressing for better premises. As a member of the Students' Representative Council, Robert was one of the leaders. He was part of the delegation which presented their views to the acting Principal, and he was prominent in organising meetings and protest action. The students began to boycott their lectures and threatened that if there was no positive action they would boycott the exams at the end of the year.

Armed guards were sent into the college. The students called a meeting of parents to explain their position, and the parents voted overwhelmingly to support them. Afterwards Derrick McBride told a reporter from the *Sunday Tribune*, 'People in that situation are going to be prey to other organisations of a military nature. It's like taking away their pens and giving them AK47s.'

Robert helped draft a petition regarding the conditions at Bechet College which was presented to the new Coloured House of Representatives. The response was swift. The Students' Representative Council was declared illegal by Parliament, the students were suspended from their classes and Robert, as one of the leaders, was banned from taking his third year exams.

He was stunned. His conclusion was simple, 'There is just no hope for a so-called Coloured person to really progress independent of the constraints of the authorities. It's designed this way to keep a person just at a certain level where they want you.

'Well, since we were suspended and banned after dealing with the issue at Bechet in a peaceful, legal manner, I decided that it can't work. You can't progress within the system.'

He decided that he wasn't going to wait to join any organisation or underground movement; he was simply going to hit back. Robert had no coherent plan; his was simply an enraged and reckless impulse. With a group of friends he broke into Fairvale High School one night and attempted to burn it down. It was a botched operation, but even so they did considerable damage. Next, through a gangster, he and a friend acquired three illegal weapons, including a small lady's handgun.

They vaguely intended to attack people associated with the system, but they didn't really know what they were going to do, except that it was going to be something startling.

Then Gordon called.

It was November 1985 and he had been gone fifteen months. On his return, Gordon contacted two people immediately: first Robert, then Anne.

There was a message for Robert one evening to contact Gordon Webster at his brother George's home in Sydenham. It had been raining hard all day, but Robert set out instantly and walked the five miles to Sydenham. George came to the door and told Robert that Gordon wasn't in; Robert ignored him and walked straight past. 'There he was!' said Robert. 'He was his usual formal, polite self, a real gent. "Hello, how are you?" he said, "take a seat." Instead, we went into his room, and I said, "I'm so glad you're back!"

'Gordon looked different. There was something about his manner – he was a lot more self-assured.

'I was so excited. I was speaking fast. I had made up my mind to put aside responsibilities, and take up others. It was a highly-charged political atmosphere, but I didn't know exactly what to do and we had no access to the ANC. Gordon came just at the right time, because I was desperate and might have done something foolish.

'Gordon had already put my name down with a question mark. We went for a walk. He was going out of his way not to get me too excited. He was acting cool, he was calm. Like always, Gordon was steadying me.

'I was ready though. He was shocked I agreed so quickly. Within five minutes, I was in.'

7

The Websters had been as mystified by Gordon's return as they had been by his disappearance. He had left three notes behind. To George he wrote, 'I'm sorry if I've disappointed you. This life is not for me. I can't take it anymore.' George thought the note a little melodramatic and wondered if he'd simply dropped out, feeling unable to cope at college. To Lucy, Gordon wrote, 'Thank you for allowing me to stay. I enjoyed it very much. I love you very much.' To his nephew Godfred, he was even more cryptic, 'I'm coming back for you one day. Everything I have is now yours. Destroy this note.'

His brother Victor told them, 'He's young, he's dropped out and he could be anywhere in the country.' One sister had disappeared for a year and reappeared with a baby. His other sister Margaret was the most worried; she thought he might be dead. His mother Agnes prayed.

Agnes reported him missing to the nearest police station at New Hanover. The policeman there told her that there were thousands of children missing all over South Africa – some of them, he hinted darkly, had crossed the border to join subversive organisations. Agnes did not believe her child could have done that.

After six months two officers from the Special Branch made the long, bumpy ride through the gum and wattle forests to visit Agnes. They asked a lot of questions: had he got in touch, where did she think he might be, was he politically motivated? Agnes was unable to help and they left, demanding that she should let them know if he made contact.

There had been no sign or word from Gordon for fifteen months when Lucy Webster dreamed that she met him walking slowly through a sports field nearby. She asked him where he was

93

coming from, and Gordon just laughed and said he was coming home. Two days later, at eleven a.m., he walked in the back door. He had come through the bushes and the mango trees of the buffer zone that divided them from the white area. Lucy was alone in the house, and she shrieked when she saw Gordon enter the kitchen. 'Where have you been?' she asked.

'Don't ask too many questions,' he replied and asked if he could have toast and bacon.

Gordon wanted to call George, but he was worried the phone was tapped. Eventually he couldn't resist it and simply said, 'It's *Gugwane*.' George came home immediately, but all Gordon would tell them was, 'I've been places.'

They all noticed how much he had changed. 'He had flowered,' said Lucy. 'He was no longer the timid, shy youngster. He was oozing with confidence and was talking all the time, though never about politics.'

Gordon planned to register again at Bechet College, but dropped that idea after travelling to New Hanover to see Agnes, who told him that the Special Branch had visited her. He told his mother that he had been in Johannesburg and was now a land surveyor. Agnes prayed and gave thanks for her son's safe return. Gordon realised that he needed to find somewhere less conspicuous to stay, and his sister Margaret arranged the rent of an outside room in the ramshackle African township of Caluza, near the African hospital of Edendale, several miles west of Pietermaritzburg.

Gordon had instructed Robert not to try to make contact, but to wait instead to hear from him. Exactly a week later, Gordon called and told Robert he would come to Wentworth that night.

It was to be his formal induction into the ANC.

Exile had changed Gordon immeasurably yet he had left South Africa with no clear idea of where exactly he was going or what he would do beyond the fact that he intended to make contact with the African National Congress. After parting with Robert in Grey Street, Gordon made his way by *kombi* and train to Mafeking, and from there he headed for the Botswana border on foot, walking several hours through the dry, sparse bush. 'As I climbed over the fence, leaving South Africa, I felt such joy,' he said. 'I felt as if I was walking into freedom.'

He was taken to the Dukwe refugee camp in northern Botswana, where he made contact with the ANC. He was offered the choice of continuing his studies or undergoing military training; Gordon said that he first wanted to further his studies. At Dukwe the refugees formed their own political classes and study groups while they waited to be processed for their next destination. After three months Gordon was transferred to Zambia, where he spent a further three months at an ANC camp at Charlestown, five miles from Lusaka where the ANC had its headquarters in exile. During the day he read and studied and attended lectures every evening with the other young refugees from South Africa. Soon, however, he went to his superiors and told them that he had changed his mind; he wished to go for military training immediately.

The lectures had concentrated on current South African politics, as well as spelling out the movement's military strategy. The recruits were told that the ANC did not intend to confront the South African Defence Force in open warfare because they knew they could not win; the strategy was to put pressure on the South African government on different fronts, by international isolation, sanctions, internal boycotts and stay-aways. The military tactic was one of sabotage, drawing white attention to black demands, demoralising the government and its white voters, and thus forcing them into negotiations.

Many of the lectures concentrated on the history of the African National Congress, and the reasons for its decision to take up arms. 'For fifty years the ANC used petitions and was peaceful, in fact was begging the government for change,' said Gordon. 'But after it was banned in 1960 it resorted to the armed struggle.'

When the British, coveting the gold mines of the Witwatersrand, contrived a war against the Boers, one of the reasons the British Governor of the Cape Colony, Lord Milner, gave for intervention in the Boer Republics was discrimination against Africans. During the war the British Foreign Secretary, Chamberlain, promised, 'equal laws, equal liberty'. Many Africans supported the British cause but at the Peace of Vereeniging which concluded the Boer War they were completely ignored, and by the Act of Union in 1910 Britain simply handed over the African, Coloured and Indian majority to the total control of the white minority.

The visionary South African writer Olive Schreiner, writing in 1909, warned that the whites, blinded by greed, saw Africans as nothing but 'a vast engine of labour'. The new South African government almost immediately passed laws to protect white workers, reserving certain jobs for them and restricting Africans to low-paid work. Blacks were forbidden to strike and black police were disarmed and put into short trousers. Special tax laws were passed, designed to force African peasants off their land so they should seek employment in the white economy in order to pay those taxes. The Natives' Land Act deprived blacks of any right to own or lease land in what were declared 'white' areas: these amounted to eighty-seven per cent of the country.

Sol Plaatje, a founding member of the African National Congress, began his epic chronicle of this dispossession, *Native Life in South Africa*, with the desolate observation, 'Awakening on Friday morning, June 29, 1913, the South African Native found himself not actually a slave, but a pariah in the land of his birth.'

The ANC was formed in 1912, originally under the title of the South African Native Congress. Many of its early leaders were respectable, and respectful, middle-class lawyers who devised petitions and wrote letters to the government drawing attention to their grievances. They seldom even got a reply. In 1943, inspired by the Atlantic Charter of Roosevelt and Churchill two years previously, the ANC drafted a document called African Claims which was sent to the government requesting, 'freedom of the African people from all discriminatory laws'. The response was an official letter of receipt.

By 1952 the ANC leader, Chief Albert Luthuli, complained in frustration, 'Who will deny that thirty years of my life have been spent knocking in vain, patiently, moderately, and modestly at a closed and barred door? What have been the fruits of moderation? The past thirty years have seen the greatest number of laws restricting our rights and progress, until today we have reached a stage where we have almost no rights at all.'

There had been constant friction between those who wished to petition and those who wished to take more decisive and radical action. In the 1950s there was a concerted campaign of civil disobedience and passive resistance, particularly against the pass laws which specified which magisterial district an African was permitted to enter or work in. Finally in 1960, after the Sharpeville massacre when police shot sixty-nine Africans at a demonstration where they burned their passes, both the ANC and the Pan-African Congress were declared banned organisations. Outlawed, both went underground.

In 1961, after fifty years of non-violent opposition, the ANC resolved to begin a military campaign and a military wing was formed, *Umkhonto we Sizwe*, Spear of the Nation.

It was this organisation, which had conducted a sporadic and ineffective guerrilla campaign lasting twenty-four years, that Gordon Webster now elected to join. He was transferred to the *Umkhonto* training base, Pango Camp in Angola, seventy-five miles from Luanda. Here, deep in the bush, he underwent a crash course in military drill and sabotage techniques, then for another three months Gordon studied engineering, tactics and politics, also learning how to handle firearms, hand-grenades and a wide variety of explosives.

In political lectures they were told that the whites were considered as an indigenous people of South Africa, and that the ANC was not fighting the whites, but the system of government. 'We were told we should avoid loss of life or exposing people to danger. It was not the policy of the ANC to kill innocent people,' said Gordon. 'I was told that the whites would form part of a future South Africa where everyone would participate as equals.'

Having completed his course at Pango, Gordon flew back to Lusaka and there was told he had been selected for a branch of *Umkhonto we Sizwe* called Special Operations. He was given his instructions: 'My mission was to sabotage transformers inside electricity substations in Natal.'

With six others he crossed the Zambesi River to Botswana in a dinghy and re-entered South Africa on foot. His other instruction had been to recruit a small group, which he was to lead, and form a cell of *Umkhonto we Sizwe*.

As soon as Gordon arrived at the McBride's home in Hardy Place, the two of them went into Robert's room and Gordon put on some reggae music, turning it up loud to drown out their voices.

'He gave me a sort of lecture, it was like an ANC induction course,' said Robert. 'He told me about the history, the set-up, how the ANC was structured. I knew a lot, but he said I must not be unclear on any issue. This was the formal recruitment. I was a member of the ANC. He told me he was working in Special Operations, so I too was recruited into the military wing, *Umkhonto we Sizwe*, in the Special Operations division. We were very close . . . he had made himself vulnerable. It was a great honour and a great responsibility for me not to let him down. He was very clear, very determined. He wanted to know if I was carrying a gun. Gordon said, 'Throw it away.' He wanted us to be clean.

'There is a lecture that lasts about six hours called MCW, military code work, and it teaches various drills like secrecy, discipline, how to change your identity, how to conceal yourself, how to become aware if you are being tailed or if anybody is surveilling your movements. But the things which are emphasised are secrecy and discipline. In fact the words used are ultra secrecy and maximum discipline. No one must know of your activities besides those within your cell, and even those within your cell should only know a limited amount of information. Obedience, carrying out an instruction without question . . . the less you know, the better for you.

'Gordon gave me a couple of plans and puzzles to test me. One was gaining access to a substation. I was more unorthodox. I suggested a rubber mat to put over the electric fence. Gordon suggested that was clumsy and it was better to use insulated pliers.

'Then there were practical details – always remember to fill up your car with petrol . . . always be early for a meeting, always have an alternative venue.

'From the beginning I realised it's possible we would have a shoot-out with the police, or when we were cornered that I could be killed or be forced to kill an enemy soldier. I was very calm, at peace. I didn't care about anything else. I had found my vocation.'

8

George and Lucy Webster seldom saw Gordon; they didn't know where he was living, and Lucy began to think it odd that he didn't telephone to announce he was coming. Gordon would simply appear at odd times, always walking through the bush and mango trees of the buffer zone and entering by the back door. He usually asked if she would cook him something, preferably a trifle pudding, and then would disappear again without answering any questions. Finally Lucy said to her husband, 'Since Gordon's been back, there've been all these substations blown up.'

George knew better than to ask any questions and changed the subject, but the next time Gordon came through the back door Lucy tackled him. 'Aren't you scared?' she asked. 'They'll kill you.' Gordon refused to discuss it, but before leaving he said, 'You must promise me one thing. You must not cry when I die. We are not killing anyone. We are doing it to wake people up.'

Beside Robert, Gordon had recruited two others: his childhood friend, Bheki Ngubane, and another young Zulu man, Welcome Khumalo, also known as 'Blackie'. Gordon had met Welcome when visiting his sister Margaret, the nurse, who lived in the township of Dambuza where she rented a room from Welcome's uncle. Gordon now asked Robert if he could find someone from Wentworth.

Robert picked a friend from Bechet who'd played with him in the college rugby team and who had joined in the attempt to burn down Fairvale High School. Dark-complexioned, sharp-featured, always smartly dressed and with short hair, Nazeem Cassiem was a Muslim. An easy-going and popular young man, he was not particularly religious but his father insisted he attend the mosque regularly. Robert gently probed Nazeem and found him ready, so he elaborately set up a meeting between him and

99

Gordon by sending them both birthday cards with the time and date for their rendez-vous.

Robert was not present at the meeting, nor at the subsequent brief training sessions that Gordon organised separately for Bheki, Welcome and Nazeem. These were hasty, sketchy endeavours, where Gordon took his raw recruits into the bush near his home in New Hanover and gave them a cursory instruction in explosives and limpet mines. Then Gordon organised a somewhat farcical simulated attack on an electricity substation, cordoning off an area by tying rope around several trees, and demonstrating a mock infiltration. The brisk exercise was rounded off with a spot of jogging. At a later stage he also showed them how to handle various firearms.

For Robert, however, a more organised programme had been planned. He was to cross over the border with Gordon for an initial introduction to senior ANC cadres; if that went well, he would return for a more extended training period.

Gordon had arranged a number of meetings with Robert to test if he were punctual, whether he observed all the necessary precautions and, as instructed, asked no questions. Once he even told him to prepare for a long journey, then at the last moment cancelled it. Robert did not question why. Then he told him to be ready again at eight a.m. on the morning of December 6 and to borrow his mother's blue Peugeot for a trip to Johannesburg. After a seven-hour drive to Johannesburg, Gordon informed him they were actually going to cross over into Botswana.

It was another five-hour drive through Ventersdorp, Lichtenburg and Mafeking; it was searingly hot as they crossed the flat, parched veld of the western Transvaal. By the time they approached the border the abrupt deep dark of the African night had fallen. Suddenly Gordon told Robert to pull off the road; he was going to cross over on foot, as they might be on the look-out for him, and Robert was to pick him up in Botswana at a prearranged spot the next morning. Robert slept the night in a Mafeking hotel and passed through the Ramatlabama border post as soon as it opened the following morning.

'Gordon told me that if he did not appear at the rendez-vous then it must mean that he had been killed or captured and I must try and make contact with the ANC to let them know, even going to Lusaka to report if necessary,' said Robert. 'When I picked him up, he told me he had been chased by a Botswana patrol at a point only about two miles from the border post. He had heard their dogs and they came close to capturing him.'

They drove into Gaborone, the dusty, dishevelled, lethargic capital of Botswana, set in the sun-blanched wastelands at the edge of the Kalahari desert. Their ANC contacts, however, were not at the agreed meeting-point; Robert and Gordon remained there for four days, sleeping in the Peugeot. 'We couldn't make contact – they had to be on the move constantly. It was a very tense period, and a very hot time for MK people in Botswana,' said Robert.

'Gordon didn't tell me what was going on. After forty-eight hours we ran out of money because Gordon had budgeted for only one day and a night. I had a bank card, so I went back over the border and got some more money so we could stay on. At one point, when we had almost no money and we had virtually run out of petrol, we stole petrol from a Peugeot which was parked next to us. I washed my clothes in a communal washing place. The nights were hot.'

On the fourth day as they slowly cruised around the disconsolate town Gordon spotted their ANC contacts speed past in another Peugeot. Robert put his foot right down on the accelerator and they followed in a Keystone Cops chase, but failed to catch up. Three hours later, still forlornly criss-crossing the few dismal streets of Gaborone they spotted them again. Once more they set off in pursuit and this time they caught up when the ANC men stopped at a dairy for milk.

They gave Gordon some money to enable them to book into the Morningstar Motel, and that night two men entered their room unannounced. Gordon introduced them simply as 'Chris' and 'Oupa' (Grandpa in Afrikaans). 'They gave me instructions, both theory and practice, on weapons. It was only half an hour but very intense,' said Robert. 'They showed me how to pack and hide things, as I was not going to be used on an operation immediately. They showed me how to make an arms cache, to put the soil down in the same way as before, how to mark it, what kind of spot to pick – safe, but accessible.

'I was made for this. I learnt it very quickly. It was hard work – they were pushing me all the time.'

Robert was then asked to leave the room for half an hour, so he took a drive and when he returned about eleven p.m. Gordon asked him whether Chris and Oupa could borrow the spare wheel of his mother's Peugeot, as they had a similar car and were about to embark on a long journey. After Robert had given them the wheel, Gordon left with the other two and did not return till the early hours. He had brought back the spare wheel, saying Chris and Oupa did not need it after all. The following evening they checked out of the Morningstar Motel to re-enter South Africa, Gordon once again crossing on foot and Robert driving through the border post of Ramatlabama.

Gordon appeared out of the bush, walking with an AK47 rifle in his hand and six grenades in a small bag. They joked and laughed a lot as they drove through the night, but Robert was exhausted. He had been trying to teach Gordon to drive, so just before they reached Harrismith in the Orange Free State Robert suggested he take over. Within minutes the Peugeot was weaving all over the road. 'I told him to pull up, and that he would just have to talk to stop me falling asleep,' said Robert. 'He began fooling around, and at one point he took out a grenade and let it roll about on the dashboard to keep me awake.'

They arrived at Pietermaritzburg at dawn and Gordon directed Robert northward away from Durban, eventually hitting a long, deserted dirt road that led over low hills, past lonely meadows, mealie-fields and vast plantations, deep into a gum and wattle forest. Robert had no idea they were close to Gordon's home at York. They stopped outside the tiny St John's church and Gordon took the AK47 and the grenades into the churchyard, asking Robert to bring the spare wheel; as soon as Robert tried to lift it, he knew the tyre had been packed with explosives.

'It was heavy, and I was very angry,' said Robert. 'I felt I should have known. When I crossed over the border I called to a soldier, a border guard, to come and search the car. Of course, at the time I had no idea there was stuff in the tyre. The guard was sitting under the tree. I called to him, quite cocky and said, "Look, come and search the car, man." It was hot and he didn't get up. He just said, "Carry on."

'I was shocked and furious. I told him he should have told me. Gordon said, "I did it to test you. You musn't ask questions. Also, if you had known what was in the tyre you might have been sweating or nervous." I changed the subject, looking for an excuse to have an argument – so we argued about the tyre. I said he couldn't just cut up my tyre and Gordon said, "I'll give you enough money for two tyres."'

In the tiny, tidy graveyard, overshadowed by the sombre forest, they removed the granite slate headstone from a grave and began packing the explosive and hand-grenades into a hole that had already been prepared underneath. Gordon was tense; they were close to his home and if anyone passed they would certainly recognise him. Robert noticed a light shimmer of sweat on his friend's face. They were transferring one item at a time, so any passer-by would think they were doing repair work; when Robert appeared with the AK47 sticking out of his jacket, Gordon shouted at him. It was mid-morning but only one car sped past, churning up a corkscrew of red dust in its wake.

Robert dropped Gordon off in Pietermaritzburg. They shook hands and Gordon's last words were, 'Forget this, forget it ever happened. Put it out of your mind.'

Robert couldn't. He felt used and frustrated. Before reaching Durban, exhausted, he had to pull over by the side of the road and do some exercises in order to keep awake. He also felt depressed: 'It was such an anti-climax. I was still tense and excited and suddenly he left me. I really felt chewed up and spat out.'

However, Robert never disputed Gordon's authority. 'Even if I felt he was abusing it, I never questioned it,' said Robert. 'Sometimes he would call me up late to pick him up. Occasionally I suspected it was social, but I didn't question him.'

A couple of weeks later, before the New Year, Robert did the fourteen-hour drive to Botswana again, crossing the border at Ramatlabama, driving deep into the wilderness beyond Gaborone. There in the scraggly, thorny veld and gritty desert outside the shanty town of Molepolole he was given a three-day course on explosives and firearms.

Robert was given his instructions: he was to establish arms caches for guerrillas entering the country and help Gordon Webster to step up sabotage operations in Natal.

9

Ultra Secrecy, Maximum Discipline: these phrases had been drummed into Robert as part of his military code work. The importance of creating a cover for himself was stressed, especially if he were travelling – in the current, tense climate two 'non-white' men travelling together would create more suspicion than a man and a woman, who would be less likely to be detained at a road block. Robert was advised to find a female partner who was willing to travel with him without knowing too much about his activities.

Gordon knew all about the plans Robert and Claudette had made for the future, and he was keen that Robert should marry. Gordon thought it would be good for Robert, that it would provide stability, and it would be good for them and their activities. But Claudette was utterly disinterested in politics and would never have consented to accompany him on mysterious trips without asking questions. Claudette was not a suitable cover at all.

As it was, she would create a scene when he had to disappear for a rendezvous and Doris remembers how she'd sulk if she wasn't allowed to go with him: 'She was very childish in lots of ways and she didn't understand Robert had to go and meet some of his comrades, so she couldn't go with him. There were many times when she would say "I'm coming," and he would say, "You can't." She used to get upset and just get up and go to walk home all by herself, at night, just to make things difficult for him. Everyone would be running after her, saying, "No, Claudette, you can't go alone, it's late, come back . . ." '

Robert finally decided to approach a person well known in Wentworth as a social worker who worked tirelessly in youth community projects. It was an unusual choice, for she had a high profile locally as an organiser of welfare initiatives and Christian improvement projects. It might have been better to have someone more anonymous, like himself and Gordon, not known to the authorities as a political activist. But he had known her slightly for some time and his instinct was that she had all the qualities required.

Greta Apelgren was twenty-nine, seven years older than Robert; she was a distant cousin of Claudette and had once been 'courted' by Nazeem Cassiem. Greta was striking, with flashes of volatile beauty. Dainty and slim – even skinny – with a sharp, tapering, delicately boned face, she had soft, dark, curly hair, chestnut-brown eyes and a glowing cinnamon complexion. Her angular face, one moment severe and drawn, could be transformed the next with a mercuric quiver of vivacity. For although Greta appeared so diminutive and frail, she had an assertive energy and spartan resolve.

The Apelgrens were a large Catholic family. Greta had six sisters and five brothers, brought up in a two-roomed house in the Assegai district of Wentworth. She had been a nervous child and at one point had suffered from epilepsy. She attended the Coloured University of the Western Cape, and in the tumultuous year of 1976 had been drawn into the student protests. She was shattered when she witnessed the police bulldoze a squatter community of about a thousand people next to the university, demolishing their homes in front of women and children in the driving rain of mid-winter. At first she turned for solace to the Bible and the church, and when she returned to Wentworth as a child welfare worker she became heavily involved in church community projects among the deprived youth of the ghetto. The violence and the deprivation appalled her, and she felt impelled to assist: at one point she participated in fourteen voluntary organisations.

But the more she witnessed the harrowing conditions, the violence and misery, the more Greta despaired. She attended meetings, organised picnics and 'coffee bars', and was instrumental in setting up the youth community centre in the former military prison; yet she felt powerless to help mitigate the grisly conditions of Wentworth in any significant way. Greta also felt increasingly constrained by the conservatism of the church. The Security Police searched her home and questioned her three times. By the beginning of 1986 Greta was confounded; the path she had followed of devotion, service and good works seemed hopeless and she could not see the way ahead.

When Robert McBride came round to visit her on the Friday evening of the second week of January that year, she assumed he wished to discuss a social welfare problem. Greta had moved away from home and was living with her sister Jeanette and her brother Eric, whom Robert had once rescued in a scrape with gangsters. Robert said he wanted to have a word in private and so they went outside and sat on the verandah.

'He came straight to the point,' said Greta. 'He said "Do you want to work with me and others for the movement?" I was shocked at first because I had never known he was politically active. Initially I wanted to laugh, but he was terribly serious. He saw I was smiling, and he said, "You must not think I am bringing you into this of my own free will, I am following instructions".

'He said my task would be to accompany him as his girlfriend or wife, so that suspicion would not fall on him. He told me I needed a driver's licence and a passport, and I asked where we would be going. He said, "I can't say but we leave tonight." I tried to question him but he would not say more. I accepted the task. I felt my time had come to be a soldier, a fighter.'

It was seven o'clock. Robert told her to pack for the weekend and he would pick her up at ten. He had spent several days at his father's workshop fitting three concealed compartments into a blue Cortina *bakkie*, or open-backed van, which Gordon had brought him. Gordon had given Robert his instructions and told him where he was to rendezvous with his ANC contacts over the Botswana border.

At first they drove in virtual silence. Greta was still stunned. Only the previous evening near her home there had been a huge explosion at the Jacobs electricity substation, on the corner of Chamberlain Road, at the edge of Wentworth. As Greta had run down to see what was happening there was a second explosion and the crowd that had gathered began scattering in panic. She saw a policeman staggering out, his clothes in flames.

'I did not dream who was involved,' she said. 'Robert had never been a member of any established organisation, like the United Committee of Concern, and when he used to come and visit my sister Penny he would never talk about politics, only school and friends.

'After we had travelled two hours I asked what time we would arrive, as I knew I couldn't ask the destination. He said we'll be in Gaborone about noon tomorrow. I was horrified – I had no idea we were going so far!' Robert was tired, so after a while Greta took over the driving. 'On the journey we talked about ourselves, our families, everything non-political really. We only once talked briefly about the ANC. He told me I would meet some people and what I should and shouldn't say to them.'

They drove right through the night and arrived for their rendezvous at midday on a lonely dirt road outside Gaborone, where they met 'Chris', who gave them money to book into the Morningstar Motel. Robert checked in as 'Michael Jones', Greta as 'Denise'. Later Chris came to the Motel to collect Robert and, followed by Oupa in another car, they drove several miles out of town to a small village; they threaded their way through the maze of houses and eventually stopped in front of three large mud huts. There they loaded limpet mines, mini-limpet mines, hand-grenades and detonators. Robert was also given another series of demonstrations on explosives and detonators. Finally he returned to the Motel at four a.m.

They left the following afternoon. 'We delayed so that by the time we got to the border, the heat would be at its hottest and the guard at the border would be too lazy to come up and check us out,' said Greta. 'And that is exactly what happened. When we came through the border there were four cars. It was Sunday, four o'clock. We stopped the vehicle and walked to the guard to show our passports, but they didn't bother to search.

'When we got to the counter I put my arm around Rob, trying to look like we were really husband and wife. At that stage Rob and I were still strangers to each other. When we got back in the *bakkie* and drove away Robert screamed out excitedly, "Yahoo, we got away!"

'He said I was his good luck charm as previously they had searched him.'

They drove all night, stopping for a rest at Warden in the Orange Free State where they sat in the van, in the dark, and talked.

'We were flirting,' said Robert.

'We talked about previous relationships, that sort of thing,' said Greta. 'He said I was not his ideal person in appearance, and I said he was not mine either as he was tall, and then quite chubby. What attracted us was not looks. But as we had survived this first experience and taken a risk together, it brought us closer.'

They arrived in Wentworth shortly before dawn and Robert dropped Greta off at her house; she was due to start work at seven-thirty that morning.

That night Robert called for her again and said he would like her to meet someone; he didn't tell her who, just that he was answerable to him. It was Gordon, whom Greta thought was painfully thin and young. They drove to the seafront and parked facing the Indian Ocean. Robert and Gordon sat in the front. 'They were making private jokes and talking in codes,' said Greta. 'He didn't say who he was or what his role was – I think he just wanted to size me up. We only sat there for a few minutes, then they dropped me home and drove off somewhere.'

Robert called at Greta's house again on Tuesday night. This time he was alone and it was a social visit. They sat up for a long time and talked. The suspense of their clandestine trip and the relief of accomplishing a successful mission drew them together.

'I initiated a lot,' says Greta.

They became lovers.

10

Soon after New Year 1986 there was a sudden spate of sabotage attacks in the Durban area. This was an abrupt change, for in terms of organised subversion Natal had been the most dormant of the provinces and even among ANC members Natal had traditionally been the most conservative. Robert's friend Jimmy in Wentworth watched approvingly, but nervously: 'As places got "fiddled" or every time we heard a loud bang, I knew who it was.'

Although Natal whites were largely English-speaking, and the province had the reputation of being historically less racially oppressive, this was not at all the case. The province, and the British, had in fact created many of the prototypes for apartheid. After the Anglo-Zulu War of 1879 the British High Commissioner, Sir Garnet Wolseley, broke up the Zulu kingdom into thirteen dependencies under approved chiefs, with the Governor as Paramount Chief. Wolseley, 'The Modern Major-General' of Gilbert and Sullivan's *Pirates of Penzance*, also instituted a pass system which commenced placing black workers into barracks, as well as imposing a regime of registration, payment of fees and the wearing of badges. Although the Zulus had been defeated, the British authorities still feared a renaissance of Zulu nationalism, of which Bambatha's rebellion in 1906 against the Natal Poll Tax Act was a brief flicker.

During the 1920s, however, the cannier officials in the Native Affairs Department realised that by encouraging Zulu nationalism they could actually put a brake on organisations like trade unions and more progressive political movements which offered a far greater challenge to white power and its economic supremacy. Gradually the policy was reversed, nationalism was encouraged, and in 1948 the state formally recognised the Zulu king.

At the same time, the disposition of the ANC in Natal had

111

always been predominantly temperate; the first President of the ANC was Dr John Langalibalele Dube, a cautious Zulu clergyman and schoolmaster who wore staid three-piece suits and a large walrus moustache. Dr Dube, much influenced by the black American educationalist Booker T. Washington, warned, 'Unless there is a radical change soon, herein lies a fertile breeding ground for hot-headed agitators among us Natives, who might prove to be a far bigger menace to this country than is generally realised today. Let us all labour to forestall them.'

There had been no change for the better, though there had indeed been a radical turn: concepts, like urban segregation, pioneered in Durban at the turn of the century, had become rigid doctrines. Now those Dr Dube would have regarded as hotheads had begun to register their outrage by placing limpet mines on transformers in electricity substations dotted all over the region. This startling campaign took the authorities by surprise, causing considerable shock and consternation.

'This is what I had been waiting for,' said Robert. 'I felt no nerves, no butterflies. I was well prepared, and this kind of thing did not worry me. I was now able to do what I was good at. This was made for me. I was born for it.'

Gordon did not take to sabotage and clandestine subversion with the same ease, despite the fact that it was he who had undergone the full military training in exile. Gordon was not a natural soldier, and sometimes it alarmed Robert.

'He could be careless. It was a mad carelessness in operations and he took too many chances even though he was better trained,' claimed Robert. 'I sometimes argued with him about that. He was fatalistic. I think he felt he could die with himself now that he was in the struggle. He would take chances and hope for the best. I told him to be careful. I was paranoid about security. But if things went smoothly he became careless. Take the limpet mine – he would wrap it in paper and put it under his arm and come and see me and say, "Tonight we are doing an op."

'It was a complete contrast to his personality and manner, which was careful and formal. He always dressed smartly, unlike me, and was always taking his clothes to the laundry. He tended to be neat and precise, and then suddenly he could be quite reckless.

'Another time we were loading the car at Margaret's house in the black township. I'd made a false compartment and he was taking the stuff out, limpets in packages. He was talking to people in the street and greeting them! A policeman passed by and looked at me strangely, because I was a Coloured in a black township. Gordon greeted him too.'

All the same, it was Gordon who exercised great restraint on Robert; Robert also obeyed Gordon's instructions unquestioningly. On their first trip to Botswana they had been sitting on the verandah of a bar when a drunk began swearing offensively at them. Robert instinctively wanted to have a go at him, but Gordon restrained him, saying, 'We must never draw attention to ourselves.'

Victor Webster, his brother, remembers, 'A white woman was very rude to us, and I got angry and was ranting and raving, and Gordon whispered to me, "Don't show your anger. You are showing your weakness." Gordon turned to the white woman and apologised, wringing his hands to be submissive, in order not to reveal himself.'

The rapport between Robert and Gordon as accomplices grew greater and more compelling with each operation.

'It seemed to me as if we were destined to be comrades, we felt like brothers,' said Robert. 'On one operation we had aborted . . . we'd gone over the fence of a substation, and I saw a guard with a shotgun, which made me push myself back over the fence. We were retreating and I felt too tired to go on, so I told Gordon to leave me. We could hear the dogs. I was armed with a pistol and my idea was to stay behind and keep them off.

'Gordon just sat down on a stone and rested his chin on his fist. "Where do you think you are going?" he said, and grinned, "Come on, let's go!"

'It made me laugh and I realised he just wasn't going to leave. He started singing an ANC song – I was so tired, but it gave me strength. I sang too. We were really terrible singers, so we drew strength from each other by showing each other a weakness.

'I got a second wind and we set off again, evading the cops. It was an invigorating camaraderie.'

113

Robert's first mission, however, had been a failure. On January 5, 1986 Gordon came to his father's workshop at Factorama with Nazeem Cassiem; first they asked if he could fix them some food, so Robert went across to his mother's take-away and got them a bunny chow. Then they asked him to drive them to the Mayville substation, a short way out of Durban. Robert dropped them there at eight o'clock and Gordon told him to drive around and return in exactly one hour. Gordon was carrying a brown canvas bag with him. Robert did as he was instructed without asking a single question, and when he returned they were waiting for him. Gordon told him that they'd had to call off the attempt to mine the substation as there was a higher electric wire fence than they expected inside the concrete perimeter wall.

The following evening, January 6, Gordon called upon Robert again. This time he told him that Nazeem was reluctant to have a second go; Gordon said he needed Robert to fill in for this mission. As darkness fell they returned to the same spot, travelling by bus. In the bush near the sub-station Gordon had already secreted a ladder and the brown canvas bag containing three limpet mines. Stealthily they approached the outer concrete wall and, placing the ladder against it, climbed over. It was ten to ten. The no man's land between the concrete wall and the inner electric fence was brightly lit.

On his four previous reconnaissance trips, Gordon had never seen a watchman, but that night in a small, secure guardroom there were two security men, Sipho Ngcobo and Delson Zangwa. As Robert, followed by Gordon, clambered over the outer wall, they spotted them.

The security men could see clearly that one intruder was carrying a pistol and the other had a leather bag slung over his shoulder. The intruders were heading in the direction of the transformers. Ngcobo pressed the alarm and Zangwa released Leonard, the Alsatian guard dog. The Alsatian raced towards the two intruders, barking furiously. Hearing the alarm, Gordon scrambled back up the six-foot high concrete wall, which was topped with barbed wire. The dog launched itself at Robert, who seized it and hurled it as hard as he could against the electric wire. As he scrambled after Gordon the Alsatian retreated back to the guard house. The alarm rang shrilly behind them. It was ten o'clock. Robert and Gordon ran as hard as they could, through the bush, away from the road. They ran back to George Webster's house in Sydenham, several miles away. It was late and no one saw them enter; exhausted, Robert fell asleep in Gordon's room and left early the following morning so no one would know he had been there.

One of the arms caches that Robert and Gordon had established was in fact in the roof of Derrick McBride's workshop. The workshop was a convenient cover, for in the Factorama unit there was often work going on till late at night. No one would be suspicious of activity there, or late night transporting of goods. Derrick McBride knew better than to ask what the two young men were engaged in and his complicity enabled them to act more freely than would otherwise have been possible.

There was another benefit: Factorama was only a couple of hundred yards from the police training college, observing the aphorism of the eighteenth-century German physicist Georg Christoph Lichtenberg, 'You can't swat the fly that sits on the swatter.'

Also nearby, in the opposite direction from the police college, was Wentworth's main electricity substation at the junction where Austerville Drive turned into Chamberlain Road. The Jacobs substation was surrounded on three sides by high concrete posts, topped with coils of razor-wire, and a green diamond-mesh fence on the fourth. Gordon had spent several nights on the roof of Derrick McBride's workshop studying the layout. He established that it was definitely unguarded.

Then on the evening of January 9, three days after the débâcle at Mayville, Gordon came to the workshop where Robert was busy preparing the secret compartments in the blue Cortina. Gordon announced they were to sabotage the Jacobs substation that night. But when Robert informed him that if he came, he would not be able to complete the concealed compartments in time for the trip to Botswana the following night, Gordon decided to go ahead on his own. He collected two limpet mines from the cache hidden in the workshop roof.

The limpet mines had red markings which indicated they were

timed to detonate an hour after the safety pins were pulled. A little more than an hour later Robert heard a loud explosion and the lights in the workshop went out; he went outside and saw that the area had been plunged into darkness. Robert crossed the yard to collect his father from the take-away and together they drove home through a blacked-out Wentworth.

Four miles inland in the white suburb of Yellowwood Park, Vincent Zimmerman, a security manager for the Durban Corporation, was just parking his car in his garage when he heard what sounded like an explosion. He looked at his watch: it was exactly 9.15 p.m. Only three nights before, Zimmerman had been called out after a sabotage attempt at Mayville, so he got a radio out of the boot of his car and began to drive towards Wentworth in the direction of the blast. As he drove he called his headquarters, but could only ascertain that Wentworth had been completely deprived of power.

By the time he arrived ten minutes later at the Jacobs substation on the corner of Chamberlain Road, the area was cordoned off, with the city police and a fire engine standing by. Zimmerman went to investigate a hole that had been cut in the green fencing at the back and there recognised a policeman, Colonel Robert Welman. They had a brief discussion and Zimmerman asked an official from the electricity department to open the front gate. As it was so dark, Zimmerman collected a powerful torch from his car and they entered the substation, followed by Mervyn Dunn, a middle-aged official from the Durban electricity department and a young policeman, Detective Constable Roelof van der Merwe.

They examined the first transformer and by the light of Zimmerman's torch they could see a huge, jagged hole in the scorched metal. Zimmerman turned to Robert Welman and said, 'Colonel, it's a limpet.'

'*Is jy seker?*' asked Welman. 'Are you sure?'

'Yes,' replied Zimmerman. 'I've seen it before.'

While Colonel Welman was studying the second transformer, Zimmerman moved across to check the third one: he shone his torch over the grey metal and could see nothing, so he called out, '*Kolonel, daardie een lyk skoon*' (that one looks clean).

It was clear they needed more light. '*Gebruik my flits*,' said Zimmerman, handing his torch to Colonel Welman. He headed for the gate to collect another one.

Colonel Welman asked Mervyn Dunn, the electricity official, to examine the damage to ensure that it had not been caused by an electrical fault. Just as they exchanged positions and Welman moved closer to the undamaged transformer, there was a roar and a meteoric flash. A sheet of flame burst over them. Dunn was hurled against a nearby wall.

At the gate Zimmerman had passed a policeman with a patrol dog on a leash: Sergeant Dudley Booyens was just about to release the dog, which was trained to sniff out explosives, when he was thrown to the ground by the force of the blast. As Sergeant Booyens staggered back to his feet he saw three figures silhouetted against the flames, running towards him. They appeared to be burning. Then he realised they were screaming.

Colonel Welman staggered past Booyens, his clothes blazing. Sergeant Booyens lunged at him and fell with him to the ground, rolling him over and over in an attempt to extinguish the flames.

Mervyn Dunn raced through the fire with what remained of his singed clothing in flames. He tore out of the substation to the grass verge where he rolled over and over and over until he was no longer burning.

Zimmerman had been hurled to the ground by the explosion; as he turned and looked over his shoulder he too saw the three spectral figures emerging in flames. One of them veered towards him, flailing hopelessly at his blazing clothes as he ran round and round in circles. It was the worst thing Detective Constable van der Merwe could have done. The air fed the flames. Zimmerman yelled at him and grabbed the young man and threw him to the ground. There was nothing to hand to extinguish the fire that still burned the policeman's body so he desperately scraped together sand, throwing it into the flames until they flickered out.

Zimmerman rushed to his car and radioed for an ambulance. He checked his watch. It was nine-forty. All the clothes had been burnt off Detective Constable van der Merwe, leaving only charred underwear; he had burns covering almost his whole body. Mervyn Dunn was badly scorched and was in an acute state of shock, he kept repeating that his car keys were missing. Colonel Welman was wandering, dazed, up and down the road, with only his flapping trousers left.

By now a large crowd had gathered on the grassy embankment behind the smouldering substation. Greta Apelgren had run down from her home, and heard that a senior policeman, Colonel Welman, had been injured. 'I didn't dream who was involved,' she said. 'My initial reaction was anger, as I thought this had been done by guys from outside the province, and I felt resentful they should come and blast our township.

'People were chanting. I heard one guy shout, "The bastard's burning." It's a very deprived area, and most people were very angry, so if a white police officer is burning it was good. Nobody felt sorry for him.'

The ambulance arrived twenty minutes after the explosion and raced the three victims to Addington Hospital in Durban. When Gordon Webster heard the news on the radio the next morning and read about the injuries, he was appalled. Mervyn Dunn had thirty to forty per cent burns. Detective Sergeant Roelof van der Merwe up to ninety per cent burns. Colonel Robert Welman was critically ill.

'I was distressed and sad and worried,' said Gordon. He couldn't understand why the limpet mines had gone off at different times: both had the same distinctive red markings. He was so alarmed that he contacted his superiors outside the country and arranged for an immediate meeting in Botswana. There he met with Chris and Oupa and explained the sequence to them; they confirmed that limpets with a red lead plate should explode simultaneously, if the pins were removed at the same time. Gordon asked if he should be recalled, but they instructed him to return to South Africa and continue his task.

Once back in Durban, Gordon conducted his own experiments to ensure the same mistake did not occur again. Before subsequent operations, rather than rely on the colour coding, he measured the width of the devices to ensure they were identical.

On January 30, three weeks after the attack on the Jacobs substation, Colonel Welman died.

11

For some time Robert had been looking for an excuse to break up with Claudette; returning from his trip to Botswana with Greta, the opportunity presented itself. He discovered that during his absence she had been to a disco in Durban with his sister Bronwyn. Robert pretended to be angry and jealous, and with sly righteousness informed Claudette that their relationship was finished.

Within a month of recruiting Greta to the cause, he had also moved in with her. She lived at 20 Maria Crescent, on the other side of Austerville Drive from Assegai, with her brother Eric and sister Jeanette, both well known in Wentworth as diligent community workers. Neither Robert or Greta formally announced they were living together, it simply happened, and Robert gradually moved all his clothes over from Hardy Place. At first the Apelgrens were disapproving, but Greta got on well with the McBrides, particularly Doris, although at times she found their argumentative spats disconcerting.

Their first months together were happy as well as exhilarating, spiced by their clandestine intimacy. The only argument they had was when one of Greta's ex-boyfriends phoned; Robert was furious but he wasn't willing to admit that he was jealous. Instead, he used their underground security as an excuse to vent his anger. He threatened to walk out, shouting, 'This has jeopardised the movement – I'll report you!'

Greta, seven years older, felt that Robert was very emotionally dependent on her. 'We did not go out much, as he did not like socialising or smoking or drinking,' said Greta. 'He only liked drive-in movies. We would go sometimes, though not regularly. We only ever went to one dance together which was a formal dance, with collar and tie and formal ballroom-type dancing. He

119

was hopeless at it . . . I had to force him to dance. He only agreed to go because we were supporting a youth organisation.'

Robert, on the other hand, thought Greta was quite naïve politically. 'She was obsessed with the struggle in a quite religious way,' he said. 'She believed that because we were right, we would win. She's willing to sacrifice much, but innocent about politics and people – she always thinks the best of people. Greta is very straightforward. She couldn't be devious, and she is very transparent if she tries.

'She has a stubborn streak; she could listen to something and simply not hear it if she didn't like it. She was also fatalistic . . . if I must die, I must die. I picked her because she was so quiet and reliable. She was also dedicated and independent. That's why I liked her. I could trust her.'

Robert continued with his ordinary life, arousing no suspicion. He and the others banned from classes at Bechet College had taken legal action, and been granted the right to take their final exams. Robert studied and played rugby for the college team. As usual he helped his father at the workshop, where they now taught Gordon Webster how to weld. Most evenings Robert was back home at Maria Crescent by five o'clock. Gordon often came over to visit them.

'I don't know what Rob and Gordon used to talk about when they were on their own, as Gordon was always too shy to eat in front of me, so he would sit in the kitchen with Robert,' said Greta. 'They used to go out several times at night, or in the early hours of the morning, mainly when it was raining. I never used to know where they went, but if I read something the next day about a particular area being sabotaged I would suspect it was them. They undertook a lot of attacks together.'

Robert was quite clear about his role as a member of *Umkhonto we Sizwe* and the objective of these missions. 'The idea was to cause the maximum amount of disruption,' he said. 'The war was a propaganda war and the effects of the substation being blown out, all the lights in the area getting cut off, and the factories not being able to function for a while – it drew attention to the ANC, let people know we were operating, hitting back. It was good for the people's morale and it also helped to recruit people for the

ANC. We knew we could not win militarily, so the other possibility was to force negotiations by bringing the government to its knees.'

Following his anxiety concerning the Jacobs substation attack, Gordon Webster had also launched into a series of further lone missions: in the early hours of January 18 he blew up two transformers at Huntley's Hill in Westville; on the evening of February 19, Welcome Khumalo drove him to the Umlaas Road substation, which Gordon broke into alone, blasting one transformer out of action; on March 2 at the same time of evening, eight o'clock, Welcome Khumalo again drove Gordon, dropping him off near the Shongweni substation in the Camperdown district, where Gordon placed a limpet on one transformer and another in the ground near the fence, one carefully timed to explode late that night and the other to detonate in the early hours of the morning, causing considerable damage and power cuts.

.The day after he blew up the Shongweni substation Gordon informed Robert they needed to make another trip to Botswana; this time as cover he suggested they take Greta and her younger sister Jeanette, who was also a social worker. At first Greta was reluctant to involve her sister, as she too had dropped out of any political activity to concentrate on community work.

'But Robert and I went through a list of the females in the area and each one was unsuitable for one reason or another,' said Greta. 'So I said to Jeanette, "What are you doing this weekend?" She wasn't doing anything, so she casually came along, and after that first trip she became very involved.'

Gordon was introduced to Jeanette as 'Humphrey Piedmont'. They drove in two vehicles, the blue Cortina van and Jeanette Apelgren's bronze Mazda. 'On that trip I discovered quite a lot about Gordon, although he doesn't speak easily and his conversation did not exactly flow,' said Greta. 'But he would be quite happy to answer and he did not question me at all. I did most of the talking. I spoke of what it meant to be doing the kind of things we were doing, and he said he felt the only alternative left was the armed struggle and sabotage. He saw himself as a soldier on a military operation.

'He felt that unless we could weaken the state with constant

121

attacks, we would not win and that the one way of weakening the economy was to give them so many things to rebuild. He saw it as weakening the state, putting pressure on it until the end result would be negotiations.

'At that point I did not know he'd had proper training, but I could guess by the way he spoke. It was surprising that he was not saying whites should be killed. He did not seem angry, he was quite calm. Many people feel that the whites are the enemy, but Gordon was very clear that a particular race group was not the enemy. I thought of him as a soldier doing his duty.'

The trip was uneventful: while Greta and Jeanette sunbathed at the Oasis Motel, Gordon and Robert disappeared in the van to meet up with their ANC contacts. They collected further armaments and Robert received a further brief training session.

'I had been under the impression that these guys in exile were having a cushy time – but these guys in Special Ops seemed to be working twenty-four hours,' said Robert. 'They were vigilant all the time. They knew they were in constant danger. The whole atmosphere was one of war. It was highly charged.

'What surprised me was that they were quite light-hearted about all the danger – crossing the border, the shoot-outs and so on. One of them was laughing to himself when he was retreating during such a shoot-out, saying, "Now this guy's got good aim – that's the way to shoot!" That was the way they coped. It was good, they gave credit to the enemy, they accepted he had strength.

'On the other hand they could be very sad when they talked of comrades who had been shot or captured. It was surprising how they could change their mood, quite paradoxical. But they were under a lot of pressure.

'They also asked us a lot about South Africa, what was happening and how things were.'

On the Saturday night the four of them went to a disco and left Botswana late on the Sunday afternoon, through the Ramatlabama border post, driving back to Durban right through the night and arriving in Wentworth at dawn.

For the next three weeks Robert was busy studying for his final exams at Bechet. It was the first time he had ever had the privacy

122

to be able to study undisturbed and he also found the military discipline had made him far more rigorous about applying himself. Robert was studying eighteen hours a day. It was a period of domestic serenity with Greta.

Robert wrote his last exam on the afternoon of March 21, a sweltering, humid Durban day. Gordon came to meet him outside the college afterwards and they caught the bus back to Wentworth together. Gordon quietly told him that he had planned a job for that night, as March 21 was the commemoration of Sharpeville Day. Gordon had also decided on an audacious target: they were going to hit the Jacobs substation for the second time.

Robert went to Jeanette Apelgren's workplace to borrow her Mazda, and then he and Gordon drove to the township of Dambuza, near Pietermaritzburg, to collect Welcome Khumalo, and then on to Caluza nearby. Gordon had introduced Robert as 'Colin' and Welcome Khumalo as 'Themba'. At Caluza they collected the explosives from Gordon's room, which he called his 'armoury room': two AK47 rifles from on top of the wardrobe, fuses and detonators from inside it and four limpet mines from under his bed.

Back in Wentworth, Robert arranged for Greta and Jeanette to pick them up at the youth club at eight. Then the three men set out on foot from the Factorama workshop to the target in Chamberlain Road. It was a still, sultry night. Robert and Welcome hid in the tall grass, armed with an AK47 rifle and a Makarov pistol, while Gordon crept up to the wire mesh and began to cut through the wire with his insulated pliars. Suddenly an alarm shrilled. The three of them raced back to the workshop.

After the previous attack on the Jacobs station, resulting in the death of Colonel Welman, the Corporation had installed an alarm system. But there were no Post Office lines available to link it up to the headquarters, so although the alarm rang out piercingly through the deserted Jacobs industrial estate, no one was alerted. At the workshop Robert handed out some pills to his flustered companions; they were Lexotan, he explained, tranquillisers that would take about fifteen minutes to work.

'He said we must take these tablets in order to get the fright out of us,' said Welcome Khumalo. 'When we had taken them we cooled down.'

By now the alarm had stopped and there was no sign that it had alerted the police. Calmed, they strolled down the road to the youth centre where Greta and Jeanette were waiting in the Mazda. Gordon did not introduce Welcome, who told him that he wanted to go home. 'We'll go home,' said Gordon in Zulu, 'but we first have to finish what we have been doing.'

'We must go back,' agreed Robert, 'no matter how the alarm rings.'

Robert asked Greta and Jeanette if they would return later. Jeanette said she had visitors at home and would be missed, so Robert told Greta to take her home and be back at the same spot in half an hour.

When they returned to the substation, Gordon handed one limpet each to Robert and Welcome, keeping two for himself; all had red lead plates which indicated that they would detonate in an hour. 'Don't forget to pull out the pin,' Gordon whispered.

He squeezed through the hole he had already cut in the green wire mesh, and as he did so the alarm immediately started again. It shrieked maddeningly in the still, torpid night. Robert and Welcome slithered through the jagged opening and placed their limpets as Gordon had carefully instructed them. Hurriedly they scrambled out again and as they began to run off Gordon asked for their safety pins. It was then they discovered that Welcome Khumalo had forgotten to pull his and activate the detonator. The alarm was still screeching with rasping outrage, but Gordon ordered Welcome to go back in and pull the pin. Robert followed him back into the substation to make sure he was not too panicked to complete the task. This time Welcome dropped the safety pin into Gordon's palm and they sprinted back to the workshop.

'The three of them were waiting in the street when I returned about half an hour later,' said Greta. 'I was supposed to take Welcome Khumalo home, but before we got onto the freeway Gordon changed his mind and said he wanted to stay with his brother in Wentworth. When we got back into Wentworth, just before Quality Street meets Chamberlain Road, we noticed all the lights in the area were out, even the street lights. I said, "I wonder why the place is like this," and none of them uttered a word even though they knew the cause of it.

'As I came down Quality Street Gordon said, "No, turn here," and that is when we saw the substation was burning. There was smoke everywhere and a strong stench of burning rubber. I was the first to speak again. "What's happened to the substation?" I asked. No one answered me. That's when I realised they had something to do with this.

'It was not just the station, but the area round it that was burning. No one said anything for about ten minutes. It was scary that it had just happened.

'After that we drove Welcome home, taking the freeway to Pietermaritzburg. Welcome was a very quiet, small man and he sat in silence the whole trip. We got back about two a.m.

'Wentworth was still in darkness.'

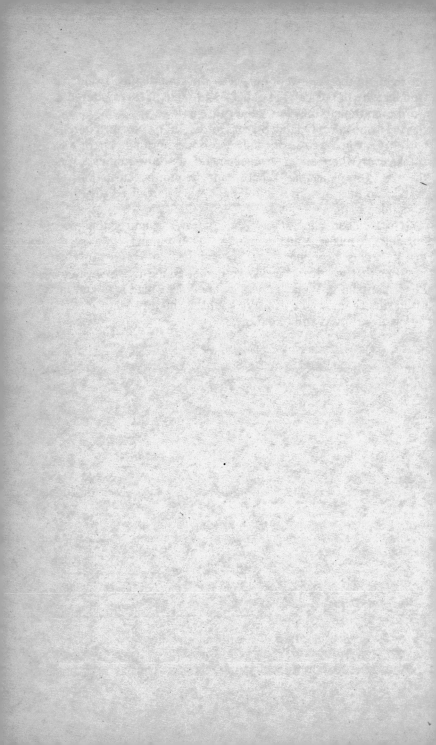

12

Unrest in the black townships continued to smoulder bitterly during 1986, frequently flaring into enraged uprisings and violent confrontations with the security forces. Youths attacked police patrols in their armoured Caspirs with petrol bombs, and stoned the white troopers. There were savage confrontations between the anti-apartheid 'comrades' and conservative black vigilantes, who were backed up and supported by the police as a surrogate force to crush the township revolts.

The fury also turned on those believed to be collaborators with the system. Black informers, puppet officials and 'sell-outs' were increasingly attacked and eliminated, often burnt alive by the 'necklace', in which a car tyre filled with petrol was placed round the victim's neck and ignited.

As the ANC gained more international recognition, the South African government stepped up its efforts to deprive *Umkhonto we Sizwe* of bases close to the Republic's border. Pressure on Botswana and Swaziland led to the ANC being expelled, while at the beginning of 1986 there was a coup within the tiny state of Lesotho to replace the pro-ANC government with a military junta more favourable to Pretoria. The South African government had also backed the rebels in neighbouring Mozambique, fomenting a pitiless civil war which so ravaged the country that its government was also forced to sign an accord with South Africa agreeing to expel the ANC. Even so, ANC attacks had increased four-fold since 1984, and during 1986 the South African Police estimated that between forty and fifty ANC guerrillas were managing to slip into the country every month.

The need for secrecy and security was paramount. Greta and Jeanette accompanied Robert and Gordon as 'cover', especially on night trips into the countryside around Durban to establish

127

arms caches. They all had code-names: Gordon Webster, apart from 'Humphrey Piedmont', was also known as 'Steve Mkhize', while Robert McBride's aliases included 'Colin', 'Douglas', 'Michael Jones' and 'Charles Franks'. Welcome Khumalo was known to some as 'Themba' and to others, more obviously, as 'Blackie'. Greta stuck with 'Denise', while Gordon picked a literary theme for his childhood companion Bheki Ngubane and bestowed the edifying pseudonym, 'Zola'. There were moments of farce. Robert told Jeanette she needed a code-name and between them Robert and Gordon came up with 'Jane', 'Helen' and 'Mary', but Jeanette was never quite sure what her alias was supposed to be; Robert proceeded to refer to her as 'Helen' while Gordon called her 'Mary'.

However, there was one immutable article of faith, the gospel of their outlaw survival. After any operation, whether it was the digging of an arms cache, or the blowing up of a strategic target, they were never to refer to that mission again.

This was MCW, the code. Only those involved in an operation should know about it, and afterwards it was to be forgotten. There was a simple edict prescribing this secrecy, an *Umkhonto* commandment: 'It's a dream that never happened.'

Two days after the second attack on the Jacobs substation Gordon instructed Robert to prepare for another trip to Botswana. They arranged to meet in Durban at Grey Street; Gordon had borrowed his brother George's roomy old black Mercedes Benz. First they took the venerably shabby Mercedes to Speedy Exhaust Services in Berea to have a towbar fitted, and then they proceeded to Rent-a-Trailer in Umgeni Road where they booked a caravan. Gordon explained that on this excursion they were going to smuggle in a particularly large consignment of explosives and armaments.

Robert asked Jeanette if she would come away for the Easter weekend, and on the cloudless, sticky afternoon of March 27 the four of them set out at five p.m. from the Factorama workshop in carnival mood. All travelled in the Mercedes, with the caravan hitched behind, driving through the night past Johannesburg, Ventersdorp, Lichtenburg and Mmbatho, arriving at the

Ramatlabama border post at three p.m. the following day. They checked into the Oasis Motel, but as there was not enough room for the caravan they had to park it at the Morningstar Motel.

'It was the same routine,' said Greta. 'We went out to meet the ANC chaps and then Rob and Gordon would disappear with them while Jeanette and I would just stay at the Motel and watch TV, swim and wait for them.'

It was not, however, the same routine at all. When Gordon and Robert were driven away by Chris and Oupa in a dusty black Ford Granada, Robert had to lie on the floor so that he would not know where they were going, and Chris took a lot of detours. The ANC cadres in Botswana had to take extraordinary precautions; they were now prohibited persons in Botswana and in constant danger. Eventually the Granada pulled up outside a spacious modern bungalow. Robert had been summoned to meet the commander of Special Operations.

Inside, he was led through a well-furnished kitchen and lounge into the dining room. Waiting for him were two men. One was an African with a stubby beard and a generous Afro hairstyle, who was introduced as 'Victor'. The other was a tall, slender, softly-spoken young Indian, whom Robert guessed to be about thirty years old, with a trim black beard and lustrous black hair that reached just below his ears. This was 'Rachid', their commander in *Umkhonto's* Special Operations.

Robert was given ANC magazines and literature to read while the others went out of the room to confer with Gordon. Then Robert was summoned into the lounge; the others were dismissed and for the following hour Rachid briefed him on his new duties. He explained codes and telephone cyphers, as well as telling him that he would be expected to continue smuggling 'equipment' into South Africa, recruiting people for the movement and carrying out sabotage missions. Rachid informed Robert that he might be required to operate all over the country but, most importantly, he said that he and Gordon were no longer to work together: Robert was to form his own cell and work independently.

Rachid called in Gordon to repeat this order. For another hour Robert was given more training, including initiation into the art of creating a secure Dead Letter Box. Rachid then returned with them to the Motel where after being introduced to 'Helen' and 'Denise' he gave them all a half-hour talk on the general political situation in South Africa.

The following afternoon, Robert and Gordon drove the Mercedes to a deserted rendezvous outside Gaborone, where they found two cars, with Rachid, Victor, Chris and Oupa. They transferred three heavy suitcases of 'equipment' into the Mercedes and Rachid told Robert that, in one of the cases, there was enough money for him to buy a car for future ANC operations.

Before they departed, Rachid gave Robert one final directive: it concerned discipline and the failure to obey instructions. If Robert should disobey a command, warned Rachid, he could have him eliminated with a stroke of the pen.

Returning to the Morningstar Motel, Robert and Gordon transferred the arms and explosives into the caravan, packing them carefully into the rear bunks under the mattresses. Then, hitching up the caravan, they returned to the Oasis Motel to pick up the bored Apelgren girls and headed for the border, arriving just as dusk was falling. They had deliberately timed their arrival, so that any search would be conducted in bad light and the officials would be more likely to be lax when the border was about to be closed for the night.

By now, Robert was getting to know the border officials; there was one in particular who was officious and painstakingly bureaucratic. However, they were in luck.

'Once one of the officials at the border had run out of petrol, and I gave him a whole drum, twenty litres,' said Robert. 'After that, whenever we came through the border and he was on duty, he'd call me to the front, even from right at the back of the queue, make some small talk, stamp my passport and wave me through.'

That Easter Monday night he was on duty. 'He was searching all the cars,' said Robert. 'I asked him if he wanted to search, but he smiled and said, "No – go on . . ."'

In the first week of April, Gordon, Robert, Greta and Jeanette had a cheerful dinner at the Roma Revolving Restaurant in

Durban. Everyone was in an expansive mood and Gordon was uncommonly relaxed and forthcoming. He even drank some wine, which was odd as he sternly frowned upon smoking and drinking.

Gordon told Greta and Jeanette that they would not be seeing him again; he was, henceforth, under instruction to 'work' separately. They were to operate as an autonomous cell, said Gordon: from now on, Robert was their commander.

To complete his unit, Robert already had his eye on a small group of young men in Wentworth whom he felt were ripe for recruitment. He had been introduced to this circle in December the previous year by Nazeem Cassiem, his team-mate from the Bechet College rugby team. They used to hang out in the tin shack at the back of Alan Pearce's granny's house in Ogle Road, and it was with some of this circle that Robert had attempted the burning down of Fairvale High School.

It was an easy-going, lackadaisical little circle; most of them were unemployed, but underneath their veneer of disdainful cool they were disenchanted, resentful and angry. There was Alan Pearce, Antonio du Preez, Matthew Lecordier, Marsden Sharpely, and an affiliated cast of irregular devotees like 'Whitey' and Virgil. Most evenings they'd meet at Alan Pearce's granny's, either in the shack or, if it was too hot, in her yard. They'd smoke *dagga* (Marijuana), listen to music, usually reggae, maybe dance a bit, but mostly just hang out and talk.

Alan Pearce was an unemployed plasterer. He had come to stay with his grandmother in order to get away from the life of a gangster. He had been a member of the Woodstock Vultures, and had been both shot and stabbed. Alan had short, curly reddish hair and was baroquely tattooed over his arms, legs, back and chest; stocky, with a thick neck and square face, he was built like a heavyweight boxer. Antonio du Preez, like all the others, could see no future in Wentworth; he felt aimless, troubled, and despite his jaunty, charming, slightly raffish manner he was prone to periods of great depression. Antonio was tall and slim, good-looking, with high cheek-bones and a freckled, sallow complexion. When he smiled, it lit up his open face and ingenious,

131

puppy eyes. Antonio was the artistic member of the Ogle Road cabal – he liked to draw, listened to jazz, and played the guitar and saxophone.

Matthew Lecordier was the enigma. His family were respectable middle-class Catholics who lived in a compact, pristine white-stucco imitation Spanish villa on Elm Street next to the Kingdom Hall of Jehovah's Witnesses. But Matthew was a feckless layabout who could never hold on to a job for more than a few months, a vaguely morose and dissatisfied charmer and ladies' man. He was sleek and handsome, always nattily dressed, although perpetually sponging for money. Matthew had an illegitimate daughter, though he was seldom able to visit her as his girlfriend's family had banished him from their house. He was quick-witted and crafty. He also coveted the good life and resented the fact that he was impeded from its attainment by his colour. He traded on his good looks and affable manner, but his indulgent ambitions were undermined by a chronic indolence.

For a while Matthew had been taught by Doris McBride, but he'd left school at fourteen and drifted from job to job. For six months he'd worked at the Wentworth Place of Safety, a home for orphans and abused children and he had been deeply dismayed to discover the wretched underworld in which these minors suffered. 'It hurt me to hear from a seven-year-old boy that his daddy was having intercourse right in front of the kids like they weren't there,' said Matthew. 'And their mummy or daddy coming home with different men or women every night, drunk. And even daddy's friends coming home and molesting them. It is very hard to bear this, it hurt me a lot. I got to thinking, it is because they cannot get things together financially, they are desperate and poor, they cannot get work, or the wages are too low, the way the situation is in this country.'

Robert concluded that this group was primed for the right approach. Cagily, he drew them out about their political feelings and expectations, steering the conversation carefully towards references to the armed struggle. It was one thing for a bunch of disgruntled unemployed youths to burn down a school; it was another proposition to blow up strategic installations.

Robert pressed harder. He began to ask them hypothetical

questions, 'What would you do in this situation? What would you do if you had guns?'

Finally he felt they were ready for a direct overture. One afternoon Robert was riding down Ogle Road and he saw Matthew Lecordier and Alan Pearce sitting on the wall. He stopped and spoke to them. It was a dangerous moment. 'I am being serious,' he told them. 'This is for real.' They asked for a week to think about it. When Robert put the proposition to Antonio du Preez, at first he was shocked. Then he said, 'Count me in.'

A couple of weeks later Matthew, Alan and Antonio came to see Robert at the Take-Away. At first Robert was distant. 'What has taken you so long?' he asked Matthew Lecordier.

Matthew told him that he had seen a picture in one of the papers of a white policeman hitting a black protester with the butt of his rifle, and it was the hatred contorting the face of the policeman that was his turning point.

It was also a turning point for Robert's new *Umkhonto* unit; as he recruited more members, the training became progressively scantier. Security was beginning to grow lax. Nazeem Cassiem boasted to his friend Gaster Sharpely that he was in the ANC and to Robert's horror Gaster Sharpely wandered into the workshop one day to enquire about joining up. Robert's friend Jimmy was so dismayed at the casualness with which Robert was drawing people into his cell that he asked him not to tell him what was going on any more. Jimmy's nerves were worse than ever, he was living on tranquillisers and was terrified the Security Police would come for him too. He begged Robert to give him back all his poetry and records. 'You're like an old man,' Robert laughed. 'Everything's cool.'

Nevertheless, it was soon apparent that Matthew Lecordier had an ulterior motive in joining up; ever dreaming of effortless affluence, he wished to get hold of guns in order to be able to carry out a bank raid.

Shortly after their induction into his unit, the new commander gave Matthew, Alan and Antonio a brief training session in the dark on the Tara Road sports field. He explained how to use a

133

hand-grenade and at the end of the session handed over two grenades which Alan Pearce took home with him to store in his granny's shed. Matthew, accompanying Robert back to the workshop, asked him for a loan. Robert told him that a loan would be possible, but at a later date. At the workshop he handed Matthew four Lexotan tablets, telling him they were to be taken quarter of an hour before an operation to calm the nerves.

Discussing potential targets, Robert had suggested the Caspir, a squat armoured patrol vehicle, which passed down Ogle Road at ten-thirty every night. Instead, Matthew and Antonio decided to attack the home of Mr Klein, a local headmaster, whom they regarded as an apartheid stooge. Mr Klein also lived in Ogle Road, in a smart glass-fronted bungalow. He was a police reservist, a member of the collaborationist Labour Party, and notorious for giving wild parties for the police at his school. ('Medium wild', Mr Klein preferred to say.) A constable would be posted at the door, and naked women could be seen running about inside. Matthew and Antonio felt that Klein represented the corruption of the Coloured establishment.

Their attack was a fiasco. They picked a moonless night; Matthew told Alan Pearce he couldn't come along as there were only two grenades. At midnight Matthew and Antonio hid the grenades in a broken air vent at the Ogle Road flats opposite Klein's house, and went and sat in the middle of the Ogle Road Sports ground in the pitch dark for the next two hours, while Matthew smoked some *dagga* and they discussed where they were going to throw the grenades and how they were going to make their get-away. The idea was not to injure Klein, but to 'scare the wits out of him'.

At one point Antonio said, 'Listen, we are just going to scare Mr Klein. We just throw the grenades outside like we planned.' Matthew didn't answer as he was busy cleaning his pipe, so after a while Antonio said, 'Listen, I'm speaking to you.'

Matthew finished with his pipe and replied, 'Well, okay, we will.'

At two a.m. they took the Lexotan tablets. Matthew pulled on a balaclava and Antonio wrapped a scarf round his face, then they collected the hand-grenades from the air vent and stood facing

Klein's glass-fronted bungalow. Antonio suddenly became frightened. Matthew pulled the pin out of his grenade, keeping his finger on the trigger to prevent it from detonating, but Antonio couldn't pull his pin out. He was terrified. 'I asked him what was wrong and he said it was jammed,' said Matthew. 'I told Antonio to hold his grenade with both hands, and I pulled the pin out.'

Then they walked across Ogle Road, and at the count of three they hurled their grenades and ran. Behind them as they slithered down the embankment and ran helter-skelter back towards the sports ground they heard the explosions and shattering of glass.

The attack was a mess. Antonio had thrown his grenade onto the verandah, to explode outside the house. But Matthew had lobbed his right through the Kleins' bedroom window. The Kleins were in bed, watching TV, as their room seemed to explode, glass falling all about them. Mrs Klein screamed, 'They're attacking us.' Both had to be taken to Addington Hospital, suffering shock and peppered with shrapnel; in addition, Mrs Klein had a broken leg. Matthew and Antonio sat in the dark for half-and-hour and watched the police and ambulances race past.

It was a bungled, dilettante effort. As commander, Robert McBride should have seen the signs; but by now he had a more pressing, personal torment than these cavalier novices.

13

On the evening of Sunday April 27, 1986, Sergeant Richard
Nxumalo had been driving with Detective Constable Dorasamy
along a deserted dirt road in the vicinity of Pietermaritzburg when
they saw a car parked on the other side, facing the wrong
direction. Sergeant Nxumalo ordered Dorasamy to pull
alongside the Ford Granada. Gordon Webster and Bheki
Ngubane (Zola) had the boot up and were preparing explosives
for an attack on the Mooi River electricity substation. Seeing the
police, Gordon shut the boot and told them he didn't have the
key. Whilst the Indian Detective Constable radioed to check if the
Ford Granada was a stolen car, his Zulu colleague Nxumalo
searched it by the light of the police vehicle headlamps; on the
ground by the boot, he discovered a brown leather bag containing
several clips of ammunition. Sergeant Nxumalo drew his revolver
and ordered his two suspects to lie on the ground, face down-
ward. While Detective Constable Dorasamay radioed for help,
Gordon and Bheki decided to make a run for it and bolted in
opposite directions. As Gordon raced towards a barbed wire
fence his spectacles fell off and he stumbled; behind him Sergeant Nxumalo shouted, '*Yima, yima*' (Stop, stop), and then fired
several shots. Gordon continued running, crashed into the fence,
tumbled over it and collapsed on the other side, punctured by
three bullets. He heard several more shots; Bheki Ngubane had
almost got across Sinathing Road when he pitched into the gravel
verge, dead.

14

In the following day's newspapers there were front page reports that one 'terrorist' had been killed and another wounded and captured near Pietermaritzburg. This counter-insurgency success was also commended in Parliament.

The police were convinced they had bagged an important adversary; great play was made of their catch on the Monday evening TV news, which announced that the captured man was in critical condition and was expected to die. The captive was in the intensive care unit at Edendale Hospital under heavy police guard, undergoing emergency surgery. Television viewers were even treated to a set of X-ray photographs which showed that apart from being shot in the right hand, the unnamed black man had one bullet lodged in his kidney, near the spine, while another was embedded close to the right lung.

Robert worried that it could be Gordon, for he was fairly sure they were the only unit operating in Natal: besides, the catalogue of explosives discovered in the boot of the Ford Granada seemed to tally with what he and Gordon had smuggled over from Botswana. But when Greta read out a newspaper account of the incident and tried to discuss it, Robert reacted moodily. 'He became very disturbed,' said Greta. 'He left that evening and did not come home for two days. When he came back, he just said, "Those were our guys." He didn't tell me who they were and he just said they were people he knew. He was very irritable after that and very quiet.'

A massive search was being conducted in the Edendale and Pietermaritzburg areas; the police had little to go on, however, apart from the fact that their enfeebled prisoner had given a name, 'Steven Mhkize'.

'I had suspected, but when I finally found out . . . for the first three hours I was devastated,' said Robert. 'I knew I had to do something.'

Then Welcome Khumalo, 'Themba' in Gordon's unit, informed Robert that he and 'Steven' had a pact: if one was taken, the other was to try and kill the captured comrade before he could be made to talk.

Themba was in an agitated state. On hearing his commander had been seized, he had panicked and hidden one bundle of 'equipment' by a railway line; another he deposited in a mealie field, without even burying it, and this haul had already been discovered. Some Zulu boys, after accidentally kicking their soccer ball into the mealie field, stumbled across the barely concealed armaments and one of the children had a finger blown off.

Welcome Khumalo didn't know what to do with all the other 'material' that he and Gordon Webster had stored around the Pietermaritzburg district. Robert took charge; with Khumalo he drove to Caluza to collect the armaments from Gordon's room and from another 'armoury' near Pietermaritzburg. The police were everywhere but they managed to transfer the armaments and explosives to the Factorama workshop.

Khumalo was in a strange, volatile mood. He had already told Margaret Webster and one of her brothers of the death pact and his obligation to carry it out. Now Khumalo informed Robert that he intended to try and enter the hospital to execute Gordon before he could be tortured. This, he said, had been their agreement. If Gordon was forced to talk, he pointed out, the consequence would be that all of them would be compromised, and the operation in Natal confounded. He would attempt to kill Gordon and then escape to Swaziland.

'When I started asking Khumalo about the hospital, he said he wanted to go and kill him,' said Robert. 'That seemed absolutely ridiculous – it was just as dangerous to go and shoot him in the hospital as it was to try and take him out of the hospital. Also, Gordon was close to me, my closest friend. There was this strong bond between us and I determined that I would organise an escape.

'I telephoned Botswana, but there was no reply. I decided to use my own initiative. In fact my orders were that if Gordon were caught I should run to Botswana. The idea of exile seemed terrible. It did not occur to me that we might fail.'

The first step was to carry out a reconnaissance of Edendale Hospital. For four days Robert went every day, driving the fifty miles in the new black Ford van he had bought with the money Rachid had given him on his last trip to Botswana. During the first visit on Wednesday morning he was accompanied by George Webster, who knew the area and was able to show Robert the layout of the hospital grounds. Robert waited in the car while George entered to try and find out where Gordon was being treated. After a quarter of an hour George returned and told him Gordon was being held in the intensive care unit on the second floor; George had also been able to ascertain that his brother was being guarded by three policemen.

Robert went the next day by himself. At the entrance he casually picked out an X-ray file from a trolley, and tucked it under his arm. He made his way up to the second floor, and walked past the intensive care unit. Outside there were three policemen on duty, one white and two black. Robert strolled to the end of the corridor and wandered back past the policeman a second time: two of them were armed with pistols, he noted, while the white policeman carried a sub-machine gun.

An escape plan was feasible, he felt, but he knew that he needed experienced help and advice. Normally he would have sought this from Gordon; instead, Robert resolved to turn to the one other person he believed he would be able to count on.

Derrick McBride had already heard about the shoot-out and capture of 'Steve Mkhize' because Robert had read him an account from a newspaper article on Tuesday morning while they had been at the take-away. Although Robert had mentioned he thought he might know this Mkhize, he had not said it was Gordon. Derrick had not seen his son for the next two days.

Robert made his appeal to Derrick late on Thursday night at home. 'Daddy, I want to talk to you, close the door,' he said. 'It's private.'

For the first time Derrick McBride learnt that his son was in

141

the ANC and a member of *Umkhonto we Sizwe*. It came as a shock. Robert explained the situation. Then for twenty minutes they had a heated and highly emotional argument.

'You must be crazy,' Derrick told him.

'It's a simple operation,' countered Robert. The idea was to take the police by surprise, disarm them and lock them up in a nearby room. 'It's a piece of cake,' Robert assured him. He explained that Gordon Webster was his only real friend, his 'bosom pal' and there were other people who had a plan to kill Webster in order to silence him.

Robert tried every argument he could, explaining that if Gordon talked, he would also be implicated. 'We're already involved,' he claimed, 'because if he talks we'll be done.'

'"You've got a passport," said Derrick, "get out of the country and that'll save you all these problems,"' said Derrick. 'I couldn't do that,' replied Robert. 'I couldn't desert a friend.'

Robert was finally standing up to his father; he challenged him to practise what he preached. Derrick McBride had his own political gospel held in front of him as a mirror.

'He said, "You have been talking for the last forty years and you have achieved nothing", and he hurled quotation after quotation of everything I had said to him since he was a growing child,' said Derrick. 'He hurled it at me.'

It was an exhausting, harrowing altercation. 'It is a situation that only a father and son can understand,' said Derrick. 'Where you have a son begging you for help and putting the position to you that you have never turned anyone away, no matter what help they have come for, for over forty years, and I am your son and I am in this predicament.'

Robert explained that he did not need his father for the operation itself; but he did, urgently, need his experience and savvy to help with reconnaissance, advice and planning. Eventually Derrick agreed to co-operate. It was a highly-charged emotional acceptance.

'He said he knew that he could depend on me,' said Derrick. 'He said, "You know Daddy, I trust you, I've always trusted you."'

'He accepted the challenge,' said Robert. 'He just wanted to

142

find another way. He was looking for a better way. He was cautioning me like a father.'

Derrick McBride accompanied Robert twice to Edendale Hospital, and afterwards he remarked sardonically, 'It's easy.'

Edendale Hospital is a chunky, unattractive eight-storey red-brick building plumped in a dip of the low, bare hills several miles south-west of Pietermaritzburg. At a distance, it is only visible from a rise, otherwise it is tucked away and approached from the road by a long, pitted gravel track beside a ten-foot concrete wall topped with barbed wire. Outside the entrance is a small market where, under rickety canvas shades, fruit sellers lay out a florid smorgasbord of bananas, mangoes, tangerines, grenadillas, guavas and pawpaws.

The hospital, as pledged by apartheid, is for blacks. It is huge, with one thousand six hundred beds. In the grounds, there are workshops with tall chimneys, barrack-like outhouses, a large nurses' home and behind the hospital, a maze of interconnecting concrete walkways with corrugated iron sides and asbestos roofs. Inside, it is crowded and gloomy. During the day in the bare, whitewashed reception area, a large number of Africans wait patiently on wooden benches. The long, windowless, dimly-lit corridors are confusingly uniform, with two-tone walls of brown and white, and brown-flecked linoleum floors; signs are in English and Zulu. Black nurses rustle by in starched white uniforms. White doctors in white coats hurry past with files under-arm. Everywhere there are clusters of Africans, many women with babies on their backs and others with tribal markings on their faces.

Round the sides of the hospital runs a narrow, sandy, roughly-pitted track with clumps of grass in the middle, and right at the back it follows bumpily alongside a tall wire fence. On the other side of this coarse trail is a tangled field of shoulder-high sun-yellowed grass which stretches as far as the small tin-shack location two hundred yards away. Clustered on the side of the nearby hill is another haggard, bleached African shantytown, but the dirt road itself is sheltered and generally unused. At night it is deserted; there is 'no light and no eyes'.

It was from this secluded point that Robert decided to launch his rescue operation.

Abruptly, however, he was forced to change his plans.

Contact had been made with some personnel who worked in the hospital, and one of them was a black doctor and veteran political activist. Late on Friday night the doctor got word to Robert that Gordon was due to be moved from the hospital on Monday. This altered the strategy Robert and Derrick had formulated. Robert was forced to bring forward the date of the operation to Sunday night.

He had already instructed Nazeem Cassiem, Welcome Khumalo, Antonio du Preez and Matthew Lecordier to be on standby. Nazeem had seemed reluctant, but at least he and Welcome Khumalo were trained in firearms. The problem was that both Antonio du Preez and Matthew Lecordier had so far had instruction only in grenades.

Antonio had also expressed reservations. 'It's a piece of cake,' Robert assured him.

On Saturday night Robert summoned them both to 29a Hardy Place for a half-hour demonstration on how to operate an AK47. There was no one at home; even so, Robert closed the door to his room and turned the music up loud. He showed them how to load, unload and cock the rifle, as well as how to manage the folding stock and use the sights when aiming. He made them practise loading and aiming.

Matthew was adept and mastered it quickly, but Antonio was nervous.

'If it's a piece of cake, then why do we need guns?' asked Antonio.

'Well, basically,' replied Robert, 'it's a threat.'

He directed them to report to the workshop the following afternoon, Sunday, at two o'clock and to wear dark clothing.

Derrick McBride did not share Robert's buoyant assurance about the hastily planned enterprise. 'What you are going to do now,' he warned his son, 'you must look out – you'll end up on Death Row.'

144

Doris and Derrick McBride on their wedding day.

Robert – 'Pepe' – on the left, with his sister, Bronwyn, and his cousin, in a freak snowfall.

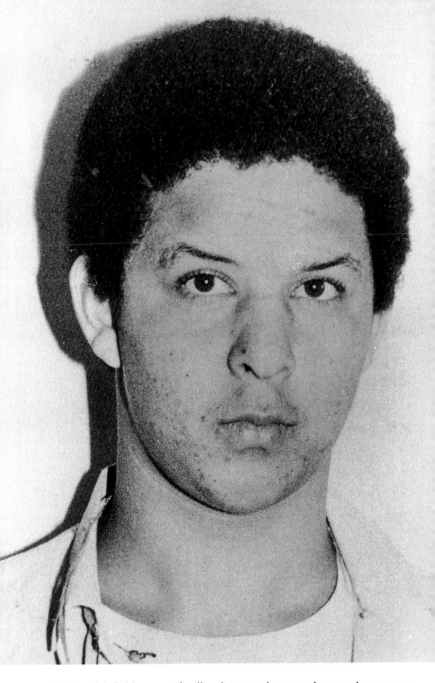

Robert McBride: most family photographs were destroyed to prevent
police identification. © *Daily News*

Paula McBride. © Ellen Elmendorp

Gordon Webster.

Wentworth storm drains: meeting place and playground. © *Daily News*

Magoo's Bar (right) and the Why Not Bar after the bombing. ©
Daily News

Robert McBride picked out on an identity parade.

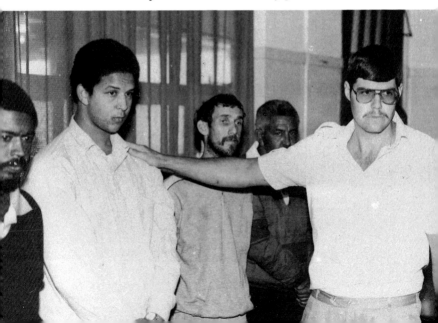

Doris McBride, in London campaigning for Robert. © *I.D.A.P.*

58a Hardy Place: the McBride family home. © *Daily News*

Greta Apelgren today.

Matthew Lecordier today.

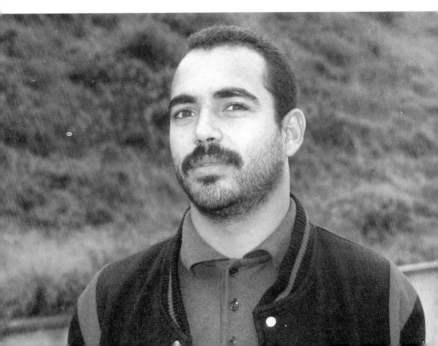

15

Greta Apelgren had no idea what was going on when Robert phoned her at two-thirty p.m. on Sunday May 4, and asked her to come down to the workshop. She had just finished cooking a lunch of curried mince, rice, green beans and sweet pumpkin, so she wrapped the food up and drove down to the Factorama workshop in her sister's Mazda.

'I thought it was just going to be a normal Sunday, where I would go down and keep him company and it would only be the two of us,' said Greta. 'When I got to the workshop there were Antonio and Matthew. It was the first time I'd seen them with Rob, and I didn't know they were his friends, but I knew them to be guys in the district who had never been to political meetings or involved in any political activities.

'After a while Themba also arrived. He seemed excitable, walking in and out with a smile on his face. I had met him once before from the Jacobs substation, and at that time I only knew him as Blackie. Robert was also walking in and out. He seemed distant and tense. When I arrived he didn't even talk to me, so eventually I started eating on my own as nobody else wanted to eat or talk. They were not even talking to each other.'

Antonio du Preez had also noticed on his arrival that Robert seemed agitated and angry. He asked Antonio the time and simply said they were waiting for someone, although to Matthew Lecordier he mentioned that it was Nazeem Cassiem who was delaying proceedings. Robert tried calling Nazeem's home, but there was no answer. Robert was concerned about Nazeem. He remembered he'd had to substitute for him back in January when Nazeem had been nervous about returning to the Mayville substation a second time.

Robert waited till three-thirty, telephoned Nazeem's home

once more, and then, without a word to anyone, strode across the Factorama courtyard to the family take-away shop. Robert had not wanted to involve his father in the actual operation in case something should go wrong. He didn't want to feel responsible for Derrick's safety or to leave the McBride family without its two men. But now that Nazeem Cassiem had let them down, a crucial breach in the plan had to be bridged. Robert explained the situation to Derrick.

'OK, I'm in,' said Derrick.

Robert called them all into the cramped workshop office. It had been arranged as if for a meeting, with five chairs drawn up facing a large blue chart pinned to the wall. On the chart Robert had drawn a sketch of Edendale Hospital and the surrounding area and roads. Robert shut the office door and explained to them that an important comrade, Steven Mkhize, had been wounded and was being held at Edendale Hospital. Their mission that night, he announced, was to rescue him.

The plan was simple: Greta Apelgren and Welcome Khumalo (Themba), were to wait at a bridge near the Edendale Hospital in Jeanette Apelgren's Mazda 323, while the rest of them proceeded to the hospital in a light blue Ford Cortina. They would approach by the unlit back road, from where Robert and Derrick McBride would enter through a hole in the wire fence, covered by Antonio du Preez and Matthew Lecordier. Robert would be wearing a doctor's white coat, and Derrick would have on a priest's dog collar and carry a Bible. After rescuing Steven Mkhize they would return to the bridge and transfer him from the open-backed Cortina van to the Mazda.

'When Robert told me what he expected me to do, at first I was shocked and I wanted to laugh,' said Greta. 'I did not know who Steve was at that point, but I knew from experience that Rob would only give you a very small amount of information. The idea was that after he was transferred to my car, we were to travel together and pretend we were lovers. I was to drive slowly back to Durban, no rushing, just acting like two normal people out for a ride. I couldn't believe he wanted me to do that, it all sounded so clandestine and dramatic.'

A change of clothing had been brought for Gordon for his

journey back to Durban with Greta. While Themba detonated a hand-grenade near the police station to draw away the police, the others would bury their firearms in a hole near the bridge.

'Then we would wipe the van down, removing fingerprints, and dump it in 'Maritzburg, all of us separating and taking public transport back to Durban,' said Robert. 'We had been told Gordon could stand. A lot depended on that. But the urgency removed all doubts.'

On the sketch he had drawn, Robert showed them the approach they would use and the layout of the hospital grounds, as well as pin-pointing the exact location where Steven Mkhize was being held. He showed each of them on the map where their position would be, precisely what he expected of them, and how long he expected each phase of the operation to take. When he had outlined his plan, Robert asked if there were any questions.

'I was nervous after Robert had finished explaining,' said Matthew Lecordier. 'I asked, "What if you people do not come out of the hospital, what do we do?" I said I was thinking of coming in to get you, or leaving, but that is why I am asking, so I know what to do. Robert said, "It is up to you to decide."'

They ran through the plan again a couple of times to make sure everyone knew their role perfectly, then Robert wished them all luck and led the way out of the workshop. He picked up a red sports bag containing four AK47 rifles, a Makarov pistol and two grenades. The meeting had taken two hours; it was five-thirty. Matthew Lecordier remembers Derrick McBride offering him a couple of pills to calm himself and he gratefully accepted them.

Outside, Derrick put on his dog collar. He was smartly dressed in slacks and a checkered sports jacket, and cut a handsome and convincing figure as a priest. The others, apart from Greta, wore dark clothing; Robert had running shoes, jeans and a black sweater. Greta wore a bright canary yellow jersey and a long, flamboyant yellow scarf wound round her head in oriental fashion. Robert handed each of the four men a hundred rand in case of emergency and to pay for their transport back.

It was a cool autumnal May evening as they drove down the N3 motorway to Pietermaritzburg. Greta and Derrick took the firearms with them in the Mazda, as a woman and a priest were the

147

least likely to be stopped, while Robert drove the blue Cortina van with Matthew, Antonio and Welcome. The motorway wound through wooded hills, quilted with emerald swathes of lush vegetation and brilliant smudges of claret, scarlet and vermilion bloom.

They arrived in Pietermaritzburg at six-thirty, and parked in the centre. Church Street was deserted. While the light was still good Robert took Derrick, Welcome, Antonio and Matthew out to Edendale and drove round the hospital perimeter, showing them the dirt road at the back. Returning to Church Street in Pietermaritzburg, Robert then accompanied Greta and Welcome Khumalo several miles out into the countryside and parked beneath a railway bridge. Welcome disappeared into the bush with a spade to dig a hole for the armaments. As Robert and Greta drove back to Pietermaritzburg he explained how long she should wait at that spot and what she should do while Steven Mhkize was being transferred.

Greta seemed nervous. To reassure her, Robert said, 'There's no risk involved. You just have to drive straight back to the workshop afterwards.'

He was talking fast. 'Everything's OK,' he promised. 'The switchboards will be jammed.'

Back in Church Street, they had to wait a few minutes; the others had gone in search of a cup of coffee. It was eight-fifteen, and dark had fallen. Robert transferred the red sports bag from the Mazda to the Cortina van. Derrick McBride produced some pills and handed round two apiece. It was the Lexotan, to calm them down.

Once again they set off towards Edendale, with Greta following alone in the Mazda. At the bridge there was no sign of Welcome Khumalo. Robert walked back to where Greta was parked and placed something in the cubby hole. 'This is for Themba,' he said. In the dark, Greta couldn't see what it was.

'At that moment Themba came from the opposite side of the road, instead of coming from the bush where he had originally jumped off,' said Greta. 'He came running out, waving his hands in the air, with a big smile on his face. Rob got hold of him and pulled him over and spoke to him . . . I don't know what about.'

Robert needed to get a move on. He wanted to be at the hospital just after visiting hours, when the police guards began to relax and sometimes played cards.

Greta watched the blue van disappear into the dark. 'Then Themba came and sat in the car with me,' said Greta. 'I don't know why he did this as Steve and I were supposed to be alone. As soon as he got in the car he started to complain that we should not be parked where we were, as it was too obvious. He said things like Steve had told him stuff about where you should not park and things like that. He became terribly anxious. The more I questioned him, the more anxious he became. Then he said we should go to the station further down and wait there, as it was safer than where we were. Then I told him that Robert had put something for him in the cubby hole, so he took it out and it was two hand-grenades. He was fascinated by them and was throwing them about. I think he was nervous. I didn't trust him so I agreed to go to the station. The station was about two kilometres from where we were supposed to park. We sat there at the station and I asked him to put the grenades back in the cubby hole. He spoke non-stop about Steve . . . then I realised Steve was some sort of commander and Themba was in his unit, as he mentioned all the things they had done together and all the training Steve had given him. He kept saying he had never met anyone like him, and he loved him.'

It was almost eight-thirty when Robert stopped the van on the uneven gravel road at the rear of the hospital. Over the tall grass they could see the lights of the African township in the distance. The road was deserted and there was not a sound in the night. Robert showed Matthew and Antonio the ramp which they would come down from the hospital. Robert put on a doctor's white coat and began cutting the fence with a pair of wire-cutters which he had bought that morning. At the last moment, Derrick decided to take off his dog collar; it made him feel uncomfortable, and he suspected that it was only liable to draw more attention to himself.

Antonio switched on the van's hazard lights and opened the bonnet so that should anyone spot the stationary Cortina in the darkened road they would assume it had broken down. Robert had cut a hole in the fence just large enough to squeeze through; he handed the wire-cutters to Matthew and told him to enlarge the hole once he and his father had gone in. Derrick put the Makarov pistol in his jacket pocket, while Robert slipped the AK47 inside his white coat. He had already cut a hole in the pocket so he could hold the rifle, its stock folded, with his left hand, keeping his right hand free. Antonio also armed himself with an AK47 and took up a position across the road, lying in the grass so that he could cover them as they squeezed through the fence.

'Then we went in,' said Robert. 'I was very cool. I had taken the Lexotan tablets, and so had my father. I felt very relaxed. Derrick looked relaxed too. We went in talking.

'Derrick is so observant. He was looking and noticing everything – he noticed that there was a trolley there. We were going along the covered walkway, and then we entered the hospital, through a ramp on the side, and we walked down the corridor, and then up the stairs.

'We were talking like doctors, mentioning X-rays a lot. We soon ran out of medical terms, so we just kept repeating, "X-ray, X-ray, X-ray . . ." '

Walking slowly so as not to draw attention to themselves, Robert and his father climbed three flights of stairs and then hesitated on the fourth landing, which led to the second floor and room 2R, the intensive care unit. With his free hand Robert pulled out a balaclava and struggled to pull it over his head, but it dropped to the floor just as a doctor came down the stairs. 'Good evening,' said Robert, keeping walking and leaving the balaclava on the floor.

As planned, Derrick went ahead to check if the second floor corridor was clear, while Robert waited on the stairs. Robert looked at his watch: it was eight-thirty precisely. He slipped the catch of his AK47 from 'safe' to 'automatic fire'.

Visitors should officially have left the hospital, but seated on a bench opposite the intensive care unit, were four young Zulu men. They were friends of Constable Edward Ngcobo and they were waiting for him to come off duty after guarding Gordon

Webster. One of them, Mlungisi Buthelezi, had been clowning about to amuse the others, pretending to take their group photo. He was chatting to Constable Ngcobo as Derrick McBride came round the corner; Derrick approached a few yards down the corridor, then turned and disappeared. Constable Ngcobo told his friends he was just going to go and have a look to see who this man was.

As Derrick met Robert at the top of the stairs, he muttered curtly, 'Abort, civilians.'

Derrick continued down the stairs, but Robert decided to have a look round the corner to check for himself. 'As I put my head round the corner, I found myself looking into the machine-carbine of Ngcobo. He froze. At that moment I knew we were already committed and that I would have to attempt to carry out the rescue mission,' said Robert. 'We looked into each other's eyes and I knew there was trouble coming. I reacted. I fired.'

A burst of automatic fire hit the floor in front of Ngcobo and a sliver of shrapnel hit his hand. Ngcobo dropped his HMC carbine and ran in the opposite direction. Derrick looked up from the stairs to see the policeman disappearing.

'He's gone!' Robert yelled back to his father. 'Stay here and see that he doesn't come back.'

As Robert raced round the corner, followed by his father, Constable Ngcobo's terrified friends got a blurred impression. Seeing a man in a doctor's white coat, Nkosinathi Nkabine simply assumed it was a white man who was waving a rifle in their direction. Siphiwe Shange was so petrified by the sound of gunfire that he thinks he remembers five, six or seven black men invading the ward. Nkosinathi, Shange, Joe Nkabine and Mlungisi Buthelezi leapt up from the bench, but as they scrambled to escape, they collided after a few yards and fell in a heap.

Robert McBride got another impression. 'The people on the benches dropped to the ground, fast, like cops,' he said. 'I thought, "Oh shit, now we're in trouble." I fired and went forward – I knew I had to go ahead.'

'My mind was clear. Everything flowed. I was in fighting mode.

'I came to the ward door. Suddenly the smoke from the firing

151

made me angry. I don't know why, and I swore. I went straight through the plastic swing doors.'

The intensive care unit was a narrow, whitewashed room with seven beds, cluttered with medical paraphernalia, oxygen tanks, ventilation tents, instrument trolleys and intravenous drips. From the information Robert had been given he was expecting Gordon to be in the bed right opposite the swing doors: the bed was empty. 'Humphrey!' shouted Robert, using one of Gordon's aliases. 'Humphrey!'

Gordon Webster had in fact been moved a couple of beds further down, but he was unable to respond to Robert's call because a white policeman was right next to him. There were only two policemen on duty that night, and Constable Johannes Visagie had come on duty half an hour previously. Visagie drew his pistol and fired; at that very moment Robert was turning and the bullet skimmed past him.

'At every step now something was going wrong,' said Robert. 'All I heard was a loud explosion. I did not have time to think. I swung round and fired. I can remember the cartridge in the air. It seemed to hang there. The policeman was wearing spectacles and he had what looked like a smile on his face.'

Visagie, winged just below the elbow, turned and ran back into the adjacent sluice room only a few feet away, slamming the door shut behind him. A couple of nurses scattered out of the room and another hid in the corner, with her hands over her eyes.

Gordon Webster waved his hand to attract Robert's attention. He was overjoyed to see Robert, but when he came over to his bed the first thing Gordon said was, 'The police will shoot.'

'What police?' asked Robert.

Gordon pointed towards the sluice-room. Robert approached the door and as he did so Visagie fired again. Robert was not sure how much ammunition he had left so he held fire as he peered round the door. He saw Visagie crouched in the far corner of the sluice room, aiming. Visagie fired and hit the door fractionally to the left of him, ripping out a fragment of the door. A splinter hit Robert and angrily he loosed off another shot, which missed. Robert pulled the door closed. The original idea had been to lock the policemen in the X-ray room, but now he had to hope that the white constable would remain shut in the sluice room, while Derrick kept guard in the corridor for his black colleague.

Gordon Webster lay naked on the bed, with two intravenous tubes inserted into his arm, one for a blood transfusion and the other a glucose-water drip. Robert had been expecting Gordon to be able to walk, but as soon as Gordon swung his legs over the bed he began to buckle, and it was clear he was not going to be able to stand. He was very weak.

Nearby a nurse who had been pushing a laundry trolley was screaming hysterically and holding her head in her hands. 'Shut up!' Robert shouted at her, and ordered her to bring over the trolley. The nurse fell silent and did as she was told. The trolley had a flat surface with a hole in the centre for the canvass laundry bag. Robert stood in front of Gordon and placing his hands under his armpits he lifted him onto the trolley, settling him into the circular hole in the centre; unable to help, Gordon was lumpenly heavy. Robert settled him on the trolley so that he was seated almost upright in the hole, his legs straddled on either side to make sure he would not fall off. Robert pulled both the intravenous drips out of his arm.

'Let's get out,' he said.

Gordon took the AK47. With both hands now free, Robert propelled the trolley through the plastic swing doors, out into the corridor, as fast as they could go.

There was chaos in the corridor; people were running and shouting, others ducked for cover. As soon as they were in the passage Gordon fired two short bursts, holding the rifle unsteadily with his left hand. There were some people on the ground, and there was blood on the floor. Robert yelled at Gordon to stop firing, and repeated, 'Let's get out of here.'

At the perimeter fence Matthew Lecordier had cut a hole big enough for two people to step through at the same time. He was becoming increasingly nervous as he was caught in a faint shaft of light from a hospital window, and at one point an African nurse in one of the wards appeared to be staring at him. After a few seconds she looked away and Matthew continued till he had cut a section of the fence right away. Then he took one of the AK47s from the red sports bag in the van and hid in the long grass near to Antonio. The night was unsettlingly quiet; all he could hear was the sound of the crickets in the bush.

'Are you still there?' asked Matthew.

'Yeah,' replied Antonio out of the darkness. 'Right here.'

From their vantage point in the tall grass the hospital was brightly lit, and at the window where he had seen the nurse he could see the heads of people as they moved about. Although only a matter of minutes, to Matthew it seemed a prodigiously long wait. After a while, he whispered, 'These guys are taking a long time.'

'Yeah,' agreed Antonio. 'I hope something hasn't happened to them.'

Suddenly they heard gun shots; automatic and single fire.

In the hospital, Derrick had been standing guard by the stairway to make sure that Constable Ngcobo did not return to cut off their line of retreat. But as soon as he heard a burst of gunfire he ran down the corridor in the direction of the intensive care unit. When he reached 2R, he looked in and saw that the bed directly opposite the door was empty. It even had a clean covering on it.

'I thought I had the wrong ward and that I should go further along,' said Derrick. 'I then ran and turned in the next corridor leading to the left. I passed two doors – the first room I passed was also empty. There was nothing in it and when I reached the second door, I heard more shooting – from behind me, the direction which I had just come. I panicked and ran back. When I entered that corridor . . . I saw people lying on the floor, two or three.'

Two of Constable Ngcobo's friends, Nkosinathi Nkabinde and Siphiwe Shange, had been wounded in the leg. A third, Mlungisi Buthelezi, lay there dying.

Derrick, the Makarav pistol in his hand, raced after Robert and Gordon. 'There were a number of people who were all panicking near the steps,' said Derrick. 'I fired a shot into the air and shouted at them to move, to move.'

154

With Derrick holding the back of the trolley, and Robert in front, they began to lift Gordon down the stairs, but as Gordon was clutching hold of the rifle with both hands he was unable to keep himself steady in the trolley basket and he began sliding forward. At first Robert, struggling backwards down the stairs, was able to support Gordon with his shoulder, but after a few more steps Gordon fell off the trolley, cushioned partly by Robert who also managed to grab hold of the rifle. Robert struggled to lift his naked, helpless friend back onto the trolley, yet after only a few more steps Gordon fell to the concrete floor again.

While Derrick went back up the stairs to make sure they were not being followed, Robert scooped Gordon up under his armpits and began to drag him backwards down two flights of stairs. Gordon clung on grimly to the AK47, his heels dragging and bumping on each step. When they reached the last flight Robert gently put Gordon down and told him that he was going back up to check what had happened to his father. Painfully Gordon crawled down the last flight of stairs.

Derrick was one floor up, following behind slowly, covering their backs. 'Come, come,' yelled Robert.

On the ground floor they found the trolley that Derrick had spotted as they came in, and between them they lifted Gordon onto it. This was a different type of trolley, with a flat top and so they were able to lay Gordon out on his back and place the rifle on the rack below. They made quicker progress now, with Derrick pushing from behind and Robert pulling at the front. They came racing down a ramp and out of the hospital into a tarred court-yard. Outside, it was dark and the air was cool; suddenly Robert felt exhausted.

Moments later they had to negotiate another set of steps. At first they tried to lift the trolley with Gordon on it, but both Derrick and Robert were tiring rapidly and Gordon slipped off once more. Robert picked him up and carried him to the top, returning to haul the trolley up with Derrick.

Patients and nurses were crowded at the windows of the hospital as the two McBrides pushed their wounded companion on the trolley the last fifty yards towards freedom. Gradually

Robert and Derrick became aware of the sound of singing and shouting. It was coming from the windows of the hospital and the nurses' home. Patients and nurses were cheering them on; they were yelling encouragement.

There were shouts of '*Viva ANC*' and '*Amandla!*'

'We could hear people singing and shouting,' said Robert. 'Then we saw a group of people in front of us, also singing, chanting, even dancing, some were ululating. Some of them rushed towards us. It was a difficult moment because they were blocking our way. Father shot in the air. It was the right thing to do, because they backed off. They started laughing; it was like a movie to them. But they backed off.'

In the nurses' home to his left, Robert realised they were singing freedom songs in Zulu. As he and his father steered the trolley down the covered walkway towards the fence, a patient came out of one of the red-brick outhouses and sullenly stood in their path. Derrick levelled the pistol at him and slowly the patient turned away and moved aside.

From his vantage point in the grass outside the wire perimeter, Antonio du Preez spotted Robert and Derrick propelling the trolley fast down the walkway. Both Antonio and Matthew could clearly hear the sound of singing and clapping.

The rhythmic chant grew louder and louder as the trolley approached the fence. They were moving so fast that Gordon fell heavily again. Robert could feel his strength failing rapidly. As they neared the fence, he shouted, 'Support, support.'

Antonio emerged from the grass on the other side of the dirt road and pushed his gun through the wire netting to give them cover if necessary. In the dark it was difficult to make things out clearly. 'I was tired, what with carrying Gordon and all the adrenalin, and I was becoming nervous that people would be after us,' said Robert. 'Antonio had a floppy green cap on and he looked like a policeman. He began pushing his gun through the fence. For a moment, I nearly shot him.'

Matthew Lecordier came through the fence to meet them and helped Robert carry Gordon through the hole in the fence. 'I saw Mr McBride was exhausted,' said Matthew. 'We lifted Gordon, one each side of him. Gordon was very heavy. He was so heavy we

156

almost dropped him. He was in pain, I don't know what he said – he was muttering things but I wasn't listening.

'He was naked and he still had part of a drip in him. He looked very weak and I could see from the expression on his face as we lifted him that he was in agony. He was moaning.'

They placed Gordon as gently as they could in the open back of the van. Matthew and Antonio climbed up in the back with him and both took off their jackets to cover him. Derrick closed the bonnet and jumped into the passenger seat. Robert started the van up and started off as fast as he dared down the coarse, rutted gravel track. He drove for a couple of hundred yards without his lights on. Behind them, gradually receding, they could hear the sound of the nurses and patients at Edendale Hospital still singing triumphantly.

16

Greta was still sitting in darkness in the car with Themba outside the darkened railway station and he was still talking ardently about Steve. Greta had no idea where they were, or how far they were from the hospital, and she was beginning to be extremely anxious about deserting their post under the bridge.

'I started to panic,' said Greta. 'Perhaps they would have returned and if Robert didn't find me there . . . so I said to Themba, "We have to go back because if Robert doesn't find us, there will be big trouble, for me especially". And he agreed, so we went back, and we passed three or four of these white police vans travelling at speed. Then he said, "I think they're going towards the hospital", so I asked him to show me this hospital – and all these vans actually went there.

'I didn't know what to do now. Either they were in trouble or had needed us to help with the second car. What should we do? So we drove up and down on that road thinking that maybe they would still come with the van, not knowing that they'd long gone . . .

'I drove past on that road maybe two or three times, but the police in front and behind us did not dream that in this car, we two were an odd couple. I mean, this coloured woman – I had an Indian style scarf – and a black guy, I mean an obviously black guy. Normally that would have made them suspicious, driving up and down. But at the same time I was worried that if Robert was in this area, and if I had deserted them, I would never hear the end of it. He would give me such hell. Outwardly I said to Themba, "Take me to the part of the hospital where these chaps could get in." And he thought I was quite crazy, but I was determined to go and check that Robert and them were not still in the vicinity of where they were supposed to cut a hole in the fence. So he took me right there, poor chap. I was so worried I even forgot that he had these hand-grenades . . . and that we were going right to the scene of the crime.

'When we got there, down this side road, it was too dark to see anything. I just saw the police cars coming out of there and riding back in, and again they didn't even bother to search us. So I asked Themba to actually go and walk up there to that place where he knew there would be a hole cut in the fence, to see if anything was there – just to go and see what was happening. Poor chap. I was in such a state, so he went. He walked up there and came back and said, no – just a lot of police and so on. So I said, "OK, let's go back to Pietermaritzburg and we can phone from there".

'He said he knew how to get back to the centre of Pietermaritzburg, and he knew of a short cut, but we landed in this white area – I don't know how – and we drove around in circles. We couldn't get out. And he says to me Steve – he couldn't stop talking about Steve – Steve taught him that if ever you are lost you must always take the left hand turns. He was just not okay. So I just took turns upon turns till eventually I came on a road out of this area, on to what looked like a main road and I just drove on it. And to my surprise I saw a sign saying "City", and arrows pointing to Pietermaritzburg. I couldn't believe it, like God was saying, "No, no, I'm here, I'm here!"'

The blue Cortina van bumped uncomfortably down the gravel back path; it was charcoal black except for the dismal lighting of the township on the hill and a faint sliver of light from the hospital. After a couple of hundred yards, Robert turned on the headlights and speeded up. When he reached the road he turned left away from Pietermaritzburg, and in case anyone had spotted them he drove for nearly a mile in the wrong direction before doing a U-turn and returning to the bridge where they were due to rendezvous with Greta and Welcome Khumalo.

It was freezing in the open back of the van and Antonio and Matthew were doing their best to keep Gordon warm. Matthew was alarmed at the speed Robert was forcing on the van. 'There was one time when we came to a bend that Rob was going so fast I thought we would tip over,' said Matthew. 'I shouted, "Watch it!" I screamed at him, "We are going too fast!"'

As they approached the bridge there was no sign of Greta in the Mazda; Robert would have been able to see her hazard lights from a distance.

'I had to decide,' he said. 'I sent a message back through father – we're going on. I didn't stop and increased the speed. Father told me to slow down so as not to attract attention. I slowed down to about sixty.

'At one point I was going to turn off the road but right at that moment I saw a road block ahead. Not wanting to create any suspicion, I had to drive straight through. It was a six-lane highway and they were putting a truck and a Caspir across to block it. We just made it through.'

Instead Robert took another turn-off which he had reconnoitered. It was a bumpy, dark side road that took them through a golf course, and saved them a couple of miles by the time it brought them back on to the N3 highway to Durban. There was little traffic on the highway at that time of night and they had overtaken a few other cars when Robert glimpsed a blue flashing light in the rear-view mirror.

The eerie, oscillating blue light was also reflected in the van's windscreen. It reminded him of the flash of a weapon firing at night.

'It looks like we're being fired on,' he said.

Derrick peered round. 'No,' he replied nervously. 'It's a cop.'

The blue flashing light gained on them. From the back Matthew passed a spare magazine to Derrick. He didn't know how to load the AK47; in the workshop that afternoon Robert had only demonstrated how to use a Markarov pistol. Robert took the rifle from his father and loaded the magazine with one hand while keeping the other on the wheel.

In the back of the van Matthew watched the police car catch up on them with horror. 'If these guys get any closer,' he remarked to Antonio, 'We've got to let them have it.'

Gordon was still conscious and had the spare AK47 which he could hardly hold. 'Don't fire unless you have to,' he told Matthew and Antonio. 'Keep your guns hidden.'

He asked if they had their rifles on automatic fire. Matthew checked Antonio's rifle; it was on the safety catch, so Matthew pushed it over to 'automatic' and told Antonio that all he had to do now was fire. The police squad car was right behind them, its winking flashlight irradiating their tense faces with a ghostly blue glow.

'We were in the middle lane,' said Robert. 'The squad car came right up on the right and slowed down to look at us. My father placed the AK on my neck, pointing out of the window, trained on them. They were staring at us. Gordon had warned Matthew and Antonio to hold their fire. We all thought: this is it.

'Then the police noticed a *kombi* to our left, so they slowed, drew behind us and instead pulled over the mini-bus.'

Robert drove so fast that they completed the journey from Edendale back to Wentworth in less than an hour.

They made straight for the Factorama workshop, transferring Gordon from the back of the van onto a mattress in the cramped workshop office. Gordon was frozen. Robert dressed him in a track suit and covered him with blankets, then they all took it in turns to massage Gordon in an attempt to stimulate his circulation and warm him up. He was so weak he could scarcely speak.

In Pietermaritzburg Greta and Welcome Khumalo made their way to the central post office where there were several telephone booths. Greta parked the Mazda on the side of the road right next to the telephones, but Themba insisted they park on the other side. The street was deserted; there was not a person in sight. By now Greta was considerably alarmed by her companion's erratic behaviour. However, Themba was so insistent that she did as he asked, and when they crossed over the road she heard him in the adjacent booth speaking to someone in Zulu. For a moment, it occurred to her that he might be reporting in to the police.

She phoned the workshop, hoping that the others had returned. Robert answered. Greta was surprised he didn't ask her where she had been; instead he curtly ordered her to come home immediately. Before hanging up, he added, 'Tell "Louis" to get rid of those things that I gave him.'

They had been on the freeway back to Durban for about fifteen minutes, recalled Greta, 'when Themba suddenly looked at me and said, "Slow down the car, I must throw these things out of the window." It was so weird because there were three lanes and I was in the fast lane on the extreme right, at top speed because I couldn't wait to get back to Durban and now this chap wants me to slow down because he has to detonate these things. So I said, "No, no, I didn't know that's how we were supposed to get rid of them."

'And he says to me, "Don't you think I should? On the white people's cars?" I was so angry I nearly pushed him out of the car. I said, "No, I'll stop by the side of the road and you can throw them into the bush." So I slowed down and pulled over to the left, and drove for a while until there was some bush and he just threw the grenades out. I was scared that just by landing maybe, sort of . . .'

When Greta and Welcome Khumalo finally pulled up outside the workshop, Robert asked Matthew to go and tell Greta to return home, then he changed his mind and went out himself. 'Robert was fuming,' said Greta. 'Furious. He told me I must go home. I didn't even ask, did you get Steve out? I had just jumped out of the car and he told me to get back in and go home. I didn't dream of explaining or questioning him. Just go home, go home now. He had that attitude. Get home. I saw him two days later.'

Inside the workshop, Gordon Webster was being treated. Pam Cele, a nurse sympathetic to their cause, had arrived with medical supplies including bandages, antibiotics and a glucose drip. She gave him an injection, dressed his wounds and before leaving she explained to Robert how to change the dressing and administer injections.

Derrick McBride had opened up the Day 'n' Nite Take-Away and brought over soft drinks, doughnuts and snowballs, small cakes with a coconut topping.

They wiped down the Cortina van to get rid of any fingerprints, and Robert parked it in Ogle Road. Robert told his father that he had done everything he possibly could and he should go home. As Welcome Khumalo was going to stay the night at the workshop, he remained with Gordon while Robert dropped Matthew and Antonio off.

'I was feeling excited to think I had taken part in something like this,' said Matthew. 'Robert said that something like this had not been done before, and we were making history. I felt proud.'

Robert stayed up nursing Gordon all night, occasionally feeding him pure orange and guava juice. As he lay awake on the mattress next to his fitfully sleeping, helpless friend, Robert realised that the next step would be almost as difficult: he would somehow have to get Gordon out of the country.

Part Three

A Dream that Never Happened

17

The news of Gordon's escape was on all the early Monday morning radio bulletins. One newspaper said the wounded guerrilla had been rescued by seven men in white coats. Greta heard the report on Capital Radio and went to work at the Child Welfare Department that morning in a daze.

'Everyone at work was talking about it, they were shocked that anyone could have the audacity to do a thing like that,' said Greta. 'I was in a state of shock. It was terrible because I didn't know if the police had any lead on Robert, and then of course with everyone talking about it I didn't know what to do. I couldn't really join in but it was difficult to distance myself.

'I just listened. I was worried about raising suspicions. If you know that you are part of something, then you feel guilty – you begin to imagine everyone knows that you know something. They talked about it all day. They were amazed at the determination, that someone actually had such courage.'

Robert was also worried. On Monday morning he slipped away from the Factorama workshop, leaving Themba to tend to Gordon while he went to a barber and had his large bushy Afro cut short. Robert spent the rest of the day tenderly nursing Gordon.

'I washed him, massaged his legs and gave him exercises because we wanted him to walk,' said Robert. 'He was very badly wounded. He had a bullet in his stomach and he needed a big operation. Gordon was terribly weak, but on the morning of that first day I got him to stand, although he could not walk. I knew that if he didn't start to walk he would begin to get even weaker.

'He was very co-operative, fighting to start walking. His spirit was strong. He was buoyed up. He kept on saying, "I must exercise again. Massage my legs again." We were talking fighting talk – Gordon insisted that I go on. I was feeling very positive.'

However, Robert realised they would have to move the wounded man as soon as possible. Gordon's picture had been shown on television and everyone at Bechet College knew how close the friendship was between them. The police were also offering a reward of two thousand rand for information concerning Steven Mkhize. On the TV broadcasts it was being said that the injured man was so badly wounded he might die anyway, but a police spokesman added that the gang who had carried out this rescue were more than likely to kill their comrade: it was known ANC policy, the policeman informed viewers, to dispatch people in order to stop them talking.

On Tuesday night, with the help of Greta and Gordon's two brothers Victor and Trevor, Gordon was driven to the black township of Umlazi, half way in the direction of Pietermaritzburg. They carried him down an embankment, using an old door as a stretcher, to the home of a black social worker known as Baby. Robert and Gordon were put in a small bare room containing two beds, a table and a wardrobe.

For two days Robert remained with Gordon, tending him. For security, Robert remained indoors and they did not turn on the light in the room. He continued feeding Gordon fruit juices, and at meal-times, first a woman and then a ten-year-old girl brought in cooked food without saying a word. Pam Cele continued to visit Gordon every evening to dress his wounds and give him injections.

Gordon had recovered sufficiently to resume giving Robert military instruction. He explained how electrical detonators worked, and how to operate more sophisticated weaponry like RPG rocket-launchers. Sometimes, to alleviate the boredom and tension, they played a competitive game of swearing at each other, a contest as to who could curse the most comprehensively.

'Gordon and Robert grew closer than brothers,' said Victor Webster. 'While Gordon was injured and needed looking after, Robert tended him like a little child. He had to do everything for Gordon, even wipe his bum. Robert would have given his life for him. Gordon would have given his life for Robert too. They really loved each other.'

By the third day the reward for information regarding Gordon had risen to ten thousand rand. The news was being broadcast on all the channels with Gordon's picture and a description of him as the commander in Natal and 'highly dangerous'. The township was also crawling with police, so after two days it was decided that Gordon should be moved.

One issue of disagreement had arisen between the two friends, however. At first Gordon had been reluctant to admit he should go into exile for a second time. After they had argued about it, Gordon eventually agreed there was no alternative; he could not possibly stay and continue operations in his present condition. However, he insisted that if he was going to leave the country, he wanted his girlfriend Anne to accompany him. Robert argued that it would be difficult enough to smuggle Gordon himself out; getting two of them over the border simultaneously would double the risk.

'I can bring Anne out later,' Robert kept telling him.

Finally, when Robert left Umlazi to go and make the arrangements for this clandestine exit, Gordon agreed he would go alone.

While Robert was making the preparations for Gordon's exit from South Africa, it was felt safer for him not to know his friend's whereabouts. In fact, the Websters transferred Gordon to another house in Umlazi belonging to a labourer called Majola, but after two days the neighbours became suspicious of the unexpected activity and began to ask questions: they suspected Majola had become involved in selling *dagga*. The arrangements for Gordon's departure had to be hurried up.

On Friday, Robert instructed Greta to hire a large caravan from a firm in the centre of Durban and at five o'clock he drew up outside 'Rent-a-Trailer' in his black Ford van. They hitched up the caravan and drove back to the Factorama workshop in Wentworth. Greta went home to pack a suitcase for them both and Robert equipped the caravan to look as if they were going on a long camping holiday, stocking it with bedding, groceries and a gas cooker. He also sealed off the compartment under one of the bunks with masonite, effectively creating a secret chamber, so that if the berth top were lifted it would look as if there was no hollow beneath.

Greta had not seen Gordon since before the escape from Edendale Hospital and she was apprehensive. All Robert had told her was that they were going to be taking another trip to Botswana. 'I couldn't imagine how it would be possible to take Gordon Webster because, according to all the newspaper reports, he was so badly injured that he could not survive without medical attention,' said Greta. 'I couldn't imagine him travelling for twelve hours, and under those conditions – some of those country roads are so bad that a vehicle rocks constantly.

'But come half past eight, his brother brought Gordon and Anne round, and we loaded him into the caravan. He was moaning and you could tell he was in extreme pain.'

Robert was surprised to see Anne, but assumed she had simply come to help Victor Webster transport Gordon. After they had settled Gordon into the caravan, Robert began to say goodbye to Anne when Gordon said, 'No, she's coming.'

Robert was annoyed but he did not quibble. He asked Anne if she had a passport and she said no. 'I had already seen there were two bunks in the caravan in which I could hide them, so I decided there was no further use in arguing about the matter and that she could go with us,' said Robert.

'I made a bed on the floor between the two bunks. I had used the mattress from the bunks in making this bed and the idea was threefold, namely that both Gordon and Anne could lie there between the bunks without being seen through the windows from the outside; the bunks would prevent them rolling around inside the caravan; and thirdly, lying where they did, they would not upset the centre of gravity of the caravan.'

Robert drove slowly. He had told Anne that if there was a problem she should shine the torch through the caravan's front window to attract their attention. He stopped several times, and then at midnight he pulled over outside the village of Van Reenen, right on the border of the Transvaal. Gordon was in pain and it was getting worse. Robert helped Anne change his dressing and

170

then he and Greta managed about two hours sleep in the cab of the truck before setting off again slowly.

It took them nearly twenty-four hours to reach the Botswana border – double their normal time. Greta was finding Robert very strained. 'He was distant, and I did most of the talking,' said Greta. 'He seldom spoke, there was no conversation or anything. I don't know what he was dreaming about.'

Robert wanted to cross the border just before eight in the evening, when it was dark and the border officials were anxious to close down for the night. They had a little time to spare, so Robert stopped a few miles from the border post and made a *braai* (barbecue). Gordon was in such pain that he could eat almost nothing. Then Robert prepared the caravan for their border crossing by making it as filthy as possible, in the hope that the customs officers would be so disgusted that they would not want to search too closely. He scattered dirty plates and cutlery from their meal, as well as old beer bottles and crisps and crisp packets, all over the interior. Then he and Greta helped Gordon and Anne into the compartments underneath their bunks; closing the lids, they replaced the mattresses, made up the beds, and then heaped clothes, newspapers and camping equipment on the top of both bunks, as well as more empty beer bottles and crisp packets.

It was completely dark by the time they reached the Ramatlabama border post. Robert and Greta walked over to the office with their passports and filled in all the forms. Just as they were coming out a woman customs official followed them and said, 'I want to search the caravan.'

Robert unlocked the caravan door; inside it was pitch black. Robert explained that he couldn't turn on any lights as he had not yet connected up the battery. The customs officer then asked if he had a torch.

'We couldn't believe it,' said Greta. 'Although Robert was shocked, he pretended to be very co-operative and said, "I'll get a torch for you so you can have a good look." I was furious. Robert came to the front and asked me for the torch and she went inside and shone the torch . . . I tell you, it's the first time I felt genuine fear. My heart was thumping.'

The woman shone the torch over the piles of clothes, cutlery, beer bottles and litter, and then clicked her tongue in disgust. She handed the torch back to Robert and told him he could lock up again and move on.

Ten miles inside the Botswana border Robert stopped and helped Gordon and Anne out of their bunk compartments. Gordon was swearing; he was in considerable distress. He told Robert he had been suffocating and had nearly coughed during the search. Anne was whooping with joy.

'We made it!' yelled Greta.

'It's not over yet,' Robert warned her. 'We have to get Gordon to a doctor quickly.'

They checked into the Morningstar Motel in Gaborone, all four booking into the same double room, Robert and Greta as Douglas and Denise Johnstone and Gordon and Anne under the name of Mr and Mrs Charles Dickens. Then they carried Gordon to Room 101; he was doubled up in pain, feverish and suffering from stomach cramps, and both he and Robert swore softly at each other. Robert immediately dialled his contact number, but a woman told him Chris was not available, so Robert asked her to take a message that Douglas had arrived and they should come quickly. Although Robert called several more times, it was not till early the following afternoon there was a knock on their door. It was Chris and Georgie.

'When they saw Gordon, their eyes were big,' said Robert. 'All the commanders had been phoning each other because they couldn't work out who had released him – especially when the newspapers had said there were seven involved in the rescue operation!

'Gordon was lying on the bed and he called out to them cockily, "Don't just stand there, come in," then patting his bed, he said, "Here."

'They were delighted to see Gordon but at the same time they were anxious about security – they feared a South African retaliatory attack because of Gordon's escape. We got straight down to business, talking over the situation. "Is that the get-away car?" they wanted to know. They decided to move Gordon immediately. They took Gordon into hiding. That was the last time I saw Anne.'

Chris and Georgie returned to the Morningstar Motel that evening and informed Robert and Greta that, for security reasons, they too should move immediately. Gordon, they said, was being tended by a doctor.

Robert and Greta were transferred to a safe house outside Gaborone and on the second day there Gordon was brought over to visit them. 'He was transformed,' said Greta. 'His face was as bright as ever. You'd never have said he was a sick man who had bullets still in his body. It was the very idea that he was free. He had improved his state of mind to such an extent that he looked as if he was actually glowing with good health.

'I thought it was a miracle that a man who was doomed to die had recovered so fast.'

Although he moved much more freely, Gordon appeared to have difficulty breathing. He told them he thought he had a bullet lodged in his lung. Gordon talked to them about Bheki Ngubane and said he was concerned that the ANC should help provide for Bheki's family.

In the house that night there was a general nervousness about security. That same day another ANC safe house only a few miles away had been raided by the Botswana police. Victor and Oupa had got away, but Chris had been caught and was due to be deported to Zambia. Robert and Greta had already been told they should leave Gaborone for a few days and head northward, possibly as far as the lake district near Maun, on the rim of the Okavagno Delta. Oupa and Victor were anxious not to stay too long, and after half an hour they said they needed to whisk Gordon away again. Robert and Gordon bade each other farewell.

'I think he was also worried about supporting Anne,' said Robert. 'Gordon's last words were, "When you came back, bring some things to sell, like *tackies* (tennis shoes)."'

18

Things began to go wrong between Robert and Greta. Robert did not want to return to South Africa, but he says the very idea made Greta nervous that he was going to abandon her.

'They did not want me to go back,' said Robert. 'But I had to return the caravan. It was in Greta's name and I did not want anything to be connected with her. Otherwise, we would have stayed.'

Greta remembers it differently. 'Robert was upset because he didn't want to go back into South Africa,' said Greta. 'He was worried the police would surely have latched onto us. Another thing was that he was so attached to Webster, and they worked so well together, that I don't think he thought he could work with anyone else . . .

'It was definitely his dream that we wouldn't return, and that we would now become fully involved with *Umkhonto we Sizwe*. One idea was that I would have to go back to return the caravan. So really my position was very uncertain. He also had the idea that I would remain with him and Eric, my brother, could fly to Botswana and then drive the van back with the caravan.

'In the end, the guys out there made the decision. As far as they could see, everything was safe. "It's no use," they told him, "you are going to go back."'

But Robert and Greta did not return immediately. Victor and Oupa suggested they disappear from Gaborone for a few days, and so they travelled northward through the dry, flat, brown landscape of Botswana. Robert was silent and irritable. He decided that going to the Okavango area was too far, and instead they drove the five hours to Francistown and booked into the Grand Hotel.

'The Grand – that was a big joke,' said Greta. 'It was quite old, there was no hot water and no blankets. We had a miserable time. Five miserable, terrible days. Robert was so disturbed. He was withdrawn. I think he was upset that he had to return to South Africa. To be separated from Webster. He was badly, very badly affected.

'He spent most of the time stuck in the motel reading books, magazines, all the ones that were banned in South Africa. I didn't know at the time what was eating him. We argued a lot because I couldn't fathom what was really worrying him. He'd get upset with me for the smallest thing, stupid insignificant things.

'I kept fighting back at him. Or I would also withdraw, not talk to him, and there would be long silences. We would both read in silence or walk in silence. For hours on end.'

Robert had written a report on the Edendale escape and his superiors had been studying it. On returning to Gaborone he was summoned to a safe house to meet a senior commander of *Umkhonto's* Special Operations.

He was given instructions to organise his unit more effectively, recruiting additional people, as well as sending Matthew Lecordier to Botswana for military training in July and Greta at a later date. Robert was also formally appointed commander of this unit.

'They told me I was going to take over from Gordon. It was a big responsibility,' said Robert. 'I knew it was going to be lonely. I had a feeling of doom. The fact that Gordon was almost killed – that made me morose.'

He was brusque with Greta on the long drive back to Durban.

They passed through the Ramatlabama border post in the mid-afternoon of Sunday, May 19. Once they had crossed over into the Transvaal, they saw a large column of army trucks packed with soldiers in camouflage uniforms. Robert was silent and distant. They drove through the night, stopping by the side of the road for a couple of hours in the Orange Free State to get some sleep. By dawn they had crossed over into Natal and Robert told Greta that he wanted her to write down some observations. He wished to make a note of all the substations on their route.

Greta was tired and wanted to relax. She asked why he required her to write these things down.

Robert immediately became irritated: 'I told her, just write it down. Don't ask questions.'

Greta also became agitated; she still felt resentful about having been told so little about the Edendale Operation. She told him that she did not want to write anything down and that anyway she had no paper to write on.

'I became upset,' said Robert. 'I told her just to write it down. I just wanted it. I saw targets there and they were suitable for me. There were so many of them.'

Eventually Greta gave in and jotted down Robert's comments on the back of an envelope: the location of substations, size, distance from the road and the number of fences it would be necessary to cross. The atmosphere between them was strained.

They reached Wentworth about ten o'clock on the morning of Monday, May 19. Robert was exhausted when they arrived at Greta's house, and he turned on the radio to listen to the news. It was startling. The South African Defence Force had carried out raids on three neighbouring countries, striking at Harare in Zimbabwe, Livingstone in Zambia and Gaborone in Botswana. The ostensible reason given by the South African government was that it was a pre-emptive strike against ANC bases in those countries, although there were no ANC casualties. The Harare 'base' they attacked had been evacuated and in Lusaka the South African planes hit the wrong target, bombing a UN camp for Angolan and Namibian refugees. In Gaborone, the only person killed was a popular local football player. An ANC house that had been hit in Gaborone was close to the one in which Robert and Greta had been staying twenty-four hours earlier.

The real reason for these raids was to sabotage the efforts being made by a delegation of seven Commonwealth elder statesmen, imposingly titled the Eminent Persons Group. On the instructions of the Commonwealth this group, which included a former British Cabinet Minister, a recent Nigerian Head of State and an erstwhile Australian Prime Minister, were attempting to mediate between Pretoria and the African National Congress. Their proposal was simple: that the ANC should be legalised, its leader Nelson Mandela released, and that in return the ANC should suspend its commitment to the armed struggle, so that both sides could begin negotiations.

The group had already met Mandela in prison and found him to be 'reasonable, without rancour and ready to seek a negotiated settlement'. On May 19 they had just flown back to Cape Town from a meeting at the ANC headquarters in Lusaka and they were about to go into a meeting with the South African Cabinet Constitutional Committee when they were informed about the raids on Lusaka, Harare and Gaborone. This military operation had the desired effect: the Eminent Persons packed their bags and flew back to London that night.

The following day the South African President was in a characteristically bellicose mood. These cross-border raids, announced P. W. Botha, were just 'the first instalment'.

'South Africa,' he threatened, 'has the capacity and the will to break the ANC.'

Robert received a call from Oupa in Botswana, instructing him to respond to these raids against the ANC. On Tuesday night he removed the weapons and explosives which had been placed in a hole in the back of the workshop and transferred them into the ceiling. The following evening, after finishing work at the take-away, Robert went across to the workshop and began to manu-facture a huge, strange, ramshackle explosive device.

He tied two SZ.6 demolition charges together, then stuck an SZ.3 charge on top using epoxy glue, afterwards also using the glue to attach a hand-grenade. He tied this bizarre concoction together with wire and sellotape, then sprayed the 15 kilogram bundle with white paint, and finally wrapped it tightly in plastic clingfilm. It was an eccentric, menacing contrivance.

Robert had selected his target: the Pine Street Parkade, a spacious, six-storey cark park in the centre of town, owned by a subsidiary of Anglo-American. He had also decided that his partner for this mission should be Greta's sister, Jeanette Apelgren. He had been instructed to recruit more people for his unit, and here was his opportunity to evaluate Jeanette. Till now she had been a passive partner, accompanying them on two trips to Botswana, and providing a cover with Greta on excursions into the countryside at night to bury arms. He had already explained to her the MCW, the military code, and this, he felt, was the assignment to test her discipline.

Jeanette had been at school with Robert. Like all the Apelgrens she had been brought up a strict Roman Catholic with a vocation to help others. In her job as a social worker she specialised in child care and marital counselling. She was a lively, attractive young woman of twenty-six, four years younger than Greta, and had been closely involved in the United Democratic Front. She was planning to write a book about the Coloured people in Natal in rural areas, and their displacement by the Group Areas Act. Jeanette had always rejected violence as a political weapon but she had been forced reluctantly to the conclusion that the only changes ever brought about were as a result of violence, and that the only voice of real protest was the ANC.

Early on Friday morning, Robert asked Greta if she would ring Jeanette and arrange with her sister to give him a lift into Durban during her lunch break. Jeanette agreed, and at two o'clock she picked Robert up outside the Checkers store at the Bluff Shopping Centre. He got into the passenger seat carrying a brown canvas bag which he placed under his legs and then he directed her to drive to the Pine Street Parkade in Durban. He did not tell her what he was going to do in town; she did not ask.

It took them half an hour to drive into the centre of Durban. The parking plaza was in Pine Street, round the corner from The Daily News and Sunday Tribune offices in Field Street, and directly opposite Woolworths. The parkade was a long, cream-coloured building with trails of greenery hanging from each level. Jeanette found a parking space on the fourth floor and informed Robert that she would have to leave in half an hour; that afternoon, she explained, she was due to remove two children from their father because he was abusing them. They agreed to meet at three o'clock in front of the take-away on the ground floor.

Jeanette went window-shopping in a smart, modern arcade near the old railway station. She lingered in a jeweller's shop, looking at engagement rings for fifteen minutes, then she bought some food and wandered back to Pine Street. Robert was already waiting outside the lifts on the ground floor of the Parkade. Jeanette did not ask him what he had been doing. But just as she was about to start the car, Robert told her to wait a moment. Quickly he got out, removed the brown bag and placed it beneath the next car, a BMW.

'What are you doing?' asked Jeanette.

'Don't ask questions,' replied Robert. 'Let's go.'

Jeanette drove off and asked no further questions, but she was nervous, wondering if it might be a bomb. As they drove out of the Parkade, she noticed Robert appeared to be relaxed. Jeanette was beginning to be frightened about what she was getting involved in.

At three-fifteen, shortly after Jeanette and Robert had driven away, a security guard at the Parkade spotted the brown hold-all bag sticking out from underneath the BMW. Unzipping it, he saw the extraordinary device inside and raised the alarm. The police were called in and the area was sealed off. The device was removed by demolition experts to the police headquarters at C.R. Swart Square, where it was detonated the following morning at ten o'clock. The bizarre contraption caused a sensation among the police demolition and security experts: they had never encountered anything like it.

Robert claimed there had been no detonator inside this home-made explosive package, and the police were unable to say whether there had been one or not. Even if there had been, it would not have gone off before the next morning and the police were stumped for an explanation as to why anyone should place a device where it would so clearly be found.

It was a propaganda exercise, claimed Robert. The intention was to show the public that all public places could be vulnerable to attack, even in the centre of the city. The second object was to give the South African police something to think about.

The device certainly baffled the police, and caused a sensation. It was widely reported on the TV and radio news and in the following day's newspapers. As propaganda, said Robert, the mission was a tremendous success.

Jeanette Apelgren heard about the unexploded bomb on the

radio news on Saturday morning. Her conscience was beginning to bother her. She said she felt compromised and contends that she went over to Greta's house to see Robert. She found them there, she claimed, both reading the account of the Pine Street Parkade scare in the *Daily News*.

Jeanette's version is that Robert said, 'You see how these terrorists are crazy, putting bombs in town.'

Robert's memory is entirely different. He never saw her the next day, he maintained, and he would never say anything like that after an operation. The rules were clear and she knew them: *It's a dream, it never happened.*

19

Exile: Gordon had not wanted to leave his country a second time to disappear into this uncertain limbo. It was only when the South African police discovered Steven Mkhize was in fact Gordon Webster, and began to broadcast this information on television, that Robert McBride had finally been able to persuade his critically wounded comrade that for all their sakes he had no option but to vanish.

Unlike most political movements, the ANC had flourished in exile. When the movement had been banned in 1960, while Nelson Mandela remained underground to organise the military wing *Umkhonto we Sizwe*, his friend and former legal partner, Oliver Tambo, was instructed by the ANC to escape abroad to build up the structures of the organisation in preparation for a long, arduous struggle.

For most political movements exile is destructive and debilitating. The political scientist, Tom Lodge, in an essay *State of Exile: The African National Congress of South Africa, 1976–86*, spelt out this predicament: 'The environment of exile politics is usually viewed as hazardous, sterile, corrosive and demoralising. Political groups which are forced out of their domestic terrain are understood to be especially vulnerable; loneliness, frustration, inactivity, hardship and insecurity generate ideological dissent, personality conflicts, and escapist delusions. Exile politicians are forced into a dependent relationship with their hosts and patrons, whose hospitality and generosity may be conditional and subject to capricious change. Survival and success in such an environment may depend on skills and talents quite different from those developed in the history of the movement before its departure from home.'

Nevertheless, concludes Lodge, 'the ANC has not been only

unharmed by the pressures and trauma of exile but has actually prospered because of it.' The ANC built up a virtual government in exile, administering a headquarters in Lusaka with an extensive network of diplomatic missions around the world. The majority of the estimated ten thousand ANC personnel in exile were members of *Umkhonto we Sizwe*, trained in five camps in Angola, but the ANC also ran cultural, educational and health services. At Morogoro in south-eastern Tanzania, the ANC managed an enormous settlement containing a secondary school, the Solomon Mahlangu Freedom College, a child care centre, a crêche, a maternity home, three factories and a large farm. The ANC ran another farm near Lusaka in Zambia, next door to a ranch owned by an Anglo-American.

Despite all this organisation, the ANC did not have the medical facilities to operate on Gordon. From Gaborone he was immediately transferred to the headquarters in Lusaka, where it was decided that his wounds were so serious that he would have to be sent abroad for treatment. He was flown to Moscow, leaving Anne behind in Lusaka.

In Moscow, he spent two months in a clinic, much of the time sharing a room with a mysterious elderly Belgian and a wounded Ghanaian general. The Russian surgeons were unable to remove the two bullets, for one was lodged too close to his spine and the other in his lung. To extract them, they decided, would be too risky and so they concentrated on recuperating Gordon as best they could, leaving the two bullets embedded in his body. After two months he was sufficiently recovered to be taken on a five-day tour of Moscow, before being flown on to East Germany for several weeks' convalescence.

On his return to Lusaka, Gordon and Anne were married.

It is at this point that Gordon resigned from Special Operations – at least that is what he later claimed at his trial. The reason, he said, was 'because of my intense disagreements with Rachid.'

On trial, usually facing the death penalty, members of *Umkhonto* are told they can put any blame they like onto their commanders abroad: fighting to save their lives, therefore, this evidence cannot be taken as gospel. However, Gordon told the court that on a trip to Botswana with Robert in March 1986, Rachid, his commander in Special Ops, instructed him to place a car bomb in Durban. Gordon refused. That was not, he objected, the policy of the ANC.

'Rachid is a blood-thirsty person,' Gordon told the court. 'That is my opinion.'

Having resigned from Special Operations, Gordon began working for military headquarters in Lusaka, involved with strategic planning and logistics. He and Anne, who had also joined the ANC, lived in a house on the outskirts of Lusaka. Early the following year, she became pregnant.

20

Robert brooded constantly but Greta could not work out why. 'After Gordon was taken away, after we had said farewell, I was touchy,' said Robert. 'I began to feel that maybe he was dead. I was depressed. Also, Greta became suddenly very dependent on me. I used to say, "We must leave the country," and she'd say, "No, you will desert me."'

Robert worked with his father at the Factorama workshop as well as at the Day 'n' Nite Take-Away, and in the evenings he often repaired cars to make extra money. In order not to arouse suspicion, he carried on as much as possible with his previous life, but Greta knew that after their last Botswana trip something had 'cracked'. Robert was detached and kept his thoughts from her; she felt excluded and anxious.

'I couldn't imagine what was driving him to be so miserable, into an emotional person who just had . . . outbursts,' said Greta. 'I didn't understand what made him so irritable and tense. I couldn't fathom it.

'After we got back to Durban our relationship was very, very poor. He hadn't wanted to return, and he didn't feel safe. And he wasn't with Webster. I saw another side to his personality . . . extremely, extremely difficult. I ultimately decided that for the sake of peace I should simply submit to everything he wanted, even if he said, "Don't disagree, don't question, don't comment."

'Our relationship had become so bad that he didn't trust anyone, not even me. And he said that if I ever betrayed him to the police and he knew about it, he would put a cold bullet through my head. He would kill me. In cold blood. I knew he meant it, simply because he was so afraid that I wasn't fully in tune with what was going on, and that maybe I would go and report him.

'He put it this way: "If ever you betray me, if ever you let me down, if you go and tell the police about me, this is what I'll do to you." It must have been just a week after we got back from Botswana. And then after a while he said, "Let's make a pact. Supposing I did it to you, would you also kill me?" I said to him, "No, I wouldn't be able to do something like that."

'He was deadly serious. I didn't believe that he actually would do it. But I realised that he was trying to say that he didn't feel safe at all. He became withdrawn, easily angered. He fought with me a lot, because I was the person closest to him. I was the target for all his frustrations. I was beginning to feel like a victim.

'Like, if I mispronounced a word, he'd get quite upset. He used to say, "You don't pronounce that word like that." "Oh well, I always say it this way," I'd say. "Why can't you say it like me?" he'd demand. "Say it like I say it!" He'd go on about it, and then he'd sulk for a long time. It was so unlike Robert. We'd fight over things like that, trivial things.

'Suddenly there were so many problems. If someone came to see me and it was a male, maybe the Chairperson of the Residents' Association in connection with some local issue, oh, when that person was gone! "Why are you seeing so and so? I don't think you should see so and so." "But why?" I'd ask, "I mean it's part of community work – I'm helping, giving them advice." "No, I don't want you to see so and so." "How do I tell him not to come here?" "No, why can't you just tell him not to come in?" "But I can't." "Look, I am telling you to tell him that."

'It was those kinds of arguments, he would be most unreasonable. I think it was jealousy. It was also suspicion, and just being unable to handle his own emotional state, I think.

'Or he'd be worried that these people were snooping. Yet they had been coming along all the time, but since the Edendale operation he'd say, "They must be coming to spy on us."'

Greta felt trapped but she did not know what she could do about it or what she could do to help Robert. 'I knew he needed support,' she said. 'No other woman would be able to give him that. We were linked by our actions, and by what we knew.

'I knew that we couldn't terminate it. I knew that there was no way out of this situation. I had to just endure it. We were doomed to be together for the rest of our lives, as long as the struggle continued and we were . . . outlaws.'

Robert had been instructed to prepare a DLB, a dead letter box, near to Durban. He selected a site on the Shongweni-Assegai road out in the countryside, at a point where the road looped back on itself; it was a deserted location, and Robert had marked a spot in the veld fifty yards off the road, hidden by the bush. First he bought a large red metal trunk from an Indian shop and then late one evening he drove there with Matthew Lecordier, accompanied by Greta and Jeanette for 'cover'.

Robert instructed the women to drive around for two hours before returning. Armed with a spade and a pick-axe, he and Matthew prepared a large hole for the red trunk, but the ground was much harder than they had anticipated and they saw the lights of the car and heard Greta toot the horn before they had finished. Robert sent Matthew to tell them to drive off again for another fifteen minutes, then they hurriedly buried the trunk and covered it, carefully planting grass and weeds over the spot as camouflage. As a final touch, Robert scattered some empty sorghum beer packets over the disguised DLB.

Since his last trip to Botswana, and in preparation for the next one, Robert had been preparing a false compartment in his Ford truck. He constructed this at the Factorama workshop, placing a wide leather-upholstered seat in the open floor behind the cab. The seat was held in position by four long bolts inserted from below, which could be removed to reveal a spacious hiding place. As further camouflage he lined the back of the truck with some old carpet.

Robert had been instructed to return to Botswana on the first weekend of June in order to collect compensation money for the death of Gordon's comrade, Bheki Ngubane; 'Zola' had left behind a girlfriend and child.

Townships all over the country were in turmoil. The revolt was reaching a raw pitch of fury. In some areas conservative and more traditionalist black groups had commenced a bitter onslaught within their own communities against the 'comrades'. At the Crossroads squatters' camp near Cape Town, bands of these vigilantes, called *witdoeke* because of the white headbands they wore for identification, launched a series of well-organised raids against camps known to be strongholds of the ANC and the UDF. Hundreds were killed and up to seventy thousand driven out, while the police stood by and watched. It marked a new and bloody phase in the escalating conflict, as the authorities increasingly adopted the tactic of colluding with such vigilantes and utilising them as a surrogate force to try and crush uprisings.

It was in this tense atmosphere that Robert and Greta once again set out for Botswana, driving all night and arriving in Gaborone on the morning of Saturday, June 7. They checked in at the Oasis Motel and Robert left a message at his usual contact number that 'Douglas' had arrived. When 'Rachid' arrived that night, he checked the bedroom for bugging devices and switched on the air-conditioner.

There were similar precautions over the next couple of days as Rachid held a series of meetings with Robert. In Botswana the atmosphere among the ANC cadres was palpably tense. One evening Oupa spent the night on the couch of their room at the Oasis Motel, and although nothing was said, they had the impression that he was on the run. Another day, when Oupa was late for a meeting, Rachid was concerned that he might have been picked up by the police. Whenever a rendezvous was arranged, strict safeguards were taken and elaborate procedures observed to ensure that they had not been followed. One surreptitious meeting was even arranged in a supermarket.

Mostly Robert met with Rachid alone; he was given fresh instructions. He was to step up his sabotage activities in Natal. The ANC, he was told, was anxious to respond forcefully to the renewed surge of repression in South Africa.

Robert was given further coaching in the construction of larger explosives, ordered to prepare more DLBs and arms caches around Durban, and arrangements were finalised for Matthew Lecordier to travel through Botswana the following month on his way to Angola for full-scale military training. But the principal emphasis of these lectures was that Robert's unit should now intensify its offensive and select bigger, more conspicuous targets.

After several days of meetings, Robert and Greta returned over the Ramatlabama border on the evening of Thursday, June 12. The van was searched, but the secret compartment was not discovered; inside was three thousand rand in fifty-rand notes, as an initial payment for Zola's dependents, as well as another large batch of arms and explosives. Robert and Greta took it in turns to drive through the night and they arrived back in Wentworth early on the morning of Friday, June 13, to discover that the government had declared a State of Emergency.

They learned the news from Penelope Apelgren, Greta's sister. She was still in shock, nervous and shaking: the police had burst into their house shortly after midnight, brandishing rifles. They arrested Jeanette and Eric Apelgren. On finding some church protest posters, one of the policemen became enraged and yelled, 'I feel like shooting you now.'

In raids across the country, the police had swooped on political activists, churchmen, community leaders and trade unionists. Under the declaration of the State of Emergency the police had been given unprecedented arbitrary powers of arrest, allowing them to detain anyone without trial and prohibit all political activity. All television coverage of unrest was banned and press reports were severely censored. South Africa was effectively under martial law.

Robert and Greta hurried to buy the local newspapers. 'CRACK DOWN', announced *The Mercury*: 'Sweeping New Powers in Force.' In making his announcement in Parliament, explained the newspaper accounts, the State President had claimed that the ANC was planning a campaign of terror and sabotage to coincide with the anniversary of the 1976 Soweto riots on June 16. 'The Government has imposed the most extensive clamp ever on freedom of speech, association and the Press in moves that are expected to have serious consequences for South Africa,' reported the *Daily News* in its front page story. 'Estimates of people detained so far vary from one thousand – as reported on South African Television – to two thousand.'

The previous evening, President P. W. Botha had gone on

television to announce this State of Emergency in an irascible, defiantly aggressive speech, dismissing the threat of international sanctions by saying that South Africa would not 'crawl before anyone'.

Botha invoked the traditional Afrikaner sense of righteous isolation and destiny: 'If we have to be dependent on our Creator and our own ability alone, then I say: let it be. We have the faith, the inherent ability, and the natural resources to ensure our future.'

The State President also sombrely and clearly spelt out his view of the decision facing the country: 'There are times in the history of nations when a choice between unpleasant alternatives is inevitable. The choice between war and a dishonourable peace is such an example.'

Robert McBride had no doubts as to which of these activities the white government was committed. 'The state,' he concluded, 'had now declared war on our people.'

21

As both Jeanette and Eric Apelgren had been detained by the police along with dozens of other activists in Wentworth, Greta was obviously also at considerable risk. As a community worker, she was too well known in the area not to be an obvious target, so it was decided she should go into hiding for a few days. Clearly it would be unwise for her to go to work and instead of taking her home, Robert drove Greta straight to her grandmother's. She would remain there indoors, they agreed, until Robert contacted her.

Robert, exhausted after his all-night drive from Botswana, was agitated, upset and distracted. He was in a stormy, reeling state. He was seething; he was incensed by the State of Emergency.

'It enraged me,' he said. 'As members of the ANC and *Umkonto we Sizwe*, we are the vanguard of the people in the struggle – we had to do something. This declaration of war on our people, I had to do something about it.'

Early the following morning, Saturday June 14, Robert went round to Elm Avenue to see Matthew Lecordier. Here the narrative diverges. In court, both later gave conflicting accounts of what they discussed at that meeting and two entirely contradictory explanations of the subsequent sequence of events.

Robert McBride's version: On the 13th I hadn't decided yet what to do. So on the 14th, the following morning, I went to see Matthew Lecordier, to discuss the situation and what we must do about it. He was also upset because his brother, Brian, is a member of a student organisation and he'd had to go into hiding. So Matthew was also in an enraged state. I left Matthew and as I drove away, I decided, "No, I am going to make a car bomb. If they want war, I am going to give them war."'

193

It was that moment, Robert claimed in court, that he decided to make a car bomb.

He said that he took two thousand rand out of the money that had been given to recompense Bheki Ngubane's dependants and caught a bus along the South Coast Road to Clarewood stopping at Gateway Motors, the first second-hand car dealer that he saw. Outside stood a number of used cars, including a 1978 powder-blue, automatic Ford Cortina. The price pasted on the windscreen attracted his attention: 1,690 rand. The salesman had some difficulty in starting the Cortina, but as soon as he had succeeded in reviving the engine, Robert agreed to buy the eight-year-old car. He paid in cash, signing as William John Hughes, as well as reeling off from memory a false thirteen-digit identity number.

'After I had purchased the vehicle I went into town to choose a target,' Robert claimed in his testimony. 'I knew it must be centrally situated so it cannot be hidden away. In West Street, in the afternoon, I saw the target that was suitable for me. It was a central building with a lot of glass plates, and my intention was to flatten that thing, destroy it.'

'That thing' was the Hyperama 'House & Home', a prominent Durban landmark. It was a major furniture and household goods supermarket with a distinctive glass front. Its stark, shimmering exterior had a huge, green fibre-glass canopy above the entrance, while on either side, high above street level, were four green flags bearing the 'House & Home' logo. The expanse of dark, gleaming plate-glass reflected the mock Gothic redbrick turrets and marble columns of a fashionable store on the opposite side of West Street.

He chose this as his target, claimed Robert, because it was in the heart of the city and if he blew up this store, shattering all that glass, the authorities would not be able to suppress the news despite the censorship. It would be a devastating propaganda blow, he said, 'and there wouldn't be a glass building left.'

Later, after dark, by this account, he then proceeded several miles outside Durban to another buried arms cache at Cato Manor and removed the entire haul: ten SZ.6 demolition charges, an SPM limpet mine, some AK47 ammunition and a

Makarov pistol. Returning to his father's workshop, he proceeded to convert the powder-blue Ford Cortina he had bought that morning into a prodigious car bomb.

Robert constructed his bomb in the boot of the Cortina: it was a makeshift, lethal device. He stacked the ten demolition charges in the recess provided for the spare wheel, and then attached the SPM limpet mine on the top. He intended using the AK47 ammunition as shrapnel, 'to shatter the windows in case the shock waves were not strong enough, because I was told there was a rumour that this thing was bomb-proof.'

There were many burglar guards – protective window bars – in the workshop, as fitting them was one of the main parts of Derrick McBride's business. Using a blow-torch, Robert cut up a number of these and added this farrago of metal to his shrapnel stockpile. He packed the shrapnel into six plastic bags which he placed underneath the explosives and then secured the whole device with adhesive tape.

Finally, he removed the arm rest in the back seat, allowing access to the boot from inside the car. Robert attached a length of black electric flex to the safety-pin of the SPM limpet mine and fed the flex through into the rear seat: this was the trigger mechanism. Simply by turning in the driving seat, he would be able to pull the flex and activate the timing mechanism.

Robert then welded off the engine number and removed the front number plate, placing it inside the car, to ensure that after an explosion there would be no identifying signs left. Fifteen minutes after the cord was pulled, the bomb would detonate. It was a powerful device, fifty kilograms of explosive. The old, powder-blue Ford Cortina was now a lethal machine.

'Well, I told Matthew to make himself available in the early evening,' Robert told the court. 'I told him we'd be meeting some ANC comrades that evening, and to dress formally.'

Robert himself changed into some smarter clothes, unusually formal for him – brown trousers, a freshly ironed shirt, a tie and a fawn-coloured jacket. He phoned Greta and told her that they would be going to a drive-in. She was not happy to be seen in public and pointed out that it would be risky for her, but Robert insisted, so eventually she agreed to try and borrow her sister's

Mazda. He also told Greta to dress stylishly, so she selected a breezily colourful outfit: a new pair of denims, embroidered with pink roses and green leaves, a paisley patterned shirt, and a vivacious, bright green jersey. She also put on a pair of long, pear-shaped earrings and a claret-coloured beret, tipped at a rakish angle.

Matthew was still dressing when Robert arrived in Elm Avenue to pick him up at quarter to eight. Matthew looked as if he was preparing for a party, with jet black trousers, a prussian blue shirt and blue suede jacket. Robert told him to come as he was, and they returned to the workshop, where they met Greta who had managed to borrow her sister's Mazda.

Robert told the court, 'I told her that we would be going to the drive-in just now, but I had to drop this car for some friends in town and she would have to follow us. I was going to stop in West Street, but she would have to wait for us in Field Street, because I didn't want her to see the people I was meeting – and I didn't want them to see her.

'We drove along the southern freeway towards town, where, as you come off it there is a bump. When I hit the bump, I commented to Lecordier that there was over fifty kilos of explosives in the back, and that's the first time I told him that this was, in fact, a car bomb.

'Well, I told him that it was a car bomb, and I was going to park it in West Street, outside House and Home. But by that time, as we were speaking, we had arrived and parked at Hyperama House and Home. So I told Matthew to pass me the number plate. It was on the dash-board of the car. And I told him, "I am going to detonate it here now. I am going to initiate the explosive device."

'He refused to hand over the number plate. He said words to the effect that I was wasting fifty kilos of explosives here . . . why didn't I take it down to the Marine Parade, because the people want white destruction. That's what the people want. So I told him – I can't remember my exact words – but I told him it wasn't the policy of the ANC to attack white people. He replied something to the effect that the ANC is out of the country, and they are not feeling it inside the country, what's happening. It's up to the

196

people to decide what target to choose. He also said, "Why must you choose this target? You are doing a disservice to the people by detonating it here." So I told him that we could get into trouble – well, I didn't use that word, I used a stronger term – for detonating the car bomb there, because it's against the policy of our organisation. But anyway, we argued for some time like this and became hostile towards each other.'

According to Robert, they argued fiercely and he kept repeating, 'It's not the policy of the organisation to attack people . . . What we are already contemplating is not ANC policy,' but Matthew insisted on a white target.

Matthew, claimed Robert, said he knew of a suitable target: a bar on the Marine Parade.

Matthew Lecordier's version: Matthew's evidence stated that when Robert McBride came to visit him on Saturday morning, the fatal decision had already been made.

Matthew was also very angry about the State of Emergency. He agrees that he probably said, 'Whitey must now pay for this.'

But, he maintained, Robert had already bought the second-hand Ford Cortina and it was at this point, Matthew insisted, he was instructed to accompany Robert that night, 'because he was going to put a car, which he made into a bomb, in town.'

Robert, testified Matthew, directed him to be ready for a mission that night. 'He also told me to dress neat and smart, like I was going out.'

At that meeting, he informed the court, Robert gave him a detailed description of buying the vehicle: 'He said that he had welded over the engine number, so that the police wouldn't be able to trace it back to him. He also said that he bought the car under a false name, and he said Alan Pearce's uncle, whom I know as Rufus, saw him buy this car. He said he'd met up with him by accident. He thought Rufus was doing a job there at the garage . . . he said to me that if anyone finds out that he bought this car, then I would know who told them about it.'

That night Robert drove him into town in the Ford Cortina, while Greta followed behind in the Mazda 323. Matthew noticed a blanket and Robert's jacket on the back seat of the Cortina:

Robert 'told me that he had got a pistol in his jacket pocket, and if the police stopped us he would tell them he'd just bought the car, and if they wanted to search the car, he was going to take his pistol and use it on them, shoot them.

'He said that there were fifty kilos of TNT in the boot of the car and he'd put a big limpet in the centre of it to set it off. He had connected a cord to the pin of the limpet, which was leading from the boot through the gap in the back seat – where the arm-rest is, and under the blanket. He said he was going to pull it to set off the limpet. We stopped in West Street, outside Hyperama House and Home.'

It was here, claimed Matthew, that Robert told him they were going to bomb a target on Marine Parade.

The Marine Parade: this was the peppy main artery of the city's holiday entertainments, an ostentatious boulevard of luxury hotels, bars, cafés and restaurants. It was a gregarious, expansive promenade that presided over the broad, well-groomed beach front and provided a dazzling view of the shimmering, sun-flecked Indian Ocean. This was the white holiday makers' Mecca: Durban's renowned Golden Mile.

It is a vacation theme-world fresh from the pages of shiny, breathless travel brochures: *Durban's famous 'Golden Mile' of hotels, beaches and seaside entertainments has grown into almost four kilometres of playground. Re-landscaped in the mid-1980s, this glitter-ing waterfront has been softened with natural greenery and colourful blooms. Motor traffic is kept back from the beach and the pedestrian reigns supreme among the open-air plazas, pavement cafés and beach promenades. It's an ideal spot from which to watch the world go by – in all its shapes, sizes and shades of suntan . . .*

It is an ersatz creation. Along the palm-fringed promenade with its canary yellow lamp posts glide small motor-driven bug-gies with pastel-striped shades – side by side, implausibly, with rickshaws pulled by middle-aged Zulus decked out in elaborate feather head-dresses and gaudy beadwork costumes. On the trim, tiled sidewalk hot-dog and fast-food carts (like the flashy 'Fudge Lady' selling candy-floss, popcorn and toffee-apples) stand beside immobile rows of squatting Zulu women well trussed-up under the boiling sun with their wares laid out on old blankets and rush mats: wicker baskets, carved wooden cutlery and the intricate beadwork of necklaces, earrings, anklets and bangles. Sweating joggers weave their way through the idling tourists – the occasional smartly-dressed Indian family, but most of them whites in shorts and whimsical T-shirts. Groups of white teenagers hang out in luminescent trunks and day-glo sun-creamed noses.

It is a microcosm of cultural mayhem: a Zulu teenager sells kitch reproductions of the sjambok, the traditional white man's whip, a shop selling imitation African curios is 'Mykonos Gifts' and the bar playing boisterous American rock music is 'The Cockney Pride Pub'.

Between the promenade and the beach is a wide expanse of landscaped grass with fountains, sweeping pastel coloured walkways, geometrically shaped swimming pools and a children's funfair with whirlygigs and ski-chair rides. The next line of immaculately drilled recreation is the orderly beach, then beyond the sunbathers and the skimming line of surfers lengthens the lazy swell of the ocean.

The realm of the Golden Mile is lined with hotels like the Balmoral, the Malibu and Tropicana, as well as tall holiday flats and sleek, tiered time-shares with palatial balconies. Further along stands the solid Edward Hotel and the elegantly thin, white Holiday Inn. As darkness marshals and the warm breeze blows in from the ocean, the globular disks of the yellow lamp posts light up, followed sequentially by a neon waltz from bars, restaurants, night-clubs and discos.

The heavy tropical night falls upon this model amusement terrarium, aglow with a zippy tracer of playful lights, glossily slipping back between the illustrated covers of yet another frisky brochure: *After a leisurely day in the warm sun at the water's edge . . . there's no finer way of showing off a golden tan than by enjoying an excellent meal in tasteful surroundings within sound of the sea. International hotels with a variety of entertainment and cuisine vie for your favours with exotic dishes . . . at restaurants along the scintillating stretch of the Golden Mile with its many attractions and amusements.*

This, then, on the night of Saturday June 14, 1986, was the end of the rainbow that Robert and Matthew – however differing their accounts – had agreed to attack: a target on the Marine Parade.

None of the three protagonists is keen to discuss the details and exact manoeuvres that preceded the placing of the car bomb. All of them, for entirely dissimilar motives, prefer to stick to the respective accounts that were given in court. Robert's evidence was that he was in such an emotional state he allowed himself to be persuaded by Matthew Lecordier to strike at a more vulnerable objective. Matthew agreed in court that he told Robert: 'I know of one hotel where people sit on the verandah.'

But he consistently maintained that Robert McBride had planned all along to park the car bomb outside one of the establishments along the Marine Parade and he only made his suggestion, 'because it would have been an easy target'. Matthew denied they had a fierce argument about the placing of the car bomb; they had only parked the Ford Cortina in West Street, which was deserted, so that they could go in the Mazda to reconnoitre the Golden Mile. Robert made the decisions, said Matthew: he was in command.

Greta had meanwhile parked round the corner in Field Street, outside the Allied Building Society. It was dark and there were only a few people wandering about in the centre of the city. A light drizzle had begun to fall. Greta waited several minutes before the other two joined her. Robert climbed into the back and told her to head for the Marine Parade. They drove in silence, turning right into Commercial Road, right again across Pine Street and then left back into West Street and straight down to the Marine Parade, where they cruised slowly past the neon bars and crowded restaurants. As they passed the Balmoral Hotel, Matthew gestured with his head; the verandah was packed with young white people at tables, drinking.

There was no parking space, so Robert directed Greta to drive back to the Cortina, and with Greta following they drove it down Pine Street towards the Parade, parking at the bottom outside a car salesroom. Robert, said Matthew, told him to wait while they went to look for a parking space again: 'and also if the police come, I must use the pistol in his jacket pocket.'

Robert told the court that as he climbed into the passenger seat of the Mazda, Greta asked if they were finished with their business. 'I told her no,' he said. 'This is the alternative meeting point with the people.'

He directed her back to the brightly lit esplanade. They cruised slowly down the Parade, but could not find a parking space anywhere. At one point, according to Matthew, they returned and Robert told him to be patient: they were still searching for somewhere to park. Eventually, as they once again drove down the Parade, Robert spotted a space on the left hand side. It was on a corner, right next to the Parade Hotel.

At the side of the hotel was Garfunkel's Restaurant, while in front, on either side of its entrance, were two of Durban's most popular taverns: on the left the 'Why Not Bar', and on the right, 'Magoo's Bar'. Robert told Greta to pull quickly into the space. She noticed he was suddenly extremely tense. Greta experienced considerable difficulty manoeuvring the Mazda into that tight space on the corner, but when she had finally done so Robert told her, 'Just wait here, I am coming back now.'

'So I got out and walked straight to where Matthew was parked and I got into the car with Matthew and we came back,' Robert told the court. 'I drove alongside where Greta was parked. I told Matthew, "Wind down the window", and I told Greta to move out. She moved out and then I parked.'

While Greta drove ahead and double-parked a little way down the street, Robert asked Matthew to pass him the number plate from the dash board, which he slotted into the boot through a hole in the back arm-rest. This was to ensure that it too would be destroyed in an explosion. Robert then took hold of the black flex attached to the explosives and gave it a hard tug. It spun back through the gap in the arm-rest and he could see that the safety pin had been detached from the SPM limpet mine: the device had been activated.

By Robert's calculations the car was due to blow up in exactly fifteen minutes. However he was anxious not to hurry in case it drew attention to themselves, so first he showed the safety pin to Matthew, who immediately began to get agitated. He told

Matthew that they must act calmly and, when they got out, to walk slowly over to the Mazda.

'We waited about two minutes so as not to attact attention,' said Robert. 'But my main interest was to get away from the car as soon as possible without attracting attention. When we got out, we walked slowly . . . and then it struck me. We had made a mistake with the calculation. Because the thing had been set for fifteen minutes, but because of the weather it might go off, maximum, in about twelve minutes, after which the police would seal off the town.'

Greta was parked about two hundred yards further down the Parade. They strolled to the Mazda as casually as they could and Robert told Matthew to get in the front. Abruptly, as he himself sank into the back seat, he felt absolutely exhausted; a surge of lassitude enveloped him as the tension of the last two days finally surfaced, leaving him sapped both mentally and physically. Robert realised they would not now get out of Durban before the bomb went off. Immediately, he changed plans.

He instructed Greta to fill up with petrol at the corner of Beatrice Street and Albert Road. This was another oversight. Before every operation it was standard procedure to fill the tank, but he had omitted to do so. If there were going to be road blocks, Robert realised, they would probably have to take many detours that night.

'Robert was in a state, he was very tense,' said Greta. 'You couldn't talk to him or question him. It was obviously too late to go to the drive-in, and by that time I was aware that this was some ANC activity. No one was talking. It was very quiet.'

As they pulled out of the petrol station, Robert checked his watch: it was nine-thirty. He quickly made another decision and told Greta to drive up Sydenham Road, towards Ridge Road. It was a steep drive, cresting one of the hills circling the city. The reason for heading in that direction was that Robert remembered there had once been a police squad-car unit there. When the bomb went off, he reasoned, the squad cars would come racing out – and they would then follow behind the police in the Mazda.

It was one of the rules of MCW: *if you follow those who are following you, they will never catch up with you.*

202

Robert instructed Greta to pull over immediately opposite a cemetery on Ridge Road. They were high above Durban, with a view over the lights of the city and the docks. Robert rolled down the window; there was not a sound. The bomb, by his reckoning, should have gone off by now.

They sat in silence for a while. 'Can you hear any sirens?' Robert asked Matthew.

'No,' said Matthew.

Greta was baffled by their conversation, Robert claimed, and she asked, 'What sirens?' It was at this point, Robert maintained in court, that he told her about the car-bomb: 'Well, at first she was shocked. I can't remember her exact words, but she said something to the effect, you know, "How can you do that? There are people . . ." She asked me, "How much time is left? How long did you set it for?" So I told her, "No, it's gone off already."'

Not one of them could explain why, when the explosion was clearly audible all over the city, they heard nothing while waiting on the hill.

'Matthew began to get anxious,' said Greta. 'He said, "We should go – we've been here a long time." Robert was very tense, he didn't say anything. He was in the back. We were sitting in the dark. There was silence and then Matthew began to panic, and so I said we should go. Robert had his arm out of the window. He was listening. He was quiet. He didn't speak. He looked very far away. He was preoccupied, strained. We must have sat there for ten minutes. I started to put pressure on him. It seemed too eerie, parked there by the graveyard. It was so dark, and I started to get nervy. I said. "Let's go". Robert didn't reply. Then he started to talk about the time and the explosion. I was about to start the car when Robert finally said, "OK." No one spoke on the way back.'

They drove back towards Wentworth, avoiding the freeway, down Umbilo Road, along the Edwin Swales Drive to the white area of the Bluff. Here Robert threw the cord and safety pin out onto the grass verge. There was no sign of any police road blocks. They approached Wentworth up Quality Street and dropped Matthew off at his home.

'No one said a word,' remembers Greta.

When they got to Greta's grandmother's house she told Robert

203

that they could not leave the car outside as it would certainly get stolen. Robert was going to return to Hardy Place for the night, so he left her there and took the car back to her parents.

'Again, we didn't say a word about that evening,' said Greta.

Matthew went to a friend's twenty-first birthday party and stayed till the early hours drinking brandy. Antonio du Preez and Alan Pearce were there, as well as Whitey and Virgil. After a while they went outside to smoke some *dagga*, and Matthew stayed till four a.m.

Greta had wanted to hear the news, but it was too late so she went to bed. She tuned into Capital Radio at six the following morning, and that is when she heard it, although she says she did not, could not, believe the news till later that morning when her sister Penny brought over the *Sunday Tribune*.

Matthew also learnt the news from the *Sunday Tribune*. When he read it, he said, and saw the pictures, he wanted to puke.

Robert read the same account. For the first time it dawned on him what they had truly done.

22

The Parade Hotel was a cream-coloured, six-storey building situated on a corner of the Marine Parade. Across the boulevard was an elevated platform fringed with shrubs, cacti and dainty palms, with a view over the ocean.

The Parade Hotel was considered something of a landmark in Durban, mainly because of its two lively bars. Behind the façade, the hotel itself was slightly rundown and gloomy, and most of its residents were either students or retired people on modest pensions, some of them former policemen or air force personnel. The upper floors were dingy with peeling walls, threadbare carpets and smudgy prints of nautical scenes, all permeated with a seedy gentility, like a faded British seaside boarding house. The hotel's renown was based strictly on its two smart, street level bars.

The smaller den on the corner of the Marine Parade, where Robert had told Greta to park, was the 'Why Not Bar', which usually attracted couples and regulars. It had an intimate atmosphere, with a bar almost the length of the small, low-ceilinged room, and black waiters in white slacks and white T-shirts hovering discreetly in the corner. A sign at the door announced: DRESS STRICTLY SMART CASUAL.

It was the other bar, however, which could boast the celebrity, and its owner claimed it was the best-known tavern in South Africa. It took its name from the grey African parrot perched in the foyer, Mr Magoo, renowned for his wide vocabulary of swear words. Outside, a cobalt blue illumination proclaimed: MAGOO'S BAR. It was altogether trendier, with large mirrors and neon signs; there was a ship-board theme in the dark wooden decor, with brass lamps and rope-bound tables dotted about the L-shaped room. In the corner was a small stage, and a much younger crowd came here for the live music. That Saturday night of June 14,

1986, both bars were so packed that many patrons were spilling out into the foyer.

It took Robert several minutes to walk back to the spot in Pine Street where Matthew Lecordier was waiting impatiently in the Ford Cortina. Greta was not at all happy to be left for so long on the corner of the Marine Parade. This was a white part of town; all the people arriving at the Parade Hotel were white, and it was quite conspicuous for an attractive young Coloured girl to be sitting alone in the dark in a parked car. After a few minutes, she was disconcerted to see a young man staring at her through the windscreen.

Brett Erasmus had arrived with his girlfriend, Karen English, at nine-thirty, having arranged to meet some friends in Magoo's Bar. Erasmus was a former car salesman who had worked for a Mazda dealer, and as they reached the Parade Hotel he saw both a smart new Venetian red Mazda 626 SLX and nearby a dirty Jamaican bronze Mazda 323. He stopped and began pontificating to his girlfriend on the difference between the two models, pointing out how filthy the 323 was compared to the shiny 626. The light was shining on the windscreen on the 323 and as he stared at it he thought for a few seconds that he was seeing a reflection of his own face.

'They're waiting for us,' called his girlfriend, bored with his talk of automobiles. 'It's getting late.'

Suddenly, with a shock, Brett Erasmus realised he had been looking straight through the windscreen at someone else. The young girl in the car was staring back at him, and their eyes caught and held each other's gaze for a moment, before Erasmus turned away embarrassed and followed his girlfriend up the steps into the hotel.

Moments later, two other white men came down the steps of the hotel and began to stare at Greta and make comments. Jan Nel, a rambunctious-looking newspaperman, was in Durban to meet an old friend from the liquor trade, Hentie Englebrecht. They had decided to look in at the Why Not Bar for a drink, but Jan Nel had just given up smoking and found the room too smoky. Magoo's was just as bad, so after just one whisky they decided to go back to their hotel.

Englebrecht spotted Greta holding onto the wheel of the stationary Mazda and gazing ahead of her fixedly. 'Look at that aunty behind the wheel,' he remarked to Nel. 'She looks a bit uptight.'

As they passed the Mazda, Jan Nel crouched down and said jocularly to the young woman, 'What are you doing here?'

She drew back, alarmed, jerking her head away. As they continued back to their hotel, Jan Nel joked to his friend that she looked very angry, as if she had just had a tiff with her boyfriend.

Brett Erasmus and Karen English, still looking for their friends, came out of the Parade Hotel; they walked northwards towards another bar, the 'Easy Beat', where they met another friend, Heidi, who suggested returning to Magoo's. There had been a brief shower earlier that evening and it was a fresh, clear night. As they arrived at the Parade Hotel, Brett Erasmus saw the Mazda 323 pulling out. His first thought was to fetch his own car and bring it closer to the hotel, but by that time another car had taken the tight parking space on the corner.

Minutes later, about a quarter to ten, a young twenty-five-year-old Durban business broker drew up on the corner outside the hotel, and double-parked for a moment to let his passengers out. He was with his new girlfriend Angelique Pattenden, and two friends, Lesley Mitchell and Gavin Maxwell. As Gavin Maxwell got out of the back door, Roger Shillaw warned, 'Watch out, don't scratch that car.' It was parked right on the corner, adjacent to the Why Not Bar: he noticed it was a powder-blue Ford Cortina.

Having dropped the others, Roger Shillaw drove on a bit till he found a parking space just beyond the Empress Hotel. As he retraced his steps, a fifteen-year-old Indian schoolboy was also approaching the hotel on the other side of the Marine Parade. Rajesh Dulcharen doubled as a flower seller in the evenings in order to earn some pocket money, and the place to sell flowers on a Saturday evening in Durban was definitely the Golden Mile. Roger Shillaw entered the Why Not, ordered a beer and made his way through the densely packed bar to a table where his friends were sitting. He had just turned to his left to make a remark when everything went dark and he was thrown to the ground.

Jan Nel and Hentie Englebrecht heard the explosion several

blocks away at the Edward Hotel. It was ten to ten. The blast was audible all over Durban. Brett Erasmus had been standing in the doorway of the crowded Why Not; he and Karen had located their friends and he was about to suggest they go and get something to eat when the car-bomb outside exploded. 'There was a hell of a bang,' he said, 'and the whole world collapsed.'

The owner of the Parade Hotel, Russell Davidson, had just elbowed his way through the Why Not with two cool drinks and had put them down on the counter in the foyer when there was a vivid flash. He grabbed the hotel manageress who was standing next to him and pulled her to the floor. 'It was yellow, and then it went darker, to an orange colour,' he remembered eight months later when giving evidence. 'And then there was a still, dead silence. Then . . . the noise started, and everything began coming down. There were objects flying all over the place. It seemed as if it carried on for about five minutes. Once the noise had settled, people were screaming and running – and there was blood and absolute chaos.'

Outside, the young flower seller Rajesh Dulcharen had been crossing the road to go into the hotel when he was blown violently backwards. He picked himself up and began to run, but he stumbled only a few yards before blacking out completely, his whole body pierced by tiny flying fragments of metal, which also punctured his stomach and lungs.

In the Why Not Helen Kearney had been serving behind the bar. 'There was an incredible roar and a green and red flash, like luminous lights going off,' said Helen Kearney. 'I was bending down behind a thick heavy steel fridge to get some lemonade when the bar blew away. It seemed like slow motion, everything being swallowed up into a vacuum, falling away, the roof, the walls. It blew the back of the bar away, right through to Garfunkel's Restaurant. Shards of glass were embedded in my head and thighs and as I was sucked through the hole I remember seeing there were people drinking in Garfunkels, Irish coffees – but there were no glasses in their hands.

'Suddenly there seemed to be nothing left standing. It was quick and yet so slow. You could actually see the wall collapsing in slow motion. For a moment there was a stunned silence, then there was screaming and crying. So much confusion . . . a bloody mess. There was skin, flesh and blood everywhere – people wandering around with their clothes scorched and half-off, blood pouring down, glass sticking out of their heads and faces, arms hanging down, saying, "What's happening?"'

In the foyer Russell Davidson, the hotel owner, staggered to his feet and began yelling, 'Get out, get out – there might be another bomb!'

He began to run outside and as usual the parrot squawked, 'Bye!', so he rushed back to fetch Mr Magoo. Outside there was chaos. Debris was scattered everywhere. Glass had shattered all over the pavement. There were charred scraps of twisted metal; bits of the cars parked nearby had been scattered hundreds of yards down the Marine Parade, and immediately outside the hotel the mangled skeletons of automobiles lay at crazed angles all over the road, flames still flickering eerily in the dark.

There were people lying on the pavement. Others wandered about in the street confused, their clothes in tatters. One man was shouting, 'Laurie, I can't see! I can't see!' Ambulances began to arrive. People had been blown through the windows of the bars. One couple had been sucked out of a car as they were passing. By the time Jan Nel and Hentie Englebrecht returned to the scene, the area had been cordoned off. It looked like a war zone, the hotel a charred, gutted wreck, with a pyramid of flames still licking four to five storeys high. Jan Nel noticed that the epicentre of the flames appeared to be on the corner, right where the car with the strange girl had been parked.

The victims were already being ferried to Addington Hospital, which immediately opened a 'disaster ward'. Nurses soon described it as 'looking like a battlefield'. Brett Erasmus and Karen English were treated at the hospital, given stitches and then discharged; they had cuts over their arms, hands, backs and faces. The ceiling had collapsed on top of them.

'I moved the ceiling out of the way and I looked towards the outside,' recollected Brett Erasmus, when called as a witness. 'I saw a burning car, I saw everything all over the place. This – the room we were in, was now totally destroyed. Everything was all over the place and immediately behind me there was a woman lying with . . . well, she was lying very still and she had one hell of a lot of blood on her. As far as I was concerned she was dead.

'Karen couldn't walk so I had to pick her up and walk out of the entrance and what was left of the revolving door. As we started walking outside we had to watch where we were walking because there were another two women lying there as well, sprawled across the pathway. I could see that they were very badly injured and they were moaning and groaning.'

He crossed the road and placed Karen in a car, and then went back to the hotel to see if he could help. One of the women lying outside looked dead. The other one was still breathing. She began to jerk, and someone tried to give her a cardiac massage. It didn't appear to be working and the man kept saying, 'She's going, she's going.' An ambulance arrived and they tried to apply a suction to the woman's mouth but as they did so she died.

Two of the women who died, Michelle Gerrard and Julie van der Linde, were friends. Michelle was twenty-eight, a commercial artist, and that night she was supposed to have gone to a cousin's twenty-first birthday, but had forgotten; the day before she had bought an airline ticket so that she could join her boyfriend in America. Julie, also twenty-eight, was a divorcee with a small daughter and had just moved into a new flat. She had gone out with Michelle to celebrate.

The third to die was Angelique Pattenden. She had been in the group dropped off by Roger Shillaw when he double-parked next to the blue Ford Cortina. She and Roger had just played a game of squash. Angelique was twenty-three; she had met Roger six months earlier, but according to the *Daily News*, the couple had decided only the previous week that they were getting 'quite serious'.

'The whole hotel was in complete darkness,' Roger Shillaw later testified. 'There were people running straight at me and trying to get out through the windows. Two young girls tried to jump through. My younger brother and I stopped these two girls and put them out of the window. There was a lot of screaming and shouting outside. I cleared the table and found Angelique Pattenden lying there.

'I tried to pick her up, but unfortunately my left arm just had no strength. I called for my brother who came back and helped me pick her up. We took her out through the window. She spoke to me on the way out. She asked me what had happened and I told her just to keep quiet, that she'd be all right.'

She died in the front entrance of the Parade Hotel.

23

Although the Why Not Bar had been the more severely hit, the press immediately began to refer to the attack as the 'Magoo's Bar Bombing'. The following day, June 15, the *Sunday Tribune* mistakenly reported that two white women and sixty-eight others had been wounded when a bomb exploded at the packed bar at nine-fifty p.m. The gruesome account of the carnage and damage mentioned that the police were looking for a short, white male in his twenties, wearing a beige jacket. Subsequent reports soon corrected the death toll to three: all white women.

Robert was horrified; he was also scared. 'I had been too exhausted to think about it on the actual night, before we heard what happened,' said Robert. 'But the next morning when I read the newspapers, and I was alone for a while, then it really hit me. The people, the sorrow . . .'

Greta reacted more calmly. That Sunday afternoon her parents and other members of the family came to visit her grandmother. 'All they could talk about was the bomb,' said Greta. '"How terrible, how shocking, those poor white people." They kept on saying they couldn't imagine how anyone could do something like that.'

Greta did not say a word until her grandmother remarked, 'I am sure a white man did it.'

'Why wouldn't a black have done it?' asked Greta, irritated. 'I mean, they're angry.'

'Even if black people did it,' replied her grandmother tranquilly, 'I am sure a white person was behind it.'

Greta realised there was no turning back now. She felt like an outlaw. She also thought it was too dangerous for her to stay in Wentworth, so she wrote to the child welfare department and told them that she would not be coming back to work. They knew the police had been harrassing her and her family and she explained that it was too risky for her to remain in Durban as, like her sister Jeanette and brother Eric, she was also in danger of being arrested.

Then she phoned Robert and told him she was going to go to Johannesburg. 'He agreed,' said Greta. 'He was disturbed about what he had done. He felt very upset. He was agitated and distressed. My sisters packed my clothes. I told them I would not be coming back. They didn't ask me any questions.'

Greta left for Johannesburg on Monday, June 16. That morning the *Natal Mercury* reported a massive police investigation was underway. The names of the three dead women were announced and the Deputy Minister of Information, Mr Louis Nel, told the newspaper, 'Western interest groups and others outside our country who pamper terrorist organisations must take note of the unscrupulous nature of terrorism.'

The Commissioner of Police, General Johan Coetzee, confirmed that the explosives had been of Russian origin and said, 'As in the past, this indicates that the ANC is probably involved.' However the ANC, said the newspaper, had no comment on the explosion. The Bureau of Information was quoted as assuring the South African public that the South African government was in full control of the situation and that there were no grounds for fear.

Reports gave detailed accounts of the scene of destruction along the Marine Parade. Glass and wreckage were everywhere, strewn hundreds of yards from the hotel, where shredded curtains billowed out of twisted window frames. An entire wheel had been found floating in the Rachel Finlayson swimming pool on the other side of the street, and it had not been able to re-open till midday on Monday as it had also been filled with glass, tyres and scraps of metal. The windows of all the surrounding flats had been shattered.

Among the injured, whose number was finally set at eighty-nine, was the Durban City goalkeeper, John McKenna, from Liverpool, who told the *Star* newspaper of Johannesburg, 'This has not put me off South Africa – it could happen anywhere.'

The local Durban paper, the *Daily News*, quoted a government

214

source as speculating that the explosives had probably been smuggled into South Africa from Tanzania, through Mozambique and Swaziland. Brigadier Leon Mellet, the spokesman for the Bureau of Information, estimated there had been between twenty-five and fifty kilograms of explosive and said that the police had already identified the car as being a blue, two-litre Cortina GL automatic, but he gave out the wrong registration number and erroneously said it had been stolen from a panel beater in April. But in a ringing conclusion, with a menacing Shakespearean twist, the Brigadier pledged, 'The security forces are in charge of the situation and will remain in charge tomorrow and tomorrow and tomorrow.'

Captain Zenardt de Beer of the Police Special Branch was tall, thin and intense, with an angular, tapering face and a trim black moustache. His inexpressive eyes were a watery grey-green and already there were flecks of grey in the thinning, dark hair and old-fashioned sideburns. Apart from a boyish cow's lick in his hair, de Beer looked a great deal older than his years. He had a distracted, wary manner and spoke with a slow, dour seriousness and no hint of humour. He did not look like a man who in fact regularly jogged, swam and played cricket. Although his neck at the open V of his shirt collar was mottled and leathery from the sun, the Captain's face was unnaturally pale, with an unhealthy, waxen glaze, like marble.

His paternal ancestors, the de Beers, had emigrated to South Africa in the seventeenth century, while his mother's family were descended from French Huguenots. His parents had moved from Pretoria to Broken Hill in what was then Northern Rhodesia, where his father worked on the copper mines and where Zenardt de Beer was born. Shortly afterwards the de Beers moved on again to Lausanne in Switzerland for two years, so when Zenardt and his two older brothers returned to South Africa they were known at school as 'the Frenchies'. The de Beers settled in Kokstad, a small town in southern Natal, close to the border with the nominally independent 'Bantustan', the Transkei.

The family were close, and staunch members of the *Nederduitse*

Gereformeerde Kerk, the Dutch Reformed Church, the largest of the three powerful Afrikaner Calvinist Churches in South Africa, which had played such a dominant role in the formation of Afrikaner nationalism, as well as in formulating its 'Christian Nationalist' ideology and apartheid policies. The de Beers, however, were not well off and Zenardt had to leave school at sixteen before taking his matric. He was admitted to the Police College in Pretoria, and not long afterwards the matriculation became a mandatory requirement for entry. He completed a year's course in Pretoria, simultaneously gaining his matric, and at the age of eighteen he was given his first posting; to a police radio station in Durban, logging complaints and sending out patrol cars.

After two years Zenardt de Beer was transferred to Durban Central, where as a police-van driver he was himself sent out to attend complaints. He spent another four years in the Durban CID on the housebreaking unit before applying for the élite police division, the Special Branch – South Africa's security police. The Special Branch were responsible for the surveillance, arrest, interrogation and prosecution of the state's political opponents. They had wide powers of detention, and effectively could incarcerate anyone they saw fit for as long as they liked. It was the Special Branch who interrogated political prisoners, frequently torturing them; prisoners who died in their care during interrogation were routinely said to have 'thrown themselves' out of windows at police headquarters.

Zenardt de Beer was accepted by the Special Branch in 1978 and promoted to sergeant. He was sent on a special security course in Pretoria, dealing with all aspects of undercover work: investigation, surveillance, recruitment and the handling of informants, agents and infiltrators, as well as firearm practice. He was issued with a 9mm Beretta. He loved his work in the Special Branch; by 1986 de Beer had risen to the rank of Captain.

He found this specialised political work particularly absorbing because, 'You deal with people with other motives – people who are ideologically motivated.' He disliked the term 'Security Police', he said, because it made them sound, 'like some kind of Nazi infantry'.

The other buttress of the Captain's life was religion. Zenardt de Beer had turned his back on the *Nederduitse Gereformeerde Kerk* and, influenced by his wife, had joined the Old Apostolic Church. This was a break-away sect of the New Apostolics, the group in which Derrick McBride's brother Spuddy was a minister. Captain de Beer had been accepted after the laying on of hands by a 'living Apostle'. In South Africa, there were four such Apostles, the highest rank in the sect – achieved through prophecies, visions and dreams. The Captain himself preached regularly to his local congregation.

If people did not obey the will of God, he believed, there would be anarchy upon earth. The Old Apostolic was a church of discipline. 'It is a church of obedience,' professed de Beer. 'If I disobey my parents that is a sin. If a government brings out a law and you transgress, that is a sin. All disobedience is a sin.'

For the past three years Captain de Beer had been deeply immersed in the huge United Democratic Front treason trial. This was only the second trial of its kind, in which the State had attempted to convict its political opponents of treason. The first trial in 1956 had attracted international attention when the state put 156 opponents including Chief Albert Luthuli, Nelson Mandela, Walter Sisulu and Oliver Tambo in the dock. That case had dragged on for four years before all the defendants were finally discharged. The state was now trying to convict sixteen prominent members of the United Democratic Front, including its co-Presidents Archie Gumede and Albertina Sisulu, of treason.

It was the state's case that the UDF was pursuing a revolutionary strategy, including non-violent actions and mass mobilisation 'which could nevertheless be seen as consciously contributing to the promotion of the violent aspect of the revolution.' Most antagonists of the government believed that this expensive, drawn-out court case was a strategy on the part of the state to immobilise the extra-parliamentary opposition and remove a number of prominent black and Indian leaders from circulation. Captain de Beer had been one of a large team of Special Branch officers involved with the case, and much of the past three years had been spent in Pietermaritzburg where the trial was to be heard in the Natal Supreme Court. The case was accompanied by a great deal of publicity, especially after some of the accused sought asylum in the British Consulate in Durban.

The treason trial finally commenced on May 20, 1986, but the state's case was already in disarray three weeks later when Captain Zenardt de Beer was recalled from Pietermaritzburg to Durban to take command of a major investigation. Captain de Beer was just thirty-one, exceptionally young to be entrusted with such a prominent, publicly sensitive case. He was to be in command of a massive man-hunt, one of the biggest in the history of South Africa.

Captain Zernardt de Beer directed the formidable search for the car bombers from the police headquarters at C. R. Swart Square, named after the first President of the Republic of South Africa. It was a tall, thin, impersonal building set in a flat, open area near the Durban Drive-in and opposite a rugby field. Security was tight, and outside there were concrete look-out posts. At the entrance, as in many public buildings, were pictures of limpet mines and grenades, with the warning: TERRORIST WEAPONS, LOOK AND SAVE A LIFE. Even the calendars were decorated with pictures of anti-personnel mines and hand-grenades. Captain de Beer's office was on the thirteenth floor, the Special Branch command centre. In the distance, facing east towards the ocean, shone the tall white towers of Durban's most palatial hotels along the Golden Mile.

The Captain found himself faced with an imposing work schedule. He began studying all the cases of sabotage in the region over the last few years; he ploughed through mounds of paperwork, visited the scenes of all known guerrilla attacks, studied thousands of photographs of political activists and ANC suspects, examined the types of explosives used in all cases of sabotage. It was important to establish if the sudden burst of ANC activity around the Durban area was the work of one unit and if there was any discernible pattern. But as the evidence piled up, he could not tell if there was any linking plan to all these attacks.

The Magoo's Bar bomb generated a tempest of publicity and de Beer soon stopped reading the papers. He felt pressurised, not only because there was so much publicity, but also from the constant attentions of his superiors. White South African public opinion had been outraged by this bombing. The shock was all the more traumatic because it had been an assault on young South Africans right in the heart of the country's leisured sanctuary, a pristine landscape of paved, pastel walkways and facsimile plazas, their own theme gardens of Babylon. The Golden Mile in many ways epitomised the middle-class white South African dream: a gregarious trilogy of fun, sun and sport. That the three victims were all attractive young women also caused a deeper, more resonant shock throughout the country. It also profoundly unsettled Captain de Beer and redoubled the burden on him to produce a suspect.

He was getting pressure from all sides, including his head office in Pretoria. Sometimes de Beer was managing to get only a couple of hours sleep a night. Normally he and his wife would attend the Old Apostolic church every evening, but that routine had to be completely sacrificed, as did all family activities with his son and daughter. His wife, who also worked at police head-quarters as a typist, understood his single-mindedness.

Zenardt de Beer found inspiration in his faith. 'I am the church, it is within me,' he believed. Zenardt de Beer was in no doubt where his duty lay: 'The government has been placed there by God. I believe I must be obedient to Caesar. Therein lies my salvation.'

The following Saturday, exactly a week after the car bomb at the Parade Hotel, there were three more explosions in and around Durban. One detonated shortly after midnight in the centre of the city, and the other two went off in the early hours of the following morning.

Robert McBride, shaken by the deaths at the Parade Hotel, was planning on withdrawing from Natal for a period and setting up operations in the Transvaal. With this in view, he was keen to delegate more responsibility within the unit, particularly to Matthew Lecordier whom he saw as a potential commander.

Matthew was ill-disciplined, but he was brave and resourceful. It was true that he was always in need of money, and after the

Edendale operation Gordon had authorised Robert to give Matthew five hundred rand from their funds. Yet since Robert had first recruited him, he had not broached the question of being given guns again. As Matthew became increasingly involved in the unit's underground activities, that extravagant notion of carrying out a bank raid seemed to have receded. The problems of Matthew's waywardness and lack of discipline, Robert reasoned, would soon be rectified by a stint of military training. Arrangements had been made for Matthew to leave South Africa the following month in order to attend an ANC camp in Angola. Meanwhile, Robert felt he needed to bring on his unit as rapidly as possible.

That Saturday evening Matthew Lecordier and Antonio du Preez met Robert at the Factorama workshop at eight o'clock. Robert had already removed a further four mini-limpet mines, with fuses and detonators, from the workshop loft and he showed them how to prepare the explosives. 'He demonstrated everything step by step,' said Matthew. 'He told us to watch very carefully as we would soon have to do it on our own.'

Robert also told Matthew and Antonio not to simply agree with everything he said. He expected them to raise objections and even suggest missions.

He told them about the targets that he had planned for that evening: two oil containers and two oil pipelines. Matthew immediately said that he felt they should not attack too many objectives around the Wentworth area. It would look as though the operations were being carried out by a Wentworth unit, he pointed out, and this would give the police an invaluable lead.

'I accepted his objection because it made sense,' said Robert. 'He also said he knew of a target in Point Road, and I thought of the police van that parks on the corner. We had spoken about that previously as a possible target. The van parks there for about three hours and from intelligence we picked up, the police leave that place and go onto the beach where the prostitutes are.'

The first target was an oil pipeline over the Umlaas Canal, immediately south of Wentworth, sandwiched between the Meerwent Indian location and the Louis Botha airport. The pipeline rose briefly above ground in order to cross the narrow canal which ran between high concrete banks through a scrubby bush wasteland and out into the Indian ocean. It was pitch black as Antonio drove them down the gravel path alongside the canal.

'I remember telling Antonio to drive as slow as possible, because I said, "Don't touch the brake lights as someone will see them,"' said Matthew. 'Antonio never touched the brakes, but I told Rob we ought to get out of the car and walk to the pipes. Antonio drove to the beach and pretended to be looking for someone. We placed the limpets under the elbow of the pipes, face up. Then we walked back along the main road, acting like we were drunk . . . a show for people in cars. After three or four minutes, pretending to thumb a lift, Antonio picked us up. Again, I told Antonio not to hurry and we returned to the workshop. Rob asked me to get one of the limpet mines. I did this and got back in the car. We went to the container just off Hime Street . . . we thought it was an oil storage depot.'

In fact the huge steel containers stored vegetable oil. They were situated in the heart of Wentworth's industrial area, parallel to Chamberlain Road, where the substation had already been hit twice. Robert instructed Antonio and Matthew to drive round the block while he approached the perimeter of Industrial Oil Processors with the limpet tucked inside his coat. There was a six-foot concrete wall topped with coils of razor wire; on the other side, Robert could hear the sound of two men talking in Zulu, whom he assumed were security guards. All the same, he pulled the safety pin and, jumping as high as he could, he pushed his hand through the wire and placed the limpet against the steel tank. The magnet made a loud clang as it struck and the voices on the other side of the wall went silent. Robert hurried away. As he reached the corner Antonio and Matthew drove into view.

They returned to the workshop to pick up the final limpet – the target this time was in the centre of Durban. Matthew had volunteered to place the explosive. They took the freeway into the city and it was nearly eleven p.m. as they approached Point Road, when Matthew suddenly suggested they should buy a carton of milk.

'I felt sure the limpet would fit into a milk carton . . . a good way to hide and carry it,' he said. 'That part of town is busy till late, so we stopped at a shop in West Street and I went in with some money Rob had given me. I bought a couple of packets of crisps and a litre of milk. While driving we drank what we could. At some lights a police car stopped alongside us. They had a couple of dogs in the back. I just looked at them from the back and I was really nervous then, though I don't think it showed. The cops drove off and Robert made a joke about us being right under their noses.

'We drove a little further and Rob told Antonio to pull over. He got out and poured out the rest of the milk. We pushed the limpet in and it fitted. Then we continued driving till a block before West Street. I was to get out and walk. Rob pulled the pin out. I think I told him to leave the straw in the milk. They were going to drive off and wait for me round the corner, and as I got out of the car I made out I was drinking the milk.'

According to Robert the plan had been for Matthew to place the explosive in the empty police van; later Matthew maintained that it had been to put it in an empty bin outside the Copper Shop, a gift and curio store. As he walked down the road, Matthew saw there was a policeman sitting in the stationary police van. Pretending he had finished the carton of milk, he casually placed it in the bin outside the Copper Shop.

'I wondered, "Has this policeman seen me doing this?"' he said. 'I thought the best thing to do would be to walk towards the Addington Hospital, so that I would not be going straight back to Robert and Antonio.

'I walked for about ten minutes and went to where the bus terminus used to be. I asked a guy parked in a taxi what the time was and he said eleven-twenty or eleven-thirty. I asked him if the buses were still leaving and he said I had just missed one. I knew that was the last bus to Wentworth, so I asked him, "How much to Wentworth?" He said about fifteen rand. I said, "No, never mind," as I only had three rand on me. I did not know what to do, as I knew Robert and Antonio must be worried.

'So I called my girlfriend Nicole to pick me up. She argued, saying, "Where are your friends?" She was annoyed because the weekends were meant to be our time together and I had not spent time with her. I'd told her I was going to meetings. She did not know what I was doing. She was annoyed with me for calling so late. It was nearly midnight. I told her the police broke up our meeting and she said, "Oh, those are the sort of friends you have." I was getting worked up. I said, "If you don't want to do this, forget it!" So she said OK.

'While walking towards West Street I noticed a lot of police, probably because of the car bomb last week, I thought, so I decided the best thing would be to go to the benches outside the public toilets in West Street and wait. While sitting there I heard the blast. It was the first time I had heard the blast of a mini limpet mine. For something so small, it made a very loud bang.

'I sat there thinking, where is Nicole? Then I heard sirens. Nicole arrived about one minute after the bang. I was very pleased. She saw all the police lights further down the road and wanted to see what was going on. But I said, "No, just take the first right out of here – I want to go home." When we got home to my dad's place, we sat outside in the car and I lied to her about the meeting that night. I invented all sorts of details. She was still cross with me . . . suddenly I saw Rob drive by and I told Nicole to step on the brake so he could see the lights flash. Rob stopped and I thanked Nicole and told her to go. Rob opened his window and asked what happened. I explained how I thought the police had seen me and all that. Robert was pleased with me. He said, "Does Nicole know anything?" I said no, I had lied to her about a meeting. He was very pleased with my handling of the situation.'

A few days later Robert called Matthew and Antonio again to help him stockpile the Dead Letter Box at Shongweni. They drove out after dark and dug up the large red metal box which had been buried in the bush. The armaments had been removed from the workshop attic and were being placed here for the use of guerrillas infiltrating the country from abroad. There were rifles, ammunition, hand-grenades, limpets and an RPG rocket launcher.

The following Sunday another sabotage operation had been planned, but Antonio du Preez was unavailable. Rather than postpone the mission, suggested Matthew, this would be the ideal opportunity to test out Alan Pearce. Robert agreed.

'That night we did the water pipes at Westville, which run

across the highway on a little walkway,' said Matthew. 'It's about twenty minutes inland from Wentworth. We had planned this and we knew what to do. Alan and myself ran up the bank to reach the water pipe, while Robert continued driving to the next turnoff where he was to do a U-turn and come back on the opposite side. The pipes were lagged so there was no place that the magnet could grip. When we got up onto the walkway we placed one on top of the pipe and then ran across to the other side where I balanced the other limpet on top of a big valve. We left it like that and ran down the bank, where Rob picked us up.

'The limpets were set to go off at six a.m., before the morning rush hour. This would cause a disruption to the traffic. Anyway, we drove off. I don't think I saw Robert again after that operation. He disappeared.

'I got worried when I did not hear. I never saw or heard from him again.'

Robert had followed Greta up to Johannesburg, where she had rented a small flat under the false name of Jacobs in the bohemian and multi-racial high-rise district of Hillbrow.

Greta found Robert much changed. He was obsessive and morose, and he would flare up angrily for no apparent reason. 'Our relationship was getting worse and worse,' said Greta. 'He suffered from depression. He'd cry at night, he couldn't sleep. Sometimes he'd read all night.'

For his part, Robert felt Greta was unable to respond to him. He was also concerned that after giving up her job, she was becoming even more dependent on him. They argued over nothing, and yet he did not know how to stop this disintegration of trust. Even when they made love, he felt Greta was unresponsive. 'It was like she was doing her duty,' he said.

At first they were nervous about going out during the day, so they stayed in the small flat. The atmosphere became fretful and claustrophobic. Robert was nervy and monosyllabic. He read much of the time. Greta remembers him immersed in the chunky paperbacks of the South African thriller writer Wilbur Smith: escapist fantasies about larger-than-life heroes, often handsome white hunters tracking big game and battling against evil in the throbbing Dark Continent. But most of all Robert read the newspapers, scouring them for any reference to the Magoo's Bar bombing.

'I didn't even want to think about the incident – I had blocked it out of my mind,' said Greta. 'If there was a newspaper report, I'd skip over it. I didn't want to face it or dredge up the bad memory.'

Robert on the other hand was obsessed by it. He seemed haunted. He was harrassed by bad dreams: 'I felt I was in a big open space, but everything was pressing down on me. The enormity of it all! I felt dizzy – unreal, as if I had woken up after dreaming, and wasn't where I thought I was – stunned by a collision with reality.'

Robert could not shake off this feeling of horror: 'I was in a state of shock. Before, I was just carrying out an operation – the effects only hit me later, when I was not hyped-up. Then the emotions came in and I felt bad. I felt terrible. I felt disgusted with myself and ashamed. I felt I would never be forgiven.

'Before I was doing it for the army, for the freedom of the people. The very planning and the act of placing the bomb distanced me. It was mechanical. It was like the bomb did it . . . and I only pulled the pin. At the time it was quite practical – something to carry out. Afterwards I realised the enormity of the whole thing. The humanness of the suffering came to me. If they had been soldiers it would have been a legitimate target. Civilians were not a legitimate target. Because they were women I felt it all the more. I felt I was stooping to the same level as the enemy. I was worried all the time. I was irritable and upset.'

They went out at night and walked the streets, and sometimes they went to see a film. Greta determined to try and continue as normally as possible, but almost nothing would bring Robert out of his morbid introspection. They bought a cassette player and Robert listened to reggae music. Occasionally the gloom would lift briefly and he'd dance in the flat. But these moments never lasted.

'He seemed to get upset over the slightest thing and he would withdraw into silence,' said Greta. 'I used to fight back and then we'd have big arguments over silly things. The tension was terrible. I told him I wanted to leave and go and stay with my aunt in Eldorado Park. He'd agree . . . then disagree.'

They still observed the cardinal *Umkhonto* rule never to discuss an operation. But to Robert it was no longer 'a dream that never happened'.

One afternoon they went out of Johannesburg into the veld. It was mid-July, winter in the southern hemisphere, a sunny golden day: a lucidly clear winter's day with a cloudless, glacially azure sky. They walked through the tall, dry, corn-yellow grass of the high veld. It was one of those serenely luminous winter days when sounds carried miles in the stilled calm, and although the veld appeared lifeless they could hear muffled voices from afar. The air was fresh and moist, the light translucent. They made love; afterwards, Robert felt subdued.

'I opened up,' he said. 'I told her how I felt. But Greta defended the action. I was shocked. She said, "No, that is what the whites have been doing." I was sad. I said, "No, even our own people will not defend it."'

In the second week of July Robert informed Greta that he wished to return to Wentworth for a flying visit. She was under the impression he intended to pass on some final instructions to Matthew Lecordier and Antonio du Preez.

'He wanted me to come, but I did not want to go . . . I also insisted on keeping the car in Johannesburg,' said Greta. 'We had a terrible argument. Eventually, though, I agreed to go.'

They set out in the Mazda 323 on Friday morning, July 11, heading south-east on the N3 past the stumpy mine dumps on the outskirts of Johannesburg, and through the ranging sweep of the Transvaal low veld, uninterrupted miles of mealie fields, sunflowers and the parched yellowing grass pastures where lean cattle grazed with officious white tick birds on their backs. The grey strip of the road stretched for empty miles ahead through the grainy, russet plains of the Orange Free State, dotted with flat-topped ochre hills in the distance, and as dark fell they reached the greener peaks of Natal, where the tree-covered hillsides were speckled with African kraals and white thatched huts.

It was eight p.m. by the time they reached Durban. Greta

226

phoned her parents' house from the public booths near the City Hall and her younger sister Belinda answered. 'The police have arrested Nazeem Cassiem,' she said. 'You mustn't come home.' Robert was not too concerned. 'It's probably just part of the State of Emergency,' he told Greta. 'Don't worry, they're picking up everyone and anyone.'

But when Robert phoned the workshop his father told him that the police had been round looking for him that afternoon. It was the Special Branch, warned Derrick.

Robert phoned home and spoke to Doris. 'Don't come home,' she begged. 'It's too dangerous – the police also searched here. They gave it a good going over.'

Doris was anxious that Derrick should not remain in Wentworth either. She told Robert that she wanted him to take his father back to Johannesburg. Derrick, however, was not so easy to persuade. 'I had to convince him,' said Doris. 'I told him to go.'

Robert reminded his father to bring his passport and they made a rendezvous in Major Calvert Street. In the circumstances it was too risky to stop by, even for a moment, at 29a Hardy Place. Robert and Greta took the freeway to Wentworth, picked up Derrick McBride, and drove straight through the night back to Johannesburg, arriving just before dawn.

From a public phone booth, Robert phoned his ANC contacts in Botswana: it was time, they said, for him to leave South Africa.

They planned to depart from Johannesburg and cross over the border to Botswana that week. But on Tuesday night their car was broken into. A window was smashed and one of the doors damaged. Derrick and Robert decided not to travel with the car in that condition and postponed their departure another twenty-four hours. Instead they agreed to travel to Nigel, a small town thirty miles south-east of Johannesburg, where they could stay with Derrick's older brother, Leslie McBride, and have the car repaired the following morning. Then they would set out for the border.

At nine o'clock that evening, Wednesday July 16, from Leslie's home in Alra Park, they made a reverse charge call to Doris McBride in Wentworth. Doris was not in, but they spoke to

Bronwyn, who assured them there had been no problems. Don't worry about us, she said.

That night Derrick slept in a spare bed while Robert and Greta camped in the sitting room, Greta on a couch and Robert on the floor. At six a.m. they were woken by a commotion outside.

'Sounds like gangsters,' remarked Derrick.

Sleepily Robert opened the front door. He found himself facing an armed police officer. He slammed the door shut.

There were bright lights outside. Greta peered through the curtains. In the murky dawn the street was incandescent, a blinding, luminous, colourless glare, like floodlights. Everywhere she looked, silhouetted outlandishly in the burnished glow of headlamps from police cars and vans, were uniformed policemen – in the yard, on the road, on the rooftops. She noticed they were all armed.

'I walked slowly back to the couch, feeling that long hands were reaching out to grab me,' said Greta. 'My feet felt heavy. I felt numb.'

'*Maak oop,*' shouted a voice in Afrikaans, 'Open up. *Polisie!*'

Robert opened the front door. The police officer, a captain, had his rifle trained straight at him. '*Moenie beweeg nie,*' said the captain. 'Don't move.'

Part Four

Among the Weedkillers

24

After their arrest Robert McBride, Derrick McBride and Greta Apelgren were driven at high speed to the town of Harrysmith in the Orange Free State, where they were handed over to Special Branch officers from Durban. All three had balaclavas placed over their heads, twisted back to front so they could not see, and their hands were handcuffed behind their backs. Inside the thick woollen balaclavas they sweated profusely.

They arrived in Durban in the early evening. After being photographed and fingerprinted, they were transferred to the thirteenth floor of C. R. Swart Square. In separate rooms their interrogations began at ten p.m. and lasted till dawn.

'In the first hour after being arrested they had hit my nose and it was very swollen,' said Robert. 'They were choking me with my parka jacket and asking my *Umkhonto* name. "I don't know what you are talking about," I said. One cop said, "Slim, man – clever one, this." I refused to speak Afrikaans. At C. R. Swart they choked me again and I got faint and fell.'

Next door Greta could hear them shouting at Robert. They were also yelling at her. 'I had to force myself to remember they were just men, human beings,' said Greta. 'I could hear them swearing at Robert next door, both in English and Afrikaans, calling him a fucking terrorist. After fifteen minutes Captain de Beer came in and screamed, "Why have you got her next door?" So they moved me to the fourteenth floor, and continued the interrogation there. They seemed to know a lot.'

Robert was still handcuffed behind his back, and the handcuffs were attached to a bar so he had to stand on tip-toes all night while they questioned him. He felt faint and his throat was very dry. It was clear the police already had a considerable amount of information. 'I admitted to the Edendale incident when I couldn't take any more,' said Robert. 'I only mentioned my father, me and Nazeem Cassiem.'

The following morning Robert and his father were taken under police escort to the Factorama Workshop which the police intended to search. Bronwyn was working at the take-away and saw them arrive with about twenty policemen. She ran to fetch her mother. Doris arrived breathless, appalled to find her husband and son under arrest.

'The police were climbing all over the place and breaking things,' she said. 'Robert's handcuffs were so tight that blood was dripping down. I objected, but the police said they were stuck, so I made Derrick open them with tools from the workshop. After that, they did not allow me to speak to Robert or Derrick.'

Father and son were confident the police would find nothing. From Johannesburg a couple of days previously they had phoned a young friend and asked him to remove the 'pawpaws'. However, the young man had lost his nerve and they were horrified to see the police emerge from the attic with armfuls of armaments and explosives: AK47 rifles, the Makarov pistol, hand grenades, mini-limpets, SPM limpets, landmines, as well as ammunition, timing mechanisms and detonators.

'When I saw the arms, I did not show how I felt,' said Doris. 'They said, "You see what your son has been doing." I said nothing. The police were there the whole day, searching. Robert told them that Derrick did not know about the equipment, and the police kept saying to me, "Look what your son's got here!"

'They did not allow me to speak to either Robert or Derrick. I had to get medicine for Derrick from the doctor, as Derrick has epileptic fits and diabetes.

'The next time I saw Derrick was four months later.'

The interrogations continued every day. The police worked in teams, and Captain Zenardt de Beer was responsible for collating every scrap of information. Interrogations were conducted in small, drab, cream and dun-coloured offices on the thirteenth and fourteenth floors of C. R. Swart Square. For the first week there were often five or six Special Branch officers present at each interrogation.

'As you passed the other interrogation rooms you could hear the police screaming at the other detainees,' said Greta. 'They screamed at you all the time. Insults about the ANC, personal insults. They were very angry and irrational. "You're just a pawn," they kept shouting.

'Sometimes they would play me a tape of Robert. They shoved a pocket recorder right against my ear, so I could hear them shouting at him. They also said they were planning to kidnap my nephew Christopher and hold him out of the window till I talked. They forced me to squat and hit my thighs with a clothes brush, and made me hop back and forth. A captain said, "We don't do any violence, we are the senior guys – we leave that to the juniors."'

When she had her period, they stripped her naked and made her bunny hop up and down the room while half a dozen young white officers jeered and shouted insults.

Robert was giving away as little as he could. Confronted with a written list that had been found in the workshop attic, he confessed to the Shongweni arms cache and took the police to the spot. There, buried in the veld, the police uncovered the red trunk containing rifles, hand-grenades, mines and the RPG rocket launcher. They also showed him a photo album of over five thousand photographs of suspected ANC personnel; he was relieved to see that they did not include Gordon's wife, Anne.

'I told them bit by bit, but withheld a lot – in particular I covered for Gordon,' said Robert. 'They'd say, "Your friends are letting you down." Or they'd bring a cassette of Greta crying, saying, "No, no, no!" Another officer came in and said, "The old man is sick. He's jerking on the floor. If you don't talk, he won't get his injections." They arrested my mother and told me – that was the worst. They played a tape of her talking to a warden and said, "You are denying her involvement, but she's talking." But from the information they had, I knew it must be Matthew talking.'

'For seven days I refused to surrender,' said Greta. 'Then they showed me Matthew's confession, and they read parts of it out.

They told me what various people had said, and they threatened to use the stun gun . . . electric shocks.

'They were going off for a *braai* to celebrate having captured the unit and afterwards they said they were going to use the stun gun. I used to suffer from epilepsy. I was terrified. I decided to co-operate and told them when they came back from their *braai*, and I made a statement.'

Matthew Lecordier had in fact been arrested two days after them. He had been smoking *dagga* that Friday afternoon with Alan Pearce, Whitey and a couple of others in a house in Ogle Road, when they had seen some youngsters go past and Alan suggested they go outside and check the young girls.

'I looked out from behind the building and saw a police car,' said Matthew. 'I pulled my head back and said to one of the guys, "Solly, go and see what is happening there." He came back and said P.C. George got out of the car, and Alan threw the *dagga* away into the grass. Solly heard P.C. George say, "It's OK, we're not here for that stuff – we are here for you, get in the car." At that point I thought, this is it, they know about the group.

'I went down with Whitey to Alan's granny. I was feeling bad. I thought she should know, so I told her the police took Alan, though I could not tell her why. I was confused. I walked around with Whitey, smoking *dagga*. I went home late that night, about ten or eleven. I just didn't know what to do.'

Matthew had not heard from Robert for two weeks. He had been given no instructions about what to do in an emergency and he had no idea where the others had disappeared to. Now, faced with imminent arrest, he did not know where to turn: he felt paralysed.

'I lay on my bed, fully dressed,' said Matthew. 'About three o'clock that night, the police came. They banged on the door. My father said, "Who the fuck's that?" "Police!" they said. I got off the bed and ran into my mum's room. I went under the bed and hid.

'My dad opened the door. The police went right past and straight to the boys' room. They knew what they were looking for and what room to go into. I heard them say, "Where's your son, he must be here somewhere?" There were fifteen to twenty policemen, all white, in uniform. They searched and didn't find anything. They were about to leave and my mum was quietly asking me what was going on. She was in a state of shock. This cop walking past the door looked at my mother's bed and he came in and shone the torch under the bed. He cocked his gun in my face and said, "Get out you bastard." He pulled me out and dragged me down the passage. I was lying there, guns pointing at me. They searched me thoroughly. He grabbed my private parts and squashed them.

'They handcuffed me, and asked, "Where's the hand-grenades? We know you have them." My parents came to me and said, "If you know anything, tell them." All they found was some *dagga* in my jacket. They took me and my brother to the car, speaking in Afrikaans. I could hear, though. He was saying, "Reverse the car and put that man's head down." As I came out I could see a figure in the car. I do not know who it was, it could have been anyone, maybe even a policeman. They began threatening us in the car, things like, "We're going to fuck you up, where is the fucking stuff?"'

Matthew was questioned for several hours at C.R. Swart Square, and then taken to Brighton Beach police station, where he was placed in a cell stinking of urine. There was only a mat on the floor to lie on, but that also stank, so he huddled in the corner until they came again for him at six the next morning. He was taken back to C.R. Swart Square, where he was interrogated by half a dozen white Special Branch officers.

'They handcuffed me to a chair,' said Matthew. 'Different officers kept coming in, each one with something different to say. They were swearing at me, because I was denying everything, like they said, "You fucking killed our daddy." They called him their daddy, Colonel Welman, the policeman who was killed at the substation. "And we're going to fuck all your family up. As for your son . . . we're going to fucking kill him, you fucking Coloured bastard."

'They assaulted me physically, kidney blows they call it. It was painful, also slaps on the face. I wet myself in the chair.

'It went on like that and after four or five hours, I broke.

'I felt, what's the good of lying when they have got me, right in a corner. They even told me, "You're going to hang. You know, you think you're putting things right in this country, look where you are now. We're going to fucking hang you." I felt, no, let me give it to them. I felt I couldn't take it anymore. When they broke me, they asked me to tell them like I was telling a story, to tell them what I did.

'I was tired. I was in a state and there were so many people talking to me, a different policeman would come in, then another, there were so many in the office, and I couldn't go on like that. I admitted everything, my part, and what I knew the other guys did. At that point I told them everything.

'Then they took me to the magistrate, and at the magistrate's it was, "Sit down and tell me your story." There were policemen sitting there. The police had said to me, "You do not have to tell the magistrate that we insulted you or that we used this kind of language with you." The magistrate asked, "Were you forced to make this statement, were you insulted in any way, physically or otherwise?" And I said no. I sat and I told him like I was telling a story.'

25

By the following week the police were triumphantly announcing the capture of an ANC unit in the press. No names or details were given at first, but anonymous senior policemen were quoted as describing the arrests as 'damn good police work'. It was left to the Minister of Law and Order, Mr Louis le Grange, to say that the arrests had been made in connection with the blast at the Parade Hotel on the Durban beachfront.

A few days after that, a headline in the *Daily News* proclaimed: 'Car bomb: no whites among those held.' The story reported that the Bureau for Information were dismissing as nonsense persistent rumours that a white man was being held in connection with the Marine Parade explosion. Brigadier Leon Mellet, the director of the Bureau for Information, told the newspaper, 'I want to make it clear that no white person has been arrested in connection with any of the bomb blasts in Durban or anywhere in the country.'

Soon the Minister of Law and Order, Mr Louis le Grange, was crowing, 'During the past few weeks we have hit the ANC for six and we have broken their back.'

A security police spokesman then announced that one of their detainees was a person named Robert McBride, held in conection with a number of sabotage incidents, particularly the escape of Gordon Webster from Edendale Hospital and the explosion at the Parade Hotel which had killed three women. The *Daily News* wrote, 'Minister of Law and Order, Mr Louis le Grange, yesterday revealed in an exclusive interview with the *Daily News* the painstaking path of the detailed investigation which led to the arrest of the ANC cell apparently behind all the major bomb blasts in the Durban area recently.

'He described the build-up of clues as small as a single fingerprint on a hospital bed which has put those behind Durban's killer bombings behind bars.'

The Security Branch had also swiftly picked up Antonio du Preez and Welcome Khumalo. Jeanette Apelgren was already in jail, having been detained immediately after the declaration of the State of Emergency. But it became clear that the very first member of the cell that the security police had detained after the Parade Hotel bombing had been Nazeem Cassiem.

Mrs Margaret Apelgren, the mother of Greta and Jeanette, was a gaunt, diminutive woman. After Greta had been arrested they came to search her tiny home in Assegai Road. They carried guns, and when they questioned her, she cried. They said, 'Mrs Apelgren, do you know your daughter is being held under Section 29? Listen, your daughter is an ANC terrorist.'

'Look, I have twelve children,' she told them. 'I brought them up in two rooms.'

When the police went, she put up a picture of the Virgin Mary, 'and we prayed to Our Lady to put her arms around Robert and Greta.'

Mrs Apelgren accompanied Mrs Cassiem to C.R. Swart Square to deliver clothing and toiletries for their children. Mrs Apelgren was in tears again and Mrs Cassiem told her she must not cry. Mrs Cassiem handed over a prayer mat.

'*Wat is dit?*' asked the duty policeman, suspiciously.

'My son needs to pray,' explained Mrs Cassiem.

The policeman was unwilling to accept it. 'These tears mean something,' Mrs Apelgren told him. 'You people have forgotten God.'

The policeman stared at her, then shrugged. 'You know,' he said, 'I could arrest you.'

Captain Zenardt de Beer had immediately discerned that Robert McBride was the commander of the unit. It was clear that he would be the one with all the information, the others merely knew segments, and it was only McBride who could fit all the details together and link the different operations. But he was proving defiant.

During one early interrogation, when told he was going to hang, he put on a front of bravado that he did not feel at all. 'I am ready to die,' he said. 'It's my sacrifice.'

His interrogators regarded this kind of revolutionary rhetoric as a corny opening gambit which they would soon break down. 'Don't you want to survive?' they asked him, and Robert replied, 'If one joins the armed struggle, and still survives, one should regard one's survival as a fringe benefit.'

It was a stilted statement, almost as if it had been carefully rehearsed. The captain in charge of the interrogation wryly remarked on his philosophical attitude. He was confident it would soon disintegrate. 'I would have thought that you are of the type that would want to survive,' said his interrogator confidently.

Robert tried to gauge how much they knew. He was particularly anxious to conceal as much information as possible regarding Gordon's actions, as well as the fact that they were both involved in *Umkhonto we Sizwe's* Special Operations. At first his interrogators insisted Gordon Webster had also been captured, but Robert swiftly realised this was a stratagem. To explain a number of operations, he invented a comrade named Mandla.

It was a poker game: the Security Branch letting snippets of information drop to persuade him they already knew more than they did, and that the others were talking. Robert meanwhile attempted to keep them at bay by telling them only what he couldn't hide, or that which he felt could do no harm. When they played him a tape of Greta crying, he divulged more information to try and ease the pressure on her. Finally, they showed him Matthew Lecordier's statement.

Robert McBride then agreed to write a statement.

He was being kept in solitary confinement in a small local police station some miles out of Durban, from where he was driven under armed guard every day to C.R. Swart Square. He had been provided with a blue biro and paper with which to write his statement. Later the commander of Bellair Police Station, Warrant Officer Wilhelm Schreuder Louw, was astonished to discover Robert had written a series of huge slogans over the grimy walls of cell C5. They were not the usual swearwords or prisoners' girlfriends' names. The largest, in block letters, declared: VIVA ANC.

There was also a drawing of a spear and banner, the ANC emblem, with the words: THE PEOPLE SHALL GOVERN. Next was a list: ROBERT MCBRIDE ANC FREEDOM FIGHTER 1986, PEOPLE'S HEROES UNDER MY COMMAND: DERRICK, GRETA, JEANETTE, ANTONIO, MATTHEW. WE SALUTE YOU. There were the names of Biko and Timol, another political prisoner who died in police custody, accompanied by the slogan: THEY CAN KILL THE MAN, NOT THE IDEA, THEY DESTROY MY BODY, NOT MY MIND.

The final scrawl declaimed: THE STRUGGLE CONTINUES.

26

In the first days of detention, especially after being kept on his feet all night with his hands handcuffed behind his back, Robert had considered trying to commit suicide. 'But I was too much of a coward to do that,' he said, 'So I decided to escape. No one knew where I was, and I knew I was going to have to do it myself.'

The police station was situated several miles south-west of Durban in the spacious, hilly white suburb of Bellair. The station itself was fortified with a high wire fence, floodlights and an armed policeman at the entrance. Across the busy road was a railway line hidden behind a grassy embankment, and beyond that towards Durban, visible in the blue-grey distance on another hill was the tall spire of the university.

'They used to take me for interrogation every day to C.R. Swart, and I was always looking, thinking of escape, noticing the layout,' said Robert. 'The cell was like a dungeon, on a lower level, the cells were away from the main charge office where the keys were kept, and the passage key was kept by the duty officer.

'I began to be friendly with one particular guard. We used to talk. He was the same age as me, and he wanted to understand how I had become involved. But every time an opportunity came to overpower him, I couldn't do it . . . I just didn't have the spirit. To psyche myself up I began insulting myself, saying, "You're chicken, McBride!"

'Then one evening this guard came into the section and I knew he had the key. I called him to the cell. I realised I had to do it now. I knew I just had to show that I was not beaten. I told him I wanted to brush my teeth. I was terrified. Shall I be able to do it? I wondered. Also, he'd been so nice to me. No, I must do it, I told myself. I walked up to him. He knew I was going to do something. I started talking, you know, just saying anything, chatting, and I put my hands out, like an open gesture. But he was suspicious. I could see it in his eyes. I threw a punch at him. He slipped and it glanced off the right side of his face. He fell. I ran out and grabbed the key off the table. Behind me he was blowing the whistle hard and shouting. There were two keys. The first did not open the iron grille gate. The second did – the gate opened and I raced out.

'There was a short passage that led to the back yard of the station, and suddenly I was faced with an eight-foot tall gate. As I climbed over the gate and jumped down on the other side, I hurt my leg. I forced myself to limp. Across the yard there was another wall, about six feet high. I ran and jumped, vaulting over the wall, and landed on the grass on the other side on my hands with a terrible jolt.

'There was a guard standing outside the station, with a gun. I thought he was going to shoot me, so I just lay there.

'The alarm was going, and after a few moments I realised he had not seen me. I crawled away and climbed over two house fences. A dog was barking. I crawled through another fence and as I came out to the road I started walking. A police van screamed right past me. I was walking downhill, keeping in the shadows. Then I saw this black guy, sitting in his car, waiting for his girlfriend, a domestic from the house nearby. I went up to the car. I thought, I'll take the risk. I was desperate. I appealed to him: told him I was in the ANC and was about to hang. He wound up his window.

'The police van made a U-turn. I hid in a hedge. There were some white people sitting out on the verandah having supper. I could hear the man talking about sport. Then the van passed. I continued downhill. There was a black girl, about thirteen, walking along and I asked her which was the way to the highway and she showed me. Once on the highway, I could make up my mind either to head for Wentworth or Sydenham. I could hear the police van coming up behind me.

'There were some roadworks there, and a big sand-sifter, so I dived under that. The van stopped and the cops questioned a white couple, who were watering their garden. I'd walked right past their hedge, but they hadn't noticed me.

'I continued down towards the highway, then crossed to the island in the middle of the road. I had to loosen my shoes as my feet were so swollen. I didn't try to hitch as it was getting dark and I wouldn't be able to see if it was a cop car. There were two people ahead who were hitch-hiking and I saw a cop car stop by them. It was only thirty metres in front of me. The police took out a dog. I was crouching behind the crash barrier; it was uncomfortable because there were thousands of tiny pieces of glass on the ground.

'The cops moved off and I went through a gap in the fence and sat for a while in a storm water drain. I was exhausted. Then I heard the sound of a helicopter. So I carried on walking and got onto the railway line.'

Captain Zenardt de Beer lived due west in the adjoining white suburb of Malvern, high in the hills surrounding Durban. It was a more modest suburb by affluent white standards, with smaller, plainer bungalows, and diminutive squares of garden hedged by rhododendrons. The streets were a mixture of Afrikaans and English names. Small boys in shorts and short haircuts played on the long strips of grass verge, or cycled and skate-boarded in the deserted roads. Captain de Beer's home was unassuming, a low apricot bungalow in a small cul-de-sac with the unlikely name of Byron Place, opposite a starkly modern Dutch Reformed Church. There was a small covered porch with rounded arches and in front lay a petite tiled yard encircled by a low, salmon-pink wall.

It was seven-thirty. Captain de Beer was having supper at home when he was telephoned with the news that Robert McBride had escaped. The Captain raced out to his car and began driving in the direction of Bellair, while over his mobile walkie-talkie he directed squad cars to various strategic points. He ordered units to stake out all the known addresses that McBride might conceivably head for. Zenardt de Beer himself decided to make for the railway line and headed for the Poets Corner station.

The escaped prisoner was hobbling as fast as he could down the deserted railway line. There were high banks on either side with tall, tangled grass. Dark was falling fast. The line weaved and curved round the hilly suburbs. Robert knew that his best hope was for a train to pass. They were forced to take the bends so slowly that he would have ample time to board and hide. This was Captain de Beer's fear.

'I was about to go under a railway bridge,' said Robert. 'There was complete darkness just ahead. Then I heard a two-way radio. I waited. The radio was switched off. There was silence. On one side was a steep, grassy bank and on the other a road. There was not a sound for about thirty seconds, then a voice said, "McBride, stand still."

'I went into a crouching position. A cop was on top of the bank, pointing a gun. It was Warrant Officer Posthumus. He was coming closer. I decided to make a break. The railway line was between us and I was praying a train would come past. Then a car came up the hill on the road. Its headlights were bright. I made a dash. There were five shots. I thought: this cunt can't shoot. I ran straight for the car. I thought they wouldn't dare fire at the car. The car hit me on the side . . . I sort of bounced off. I kept running; he kept firing. I felt a tug on my foot. It was like a sharp jerk, but I kept on. I realised I'd been shot.

'Then I fell. I started crawling through a hedge. Suddenly there was an Alsatian in front of me. Frantically I tried to scramble back out. Someone shone a torch in my face. A cop put his foot on my chest. He said, "*Ja*, McBride." He had a hand-carbine.

'Posthumus came running up. He was fat. "Did I get him? I thought so!" He started to kick me and so did the other cop. In about a minute it seemed like there were thirty cop cars on the scene, all their headlights glaring. Other cops started kicking me.

'Back at C.R. Swart, a brigadier put a gun between my legs and said, "You should be shot in the balls." I tried to grab him and he said, as he squeezed my balls, "You are going to hang, McBride." They took me to hospital after about four hours. The bullet had gone right through my foot.'

244

27

In Lusaka at the ANC headquarters where he now worked in logistics and military planning, Gordon Webster had been profoundly shocked to hear of his friend's arrest by the South African police. After his escape from Edendale Hospital, Gordon felt that he owed his life to Robert.

'I was overwhelmed, tormented by his capture,' said Gordon. 'I was obsessed by the need to get him out.'

He began to campaign among influential exiled personnel in Lusaka to be allowed to organise a rescue mission for Robert McBride. No one paid him any attention. Everyone thought it was a romantic, doomed, ill-advised notion and counselled the young man to dismiss this fixation. Besides, he himself had been severely wounded. Only his wife supported this quixotic proposal. For Gordon, 'It was a demented year.'

After his escape attempt from Bellair Police Station, Robert McBride was transferred back to C.R. Swart Square. Greta Apelgren was also being held in the cells there, though on a different floor. There were quite a number of political prisoners at the Durban police headquarters and a sophisticated communications system had been devised; Robert and Greta occasionally managed to exchange messages. Robert was particularly concerned to know if Greta had destroyed all the photographs of himself and Gordon, as he had asked her to do after the Edendale operation. He was worried that the police might be able to identify Gordon's wife from some of them.

Sometimes, with the help of common criminals who cleaned out the cell corridors, they were even able to exchange notes written on toilet paper or soap wrapping. One day a civil prisoner on cleaning duty asked her, 'Got a letter for N28?'

Greta had evolved an escape plan of her own; quickly she scribbled a letter to Robert on the back of a prisoner's property receipt, on which all the belongings removed from her had been listed. At the top she drew a scrappy map of their prison and its surroundings.

My Lusty Loveable Leopard,
I *smaak* to *vie* with you a thousand times over & over: flesh on flesh & tongue on flesh! You are my race-horse rider & I am your racehorse!

A miracle occurred yesterday (Tuesday, 04.11.86). In the morning, I prayed that I could be taken out of C.R., so that I could get a better picture of area surrounding C.R. bldg. After lunch, 3 SBs (not my usual interrogators) came to fetch me & took me for a drive to La Lucia beach!

Their motive: 'to give you a break from the cells.' (probably plotting something for me in the future). Hence the new layout of C.R. sketch! God is on our side – we are His oppressed people. I still pray daily for you: 'Father, deliver (i.e. save) R. McB. from prison into exile, for thine is the kingdom (i.e. S.A./Africa), the power (i.e. successful escape) and the glory (i.e. victory of the oppressed masses)!' You *must* say 1 Our Father daily in the morning.

That 'connection cop' (Indian) – I think his name is George; he is very likely to be on duty tonight (5.11.86) – I will encourage him to make a plan to see you . . . My main contact among the robbers was transferred to Westville for the past two weeks; his name is Bongeni, from Chesterville (robbed a bank in Maydon Wharf). However his brother (also in no.17) told me that Bongeni got bail of R7000 and is to be released today: further, he may be coming to see his brother here today.

This same Bongeni was keen to assist me in escaping, hiding in Inanda & taking me across to Zimbabwe (he has relatives there!) Bongeni has many police 'connections' here at C.R. If the door is opened for you, I suggest you take the two sheets with you + leave them somewhere on the roof or anywhere on C.R. premises, so as to give the impression that you escaped via the roof bars. Remember the problem of eye-witnesses: speak to Bongeni alone or to George alone. PTO

Which photographs were you referring to in your letter – I destroyed all Shongweni photos while I was staying at your Hardy home. When Capt Taylor took the blue plastic bag with the Instamatic Camera in, only the new pack of spools was in there as well. Nothing else!

The letter, however, never reached Robert. The prisoner carrying this hasty note dropped it. He was spotted by a policeman and it ended up on Captain de Beer's desk.

Greta's sister, Jeanette Apelgren, was completely unable to cope with solitary confinement. She became anxious and depressed and gradually she began to have terrible nightmares. She also thought she heard voices, yet she was alone in her cell. Jeanette subsequently commenced to hallucinate. At first she saw snakes all over the walls, then they were crawling over her body and writhing about in the food. There were also, she imagined, snakes slithering out of her mouth.

Matthew Lecordier was informed that the Attorney-General was considering using him as a state witness.

'I asked what would happen to me if I did decide to do this,' said Matthew. 'They said they could not guarantee me anything else but my freedom. After a couple of weeks, I told them, yes, I would stand as a state witness. I thought I was going to hang, and I thought back to how someone had told the policemen about me, and I thought I would really like to see my child again.

'When I said yes to them, I wanted to be free, although inside me I felt it wrong to stand against my comrades. We had been through so much together and I felt it was wrong. But I also thought, who was it who stood out and spoke against me? Maybe nobody did, I don't know. I thought of all of them, Robert, Antonio, Alan. And then I just thought of myself: I can't stay inside here.

'I thought of it all, although I had doubts and felt wrong, I felt someone had spoken against me, and I decided yes. They took me to see the Attorney-General again and I told him I would do it. They had only spoken to me about standing against Robert and that was the first time they told me I would have to stand against each and every one of them.'

Jeanette had also decided to stand as a state witness. At first she asked to see a lawyer, but Lieutenant Brand told her, 'In terms of Section 29, you are not allowed to have a lawyer.' She had already been informed by Captain Baker that under Section 29 they could detain her for as long as they wished. She was also informed that she could be prosecuted as an accomplice.

When her mother saw her, Jeanette was in a demented state. She was laughing and crying. Her mother pleaded with her not to be a state witness, and the police terminated their visit. Other members of the family got messages to her, begging her to reconsider. Jeanette felt it was imperative to get out of solitary confinement. She had already given the police all the information she knew, and she told them she was prepared to repeat it in court.

Jeanette knew she was running a risk; as an underground movement, *Umkhonto we Sizwe* maintained discipline by executing those regarded as turncoats and traitors. Greta, though, was fiercely protective of her sister. She warned Robert, 'If anything happens to Jeanette . . .'

In Lusaka, Gordon Webster's persistence finally paid off. He had at last found an influential ally.

28

The Deputy Commander of *Umkhonto we Sizwe*, and the army political commissar, was a lanky, bearded, scholarly man who had graduated first from Fort Hare University in the Eastern Cape (known derisively as a 'bush' college as it was for Africans only) and then from the nearby Rhodes University, modelled with colonial deference upon the British Oxbridge ideal. In 1962 Chris Hani gained a BA in Latin and English. His father had been a pedlar, a migrant construction worker and an ANC activist. While articled with a law firm in Cape Town, Chris Hani saw at first hand the impoverished conditions of the migrant workers. His political development was, unusually, also influenced by his reading of the Latin classics, particularly the struggle between the Patricians and the Plebians.

After joining *Umkhonto we Sizwe*, Hani went underground and later fought with *Umkhonto* detachments in Rhodesia alongside ZAPU troops against the Smith regime. For several years he was based in Lesotho, where he survived a number of assassination attempts before being recalled to Lusaka and appointed Deputy Commander of *Umkhonto*. Later he rose to Chief of Staff. Popular among the rank and file and close to the young militants, he was a scholar whose relaxation was Greek mythology.

Hani was more intransigent than most of the older leaders of the ANC. Oliver Tambo, the President of the ANC in exile, censured guerrillas who ignored ANC guidelines and hit 'soft' targets. After a bombing which killed civilians, Tambo said, 'Somebody was inexcusably careless. This sort of thing has the effect of distorting our policy. The failure to take precautions and to avoid hitting people who are not intended to be hit has become intolerable.' Chris Hani, however, took a tougher line and claimed such attacks helped shock whites out of their complacency: 'Their life is good. They go to their cinemas, they go to their *braaivleis*, they go to their five-star hotels. That's why they are supporting the system. It guarantees a happy life for them, a sweet life. Part of our campaign is to prevent that sweet life.'

When Hani learnt of Gordon Webster's aspiration to rescue Robert McBride, he immediately agreed to support the project. This was an important break for Gordon. So far he had come up against either reluctance or outright resistance within the ANC hierarchy in Lusaka. Gordon was an asset and they did not want to lose him; it was also pointed out that he was known in South Africa, so that infiltrating back into the country would be particularly dangerous. In addition, after all the publicity surrounding the Edendale escape, it would be a considerable coup for the South African authorities to capture him a second time. With Chris Hani lobbying on Gordon's behalf, however, attitudes changed: senior cadres began to listen seriously.

Matthew Lecordier wrote a twenty-one page statement. He was informed that this was exactly what he must repeat in court, under oath.

'The Attorney-General told me that I don't have to look at Robert and the others in court, you are answering to the judge,' said Matthew. 'I thought, if I try and back out now, these people will hang me – I did not want to hang, so I agreed to stand against all of them.'

He was taken to an identity parade at C. R. Swart Square. Robert McBride was also in the line-up: 'There were other Coloured guys and Robert sent a message along the line asking where they were holding me, and I sent the message back that I was at Brighton Beach.

'Two or three weeks later the cops told me, "Your friend tried to escape and was shot in the leg." They said, "We shot him in the fucking leg and he was lucky we did not shoot him dead." I thought back to the ID parade and I felt that Robert wanted to know where I was, so that he could come and get me. That is what I felt inside. I looked up to Robert for that. The next time I saw him was in court.'

By New Year 1987, the defence team for Robert McBride and Greta Apelgren had been assembled. Their lawyer was a fresh-faced, canny and quicksilver young Indian, Roshan Dehal, who had defended Derrick McBride a number of times in the past when the police had been harrassing him. The junior counsel was an African, Mr Marumo Tsatsi Khabele Moerane, while the Senior Counsel was a white man, David Anthony Gordon. The state, it was clear, would be looking for the death penalty.

David Gordon was Chairman of the Natal Bar Council. He had once stood as a candidate for the Progressive Party in the provincial council elections. On the walls of his elegant offices in Smith Street, he had chic abstract paintings alongside glossy pictures of his racehorses. There was also a large cartoon of himself and other Durban grandees, members of the Friday Lunch Club. He was dapper, flawlessly tanned, poised, deftly charming, with gold-rimmed spectacles and an assured manner-ism of affectionately stroking his beige bald pate as he confidently and eloquently made a debating point. He smoked untipped Camel cigarettes and dressed flamboyantly: expensive suits with red satin lining, dashing striped shirts with wide, white collars, radiantly multi-coloured ties and electric-blue braces with Mickey Mouse motifs.

His successful, prosperous practice was maritime and com-mercial; he was not a criminal lawyer. The Magoo Bar bomb was going to be an emotive and prominent case and not one popular to defend among the English-speaking liberal establishment. Nevertheless, David Gordon decided it was a case he was morally obliged to accept.

'It's easy to walk away from such a case, but as leader of the bar, I felt I should set an example of the legal principle that every man is entitled to a defence,' he said. 'I came in for a lot of criticism, on a personal level. At dinner parties people would say, "How can you defend a man like this?"'

At their first meeting, Robert McBride suggested he put up an alibi that he had been at a drive-in movie on the night of the Parade Hotel explosion. What was the name of the film? Robert couldn't remember.

'Look, what do you want?' asked David Gordon. 'Do you want

251

your life to be saved? Or is it your ambition that following the revolution they will name a road after you, as a hero of the revolution?'

It was the lawyer's impression that Robert was initially tempted by the heroic vision, and he said he regarded himself as a prisoner of war.

'That was not the act of a soldier,' replied the white man. 'You were not in uniform, and the three young women there were not combatants.'

'With the vote, these people give power to the government to kill blacks,' replied Robert. 'And then when the army and the police were killing people in the townships, they were in discos.'

'Killing is never justified.'

'Anything can be justified,' argued Robert. 'The South African Government does it all the time. The situation is unique. The fact is, people will be caught in the cross-fire.'

'There must be justice and retribution,' rebutted the lawyer.

'Only from the whites?' demanded Robert provocatively.

A fierce argument developed. 'Robert told me that all whites were the same, all whites were the enemy,' recalled David Gordon. 'At first he was suspicious of me, partly because I was white. He believed that violent revolution was the only way the movement he represented would be treated properly. I felt he was motivated in part by a disgust at his own racial group – that they had been passive too long and had accepted too much mistreatment. He felt that it was time the Coloureds *did* something. That, perhaps, is why he went on a binge of acts which over a period of six or seven months far outstripped anyone else.'

The Chairman of the Natal Bar Council disagreed fundamentally with his strong-willed client: 'I fought with him about everything – political philosophy, history, systems of government . . .'

'It was a really heated argument,' said Robert.

He told the white man, 'I do not deserve one day in prison. I did not create apartheid. They were victims, but so am I. I did not enjoy one day of the privilege that they did.'

'He saw things very much in black and white,' maintained David Gordon. 'He did not have a proper sense of balance.'

'A white person cannot understand,' Robert bitterly informed his lawyer. 'They can never be in our position. I spoke to a white priest once who admitted he had spent a lot of his life in Coloured areas, and yet he could never understand what it was like to be Coloured. Whites have a lot to lose. Liberals feed off the apartheid system. They are, on the whole, happy with white justice.'

David Gordon made it clear to him that he was not prepared to go ahead if Robert wanted to debate 'white' justice or challenge the jurisdiction of the court.

'Well, I see it from my point of view,' said Robert, slightly conciliatory. 'They lecture us, call us terrorists. The Americans called the ANC terrorists, and yet what about Vietnam, My Lai? In the second world war they bombed civilians in order to win. Look at Hiroshima and Nagasaki.'

That argument, according to Robert, infuriated his lawyer. 'Yes, but the whole of the West sides with the South African government,' continued Robert. 'When the South African forces hit the wrong house in Zimbabwe, did they speak out? That's an acceptable mistake. I mean, white races do not act with such restraint when attacking other races, but they expect blacks to behave differently. That attitude is everywhere – in books, TV, films. I understand how they think like that – they are not exposed to our suffering.'

'From the start I made some ground rules with Robert,' said David Gordon. 'One, I would not defend him if he wanted to challenge the court. Two, I was confident he would get a fair trial. Finally, and this upset him, when he suggested that I did not understand or was not sympathetic, I pointed out that my daughter and sister-in-law used to frequent Magoo's and the restaurants along the beachfront and they could easily have been there that night.'

'I couldn't fight two battles, so I backed down and became more helpful,' said Robert. 'I could see he was in a moral dilemma; he was blowing hot air. I discovered he was Jewish and I gave him the example of how the Nazis were allowed too easily to rise to power in Germany, and I said to him, "The older generation allowed this to happen here as well, because they did not oppose it."'

'I knew I was collecting a lot of his virulence,' said David Gordon. 'It was better that he vent it on me, than at the court.'

'Tell me, who is innocent in this country?' demanded Robert. 'When the SADF raids Botswana and kills civilians and boasts they've killed ANC collaborators . . . I mean, ninety-five per cent of the white males serve in the army, the police or the prison services. And that makes them collaborators. Then of course, they're all married to women, who also support this system, and so it goes . . .'

'I think he grew to trust me,' said David Gordon. 'I grew to like Robert a lot. Just before the case, he laughed at me and said, "You're just goading me, so that I'm prepared for when I testify."'

29

The trial was to be held at the Natal Supreme Court in Pieter-maritzburg; normally it would have been held in College Road in the Victorian buildings of the old Native High Court, which had a glass-fronted bullet-proof dock. But because of the sensational nature of the case and the large crowds that were expected to attend, it was scheduled for Court A in the new Supreme Court, opposite the Market Square in the centre of the city. It was to be a massive trial, with dozens of witnesses, detailed forensic and explosives analysis, as well as the Special Branch provision of intensive security throughout the hearings.

Robert McBride was listed as Accused Number One, and Greta Apelgren as Accused Number Two. They faced twenty-four counts, ranging from furthering the aims of the ANC, an unlawful organisation, contraventions of the Terrorism Act in sabotaging substations, conspiring 'to overthrow or endanger State Authority in the Republic', to charges of attempted murder and murder. It was clear that the pivotal proceedings concerned the Edendale Hospital escape and the Marine Parade car bomb.

The judge appointed to preside at this mammoth trial was a cultivated, affable figure of the Durban establishment. He was on the board of committees for the arts, and had also achieved some local celebrity as a rose-grower. Rose-growing in those sub-tropical conditions, with the hardy soil and profusion of pests, was a minor achievement, and Douglas Lennox Lyall Shearer took particular pride in his pink blossom, Bride's Dream. He had gone to Michaelhouse School, the Natal simulation of a British public school, and then he had gone on to Trinity Hall at Cambridge University, where he played both cricket and golf.

Judge Douglas Shearer was renowned as a raconteur of amusing legal anecdotes. In his younger days he had been a radio actor, and he had a fine, resonant speaking-voice. Like the defendants' Senior Council, David Gordon, he was reputed to be a bon viveur, with a liking for fine wines and good food. Indeed, before Shearer's elevation to the bench in 1968 the two of them had shared chambers. Judge Shearer lived in an attractive, shaded old colonial house in a quiet, secluded cul-de-sac on a hill overlooking Durban. He had only a few more years to go before retirement; with grey hair and owlish glasses, and a cautious, dignified manner, Judge Shearer of the Natal Provincial Division of the Supreme Court was more like an old-fashioned English gentleman from the Home Counties – what the English establishment likes to call a 'clubbable' fellow. He had a passion for music, particularly Mozart and Beethoven and the more modern romantics like Rachmaninov and Mahler.

The jury system had been abolished in the early 1960s, but for a trial of this magnitude which involved potential death penalties, the judge was required to choose two assessors. Douglas Shearer determined that he was not simply going to rope in a couple of magistrates, who he believed tended to rubber-stamp a judge's decision. He felt it was important to enlist independent legal experts and managed to persuade a lecturer in law at the University of Durban-Westville, Brian Leslie, to agree to sit with him. Westville was originally established for Indians, but today is open to all races. Many of its teachers are white, like Brian Leslie, who had also practised in the courts as an advocate. For the second assessor Shearer turned to another legal expert.

Professor John Milton of the Pietermaritzburg Campus of the University of Natal was a soft-spoken, neatly-groomed intellectual who had written a number of standard text books on criminal law, and was in the process of writing another during a sabbatical leave of absence from his university post. A humane and highly literate man, he had three years previously published a vivid and original history, *The Edges of War*, detailing one hundred and seventy-six years of frontier conflict between the white colonists and the Xhosa nation in the Eastern Cape region. For an epigraph, Professor Milton had chosen an account by Sir Andries Stockenström, Commissioner-General for the Eastern Districts, of an interview with the chiefs of the Ngqika Xhosa in August

1831: '*Some pathetic and eloquent speeches were made, setting forth the alleged wrongs of the kaffir nation during a series of years, but concluded with the most solemn promises that the peace should be maintained, "If", said they, "you will only leave us what we have left, but we know that the white man will not let us sit still, as long as we have a foot of land or a fat cow."*'

There was considerable concern about security surrounding the trial. There were even rumours circulating that Gordon Webster would return to South Africa to make a desperate attempt to free Robert McBride. The police provided Judge Shearer with a constant bodyguard. Due to the security situation in the country generally, all judges were having their homes fitted with security fencing, alarms and lighting at the state's expense, and Shearer's home was being equipped with these devices as the trial began. Several times the lights went on or the alarm went off by accident, causing the judge a great deal of inconvenience, fright and loss of sleep. Most of the time during the trial, however, he stayed in Pietermaritzburg, either at a flat, or in the Victoria Club which still flew the Union Jack, did not permit female members and displayed animal head trophies on the walls of its hushed, sombre lounge.

The security police were jumpy, and on the first day of the trial there was a bomb scare when a Saucy Sausage van backfired in the street outside. The Special Branch were also nervous about Robert McBride: he had gained considerable notoriety for his escape attempts, and they felt that he might easily make another.

Immediately the trial commenced on February 2, 1987, there was a tussle between Zenardt de Beer and David Gordon. Captain de Beer insisted the lawyer consult his client in the tiny, stifling cell below the court. David Gordon stormed in to see the judge in his chambers and complained that he could not consult his client freely in a 'dungeon'. Captain de Beer tried to convince Shearer that with McBride's record of escaping, drastic precautions were justified, and they came to an agreement that in recesses the defence team could consult with Robert in the open court where he could be watched at a distance by armed guards.

Tactically, David Gordon had worked out his strategy.

Although there was a great deal in the long list of charges they clearly could not deny, McBride and Apelgren would commence by pleading not guilty. This would force the prosecution to lead their evidence and show their hand; the defence could then work out their response once they knew exactly what the State had to back up their case. The major decision, however, he had to leave up to Robert.

The lawyer spelt out the options. If they both eventually admitted responsibility for the car bombing, it would put the judge in a psychologically more pressurised position. Greta was young, pretty, and the same age as Shearer's own daughter. David Gordon knew Shearer extremely well from the time they had shared chambers. 'He was gentle, highly cultured and enormously intelligent,' said the lawyer. 'Tactically, it would be better to say in effect to the judge, "Sentence both, the man and the woman – a woman your daughter's age. If you are not going to sentence the woman to death, you cannot sentence the man to death."

'What is your decision, I asked them? If I call Greta to testify in her own defence, the prosecution might trap her. If I do not call her and let Robert testify as to her ignorance, she may get the benefit of the doubt and be acquitted. The dilemma was: would we try to save both, or sacrifice one?

'I gave them the choice. I spelt it out to them, that I did not think they would get the death penalty, more likely twenty years, but that was the possibility. Greta was very lucky. Robert took the decision – only he would testify. He was going to protect her.'

The trial lasted two and a half months and by its conclusion there were fifteen volumes of evidence. Court A of the Natal Supreme Court was a huge, airy room with a high ceiling, redolent of judicial procedure and pomp: red carpets, Oxblood red wood panelling with yellow-wood trim, and red leather on the rows of seating for the defence and prosecution teams facing the judge's high dais. Behind them was the defendants' dock, and then the ranks of spectators' pews. Court A was packed every day with security police, reporters, inquisitive whites and dozens of supporters and friends of both the McBride and Apelgren families.

Doris McBride and her eldest daughter Bronwyn travelled up every day from Wentworth, as did the the Apelgrens. 'I had to put on a good front,' said Doris. 'The smirks on the policemen's faces kept me going. They were waiting for us to crack.'

'People in 'Maritzburg supported us a lot, and during the lunch break the Rev. Smith would make a prayer,' said Mrs Margaret Apelgren. 'But there was a split with the McBrides when they found that Jeanette was going to be a state witness. We would go and have lunch in the car park and the McBrides would say no thank you. There was a lot of ill-feeling from their faction. I heard a friend of theirs say, "This is the mother of a state witness." But I had trust in Jeanette, that she would not make things too bad for them.'

As he sat next to the judge on the presiding dais, Professor John Milton had in front of him a beige-coloured, floppy school exercise book, and he scribbled in pencil: 'Young people's trial. Accused young. Police guards all under 25 except court-orderly & senior plain clothes officers. Police young men of riot squad.'

The first witness called by the State was Brigadier Herman Stadler, introduced as an 'expert' on the ANC. He spoke in Afrikaans and for the benefit of the accused there was an interpreter; but the first could not cope with some of the technical political terminology, so there was a short adjournment until a more competent English-Afrikaans translator could be found. The main thrust of Brigadier Stadler's evidence was that ex-ANC people who gave evidence risked assassination. For a while he and David Gordon sparred over the definition of the word 'terrorist' and then Gordon pounced.

'All right,' he demanded triumphantly. 'Now do you then concede that, if that is your definition of terrorist – as a person who attacks in order to terrorise – many people in the townships in South Africa are entitled, on that definition, to regard the Defence Force and the police as terrorists in relation to them and they do so regard them?'

The purpose of the brigadier's evidence was to allow the state prosecutor, Ian Slabbert, to request that witnesses A, B, C and D be allowed to give evidence behind closed doors. In closed session, Captain Zenardt de Beer told the judge that, in his opinion, all four of those witnesses who had been part of McBride's unit and had now turned state evidence were in danger of their lives. On February 4, Shearer returned to say that he had weighed up the safety of the witnesses against the need of justice to be seen to be done, and he had concluded that their identity was already known to the ANC, whether they testified openly or in camera. 'That being so,' ruled Shearer, 'it does not seem to us that this is a proper occasion to depart from the principle that justice be administered in public.'

He did, however, leave open the possibility that the witnesses could elect to have their names withheld in press reports. Slabbert immediately asked that the first such witness be referred to as Witness A. This was Nazeem Cassiem.

Shearer informed Cassiem, after reminding the press to refer to him as witness A, that if he answered all questions frankly he would be offered immunity from prosecution. Nazeem Cassiem told the court that he was a Moslem, and he followed the Koran, praying five times a day. His understanding, he explained, was that the Koran placed an obligation on followers to rise up against oppression. 'M'Lord, if I can quote a certain passage from the Koran,' he said. 'It states that, "Thou shalt not be oppressed nor shall you an oppressor be."'

He explained his political anger and development: 'At first I felt we could achieve certain aims non-violently and then at a later stage it seemed to me that change wasn't coming about fast enough and the nature of the change wasn't in accordance with, shall I say, what I felt was needed and therefore I resorted to violence.'

Cross-questioned as to why he was now co-operating with the police, Cassiem broke down in tears. 'Within myself I wouldn't bring . . . I couldn't bring myself to killing other people,' he said, weeping.

After a short adjournment to allow him to recover, Cassiem said that in order to avoid further involvement he began evading Robert, and that was why he had not taken part in the hospital rescue of Gordon Webster. He described Robert, with whom he had played in the Bechet College rugby team, as an 'overwhelm-

260

ing personality.' He had also had a relationship with Greta some time before, venturing gallantly, 'I courted her.'

The next day he was tackled more aggressively by the defence: 'Do you regard yourself as a traitor?'

After a long pause Cassiem said, 'No.'

He admitted that while in detention he had continued to sing liberation songs in order to mislead the others, so they would not think he had agreed to turn state witness. He also conceded that in turning on his former colleagues he was betraying his guiding principles. But arrest and imprisonment had affected him dramatically. 'When I was confronted with the reality of it,' confessed Cassiem, 'I couldn't take it.'

Welcome Welela Khumalo was the next state witness. Judge Shearer again cautioned that immunity would be offered if questions were answered honestly. Khumalo testified in Zulu, through an interpreter, so softly that he had to be asked several times to speak up. Khumalo recounted how he had been recruited and trained by Gordon Webster, and given the codename 'Themba'.

He told the court of his pact with Webster, that if one of them were caught, the other should try and kill his companion before the police could make him talk. When he discovered that Webster had been wounded and was being guarded in Edendale Hospital, Khumalo explained through the mangled English translation, 'I thought of going there where "Steven" or Webster, where he is, and finish him up. And also kill or finish myself up also.'

Khumalo appeared evasive and the Judge reminded him that indemnity would be granted only after consideration of his frankness. Questioned by David Gordon on his attitude to the police and why he was collaborating, Khumalo at first tried to put a good gloss on his behaviour. Naïvely he remarked, 'It is simply because I like to give evidence. I wasn't offered anything.'

Pressed, he finally admitted that he hated and feared the police. He collaborated, Khumalo acknowledged, 'because I wasn't prepared to be arrested or detained.'

The court continued to be packed, though often with more policemen than spectators. Professor Milton jotted in his notebook: '3 heavily built Mediterranean women all dressed in similar shades of yellow, looking vaguely alike & by hairstyle, heavily made-up (black hair) rather like ladies of the night come in & sitting rather like twee sluttish canaries, accompanied by short younger girl, obviously Coloured, almost Khoi in appearance.'

On February 17, when Jeanette Apelgren was called to the witness box, Milton noticed that Greta smiled at her sister. Jeanette Apelgren was nervous and spoke in a hoarse voice, but she preferred to testify in her own name without hiding behind the disguise of a letter of the alphabet, so that everyone would know exactly what it was that she had said. After identifying herself as a social worker and the younger sister of Greta, Jeanette explained that she had been at school with Robert and that his father Derrick had helped her on many community projects.

'Personally, I have never seen violence as a weapon to achieve political objectives,' she said. 'But what I have been forced to accept is that we have only experienced meaningful change because of violence, and I am speaking from the experience of Wentworth.'

She described their trips to Botswana, a night trip to bury arms, and the time she drove Robert McBride into the centre of Durban when he placed a bomb in the Pine Street Parkade. She admitted she felt foolish about not asking him more questions, but when David Gordon suggested that she might have been drugged in prison, she denied the possibility. She ascribed her hallucinations – the plague of snakes – to the stress of solitary confinement.

Jeanette's evidence was not particularly damaging. Both sides knew that it was Matthew Lecordier's performance in the witness box which would decide Robert's fate.

Captain Zenardt de Beer was nervous. 'He was a key witness and every moment he gave evidence was dramatic,' said de Beer. 'When they are testifying, you sit on the edge of your chair, because you never know when the defence will eat them up and spit them out. When witnesses are in the box for three days they tire out. Matthew took a lot of battering.'

Matthew was visibly nervous. He knew he was the crucial witness, yet he was also acutely conscious of betraying his companions. 'When I entered the court I looked at Robert,' he

262

remembered. 'Maybe I thought inside of me by looking at him he might understand why I was doing this, not that I wanted him to, but just so that he would understand. I had my reasons, but maybe he will never see it that way. I just glanced at him, but from his look, I couldn't judge anything. I went into the witness box and while I was giving evidence against him I looked at the judge. I just wanted to get out of the witness box. If I could have run and hid somewhere I would have. I just wanted to get it over with. Inside me I wished it had never happened. I felt that I was standing against him for something we believed in.'

In his school notebook, Professor Milton wrote: 'Neat, trim, handsome, small moustache, Coloured/Malay, straight nose, small ears, black short hair brushed back.' Robert, he noted, merely stared at Lecordier while Greta smiled. After he had been speaking for a while, Matthew stared fixedly at the far corner of the courtroom and several people felt that he had memorised his evidence and was repeating it parrot-fashion. But Milton also noted: 'Speaks clearly, distinctly, good simple direct English, without hesitations, slang or circumlocutions.'

When it came to the crucial Parade Hotel bomb, Matthew said that Robert had planned a target along the Marine Parade all along. 'Absolute silence in court as witness recounts events leading up to bombing,' wrote Professor Milton. 'Witness speaks slowly, clearly, staring straight ahead. State counsel allows him to speak without much interruption.' After they had parked the Ford Cortina outside the Parade Hotel, he said, they drove up to Ridge Road above Durban in order to get a view of the explosion. As they sat there waiting in the dark, he claimed, Robert remarked, 'The Boer is going to shit tonight.'

For Greta, Matthew's evidence was a boon; it suggested that she was unaware they were planting a car bomb that night. For Robert, however, Matthew's evidence had been devastating. Thus when it was David Gordon's turn to cross-examine, after Lecordier had been in the witness box for two days, he realised that he would have to try and concentrate on the aspects which damned Robert. He was going to have to try and entirely destroy Matthew's credibility as a witness.

David Gordon began aggressively, suggesting that he,

Lecordier, had been taught what to say. Matthew hotly denied this. The atmosphere was febrile as the entire court realised that this duel could determine Robert's lot.

In his diary, Professor Milton scrawled, 'Jeanette Apelgren in gallery. Large numbers of Coloured people present, apparently members of the McBride & Apelgren families. Palpable sense of anticipation as Gordon rises to cross-question. Witness answers in steady monotone, almost mechanically, a robot-like way, as in a trance, answers embarrassing questions frankly, admitting matters derogatory of himself without hesitation. Gallery people smile at some of his answers. Day ends as Defence cross-questioning causes witness to apparently contradict himself & admit he refreshed his memory by "reference" to his "statement". Defence argues it should obtain statement.'

David Gordon had found the chink he was looking for. It was illegal to provide a witness with his statement and he went on the attack. It looked like the prosecution were coaching their star witness, as he had suggested to Matthew earlier, and Gordon angrily demanded that he should be allowed to see the statement. Captain de Beer was appalled at this turn of events; his witness could be discredited by this legal slip. The following day Professor Milton noted: 'Argument re availability. Agreed that page of statement be made available.'

Having thrown the witness off his steady flow, David Gordon tore into him mercilessly. He forced Matthew to make mistakes; Matthew became flustered and began contradicting himself. He had to admit he 'forgot' this, got 'confused' about that. He began making more and more blunders. 'I did not think clearly before I spoke about it,' he admitted, after Gordon caught him out on yet another inconsistency.

Mr C, as he was referred to in all the newspapers, said he was a friend of Robert's, but tried to claim that he only joined the unit because he was frightened of him, and then was compelled to acknowledge that Robert had only ever been helpful to him. 'I did it for money and a bit to change the system,' he said.

Matthew was forced into a succession of, 'I don't remembers.'

Gordon: 'You have a fine memory for other details?'

Matthew: 'Yes.'

Over the car bomb, however, Matthew remained firm that Robert always intended a target along the Golden Mile. He admitted that he himself had suggested one hotel, and after denying he told Robert the people wanted white destruction, he was forced to concede he may have said that and used the phrase, 'The whites must pay for the way blacks are suffering in this country.'

David Gordon: 'You see, what I am suggesting to you, Matthew, is that you have, and I am not suggesting from your point of view that it is not understandable, but you have a fixation about the Marine Parade area, sorry, I can't use the word fixation . . . That you regarded the Marine Parade area as the place where whites were at play, while blacks were suffering from oppression and that is why you chose those targets in that area, is that so?'

Matthew: 'No, M'Lord.'

Gordon: 'Now that, I suggest . . .'

Judge Shearer (intervenes): 'Did that thought never pass your mind – never pass through your mind at all?'

Matthew: 'No, M'Lord.'

Shearer: 'That thought, or something like it?'

Matthew: 'Something like it, it was whites being there, M'Lord.'

Shearer: 'Just whites being there?'

Matthew: 'Yes, M'Lord.'

Shearer: 'And doing anything in particular? Enjoying themselves?'

Matthew: 'Enjoying themselves, M'Lord.'

David Gordon: 'Yes, and you don't like the thought of whites enjoying themselves, do you? Because of the tragedy in the country, isn't that your way of thinking, Matthew, isn't that so?'

Matthew: 'No, M'Lord, I did not think like that at that time.'

David Gordon: 'But as M'Lord said to you, you thought something like that, didn't you?'

Matthew: 'Yes, M'Lord.'

Gordon: 'And at that time, on the evening of 14 June, you and accused Number One felt angry, didn't you, at what was happening in the country? Isn't that so?'

Matthew: 'Yes, I was angry, M'Lord.'

At one point, Matthew broke down and wept. But the damage had been done. Mr C had stuck to his point that Robert had initiated everything and had planned to attack a target along the Parade. He had continued to repeat the essential theme of his story: McBride was the leader, the initiator, and he carried the responsibility. Captain Zenardt de Beer sank back, relieved. 'It was dramatic and exhausting,' he said, 'but Matthew Lecordier's evidence was crucial.'

Robert remained impassive, constantly taking notes and often scribbling messages for his defence counsel. But Greta was not managing to keep up such a confident front. On February 27, Professor Milton noted: 'Greta looks strained, line of stress under left eye, eye sockets dark. Her skin colour seems darker; smiles, talks less.' On March 3, he wrote: 'Apelgren's hair-style, during previous week done in curls, now straight, in page-boy style. She looks very tired & strained as in previous week. There is a line running from inner corner of left eye, diagonally down towards the corner of her mouth. It seems like stress, but the line is quite distinct as if a tear.' On March 10, in his notebook, Milton observed: 'Last few days Greta has appeared subdued, listless, her complexion seems darker, she is slightly haggard. She seems withdrawn as if she has no interest in her case.'

The strain was also undermining Doris McBride. She travelled up to Pietermaritzburg from Wentworth every day. Sometimes as she entered the Supreme Court building, white policemen would recognise her, and whisper, 'The rope.'

Across the corridor from Court A, the trial of Derrick McBride and Antonio du Preez had begun. Doris took it in turns with her daughter Bronwyn to attend, so that one of them would always be present at both trials. They alternated: one day Doris would attend her son's trial in the morning and then her husband's in the afternoon; the following day she would sit in on Derrick's case first, then cross over to Court A for the afternoon.

30

Having discovered the state's evidence, the defence now made a number of admissions. This followed their overall tactic: Robert would go into the dock, and while admitting his participation, he would be able to reinforce the view that Greta was not that deeply involved. Then, vitally, he could present his own interpretation of events and his actions.

Right from the start the State has made this a political trial, David Gordon told the court, adding, 'M'Lord, we believe as well that it was proper for the State to do so.' He submitted that the accused's violence would have to be seen against the backdrop of violence in the country as a whole, 'That the reaction of black people, the violent conduct of black people, is the result of the violent conduct of white people.'

Ironically, in view of the lawyer's own furious argument prior to the trial with Robert McBride, David Gordon faced Judge Shearer and suggested, 'An essential therefore to this case, M'Lord, is our endeavour to understand the black mind. To understand his attitude towards violence and to avoid insofar as we are able the application of white-western approaches to a problem which is not generally speaking experienced by whites in South Africa.'

He concluded, 'Within the confines of our own city there would be people, predominantly white people, who would condemn out of hand the Parade Hotel incident and the man in the street would probably feel the accused, because of the consequences, are not even entitled to a trial, but that justice should have been popular, swift, without the trappings of legal procedure.

'Yet almost within sight – and certainly within earshot – of any explosion, there is another community in Durban who, excluding the injuries and the deaths, would applaud what was done as heroic.'

Matthew Lecordier, shortly after his marathon grilling in the dock, received a shock. 'I told the state counsel that I would like to have a newspaper, radio and books to read,' he said. 'They gave these things to me and that is where I read that Witness C was refused indemnity from prosecution.'

For some while negotiations had been conducted behind the scenes to see whether a vital witness relating to the Edendale Hospital charges could give evidence. Both policemen on duty at the intensive care ward that night had been in the witness box, neither covering themselves in glory. But the defence and prosecution united in agreeing that there was one man whose evidence regarding the death of Mlungisi Buthelezi was indispensable.

Gordon Webster, however, was an exile and an outlaw. Clearly he could not return to South Africa, and yet his testimony would be vital in the attempt to establish who shot the visitor in the hospital corridor. Secret bargaining between the two sides established an agreement that evidence could be taken, under oath, from Webster outside South Africa, and Judge Shearer authorised such a commission. There was nevertheless one major hurdle – the State was not prepared to travel to any African country. A neutral territory had to be found, and after the defence attorney Roshan Dehal flew to Lusaka for consultations, both sides accepted that the Special Commission could sit in England.

At nine-twenty on a Saturday morning, March 21, nearly seven weeks after the trial had began in Pietermaritzburg, the Commission convened in London. Gordon Webster, accompanied by a lawyer, faced questioning from both David Gordon and Deon Schaup, the deputy state prosecutor. The testimony was heard, with great formality in the presence of a British Commissioner for Oaths and an accredited shorthand transcriber. The South African state had one objective: to establish that it was Robert McBride who fired the fatal shots. Deon Schaup was a subtle, incisive examiner and he tussled doggedly with Webster over who had the AK47 at what precise point as he was being bundled away on the trolley. But with his friend facing the death penalty, Webster was determined to protect him at all costs. It was an acerbic battle of wits and Webster could not be shaken. Schaup tried to trap Gordon Webster into admitting he was testifying in favour of his comrade.

GW: 'I am testifying on what happened.'

Schaup: 'You are trying to help by saying you killed or injured the people.'

GW: 'I am telling you exactly what happened.'

In fact, in all the trials that dealt with this incident, it was never established who fired the fatal shots: Robert, Gordon or Derrick. What did happen in London, however, was that Gordon Webster managed to obtain some vital information. From the diary of the defence attorney Roshan Dehal, he surreptitiously cribbed key names, telephone numbers and addresses, principally those of Captain Zenardt de Beer and Judge Douglas Shearer.

In Pietermaritzburg, four days later, in Court A, Robert McBride finally went into the dock. So far forty-nine witnesses had been called, mostly policemen who had attended the scenes of his sabotage actions, including by chance the lieutenant who had called him 'Hottentot' while he was playing for the white Northlands rugby team.

The court was packed. This was the ghoulish drama of the trial; everyone knew that Robert was fighting for his life.

The prosecutor, Ian Slabbert, rose. He was short and stocky, with a round face, dark-rimmed glasses and a square jaw. Dark strands of hair were swept round from the sides to try and cover his baldness. He began nervously. His wife was sitting beside him at the prosecution table. While speaking, he rocked back and forth, cocking his head to one side, and making flicking, fidgety hand gestures.

Robert was impassive while he recounted his life story: the squalor of Wentworth, the gangs, his parents' frustrations. He told the court of his father's inflexible caution: 'Never trust a white man.'

While explaining in detail his own political development, his friendship with Gordon Webster, recruitment into the ANC, military training and the succession of sabotage attacks, Robert was at pains to shield Greta. At all stages he claimed she was not aware of the full extent of his operations and that he kept her in the dark as much as he could. He regarded Greta and Jeanette, he said, as 'non-combatants' in his unit, and therefore even though she had been his lover, he never gave her more information than was absolutely necessary.

'There is a saying among ANC people that if ever you have a downfall, it's going to be because of your woman,' he said. 'And I made sure that wasn't going to happen to me.'

He was in the witness box for five days, cross-questioned first by Slabbert, then by David Gordon. It was so exhausting that eventually Judge Shearer allowed a chair to be brought into the court so he could sit down. 'He came across as defiant, though not aggressive,' was Professor Milton's impression. 'As if he was saying: I am a soldier, I'm fighting a war, but I've had to do things a soldier has to do, and I'm sorry innocent people were killed, but I'm not apologising.'

McBride took this opportunity to state his position clearly: 'It is a war, M'Lord. I see myself as a soldier.

'I thought that, well, I had seen violence as a means of obtaining political equality in the country and my acts – at least most of my attacks – were intended to try to pressurise the government into negotiating with the majority of the people.'

He addressed Judge Shearer directly, 'Racialism, M'Lord – that is the enemy and it must be destroyed. You cannot negotiate with racialism.'

The car bomb was the fateful issue. Robert failed to convince the court he had intended to bomb a target where there would be no victims, the 'Hyperama House & Home', and had only been persuaded to attack a crowded white bar by Mr C.

McBride: 'M'Lord, I must also state that I was undisciplined that day.'

Slabbert: 'Here you were, the commander of the unit, the man with leadership qualities, and you allowed yourself to be

270

persuaded by an undisciplined and insubordinate member of your unit, is that right?'

McBride: 'Yes, M'Lord, but I don't know what allowed me to be influenced by him, persuaded by him, but M'Lord, there must be some explanation somewhere.'

Another explanation has subsequently been put forward. It is that Robert McBride placed the powder-blue Ford Cortina car bomb outside the Parade Hotel on the specific instructions of his ANC military superiors.

During the trial, Robert consistently protected Greta to his own detriment. But there are well-informed suggestions – not provable, or available to the court – which imply that Robert McBride was shielding not only his lover, but also his organisation. The shadowy Special Operations branch of *Umkhonto we Sizwe* does not debate its operations; neither Matthew Lecordier nor Greta Apelgren wish to discuss the critical moments in West Street, outside the 'Hyperama House & Home', when the final target was selected. Robert McBride himself is publicly sticking to the account he gave during his trial. So he took the rap.

31

Judge Douglas Shearer delivered the verdicts on April 7, 1987. He and his two assessors gave Greta Apelgren the benefit of the doubt on the most serious charge; they concluded that the state had not proved she knew about the car bomb and acquitted her on all counts relating to the Magoo Bar deaths. Robert McBride, however, was found guilty of murdering Angelique Pattenden, Marchelle Gerrard and Julie van der Linde.

Both accused were also found guilty of aiding Gordon Webster to escape, of harbouring a terrorist and helping to smuggle him out of the country. A number of counts, especially against Greta Apelgren, were dismissed. Nevertheless, Robert McBride was found guilty of furthering the aims of the African National Congress, as well as several counts of sabotage and terrorism. But there was only one issue which dominated the next day's headlines: MCBRIDE CONVICTED OF THREE MURDERS.

The trial moved into its final stage. This was the consideration of whether Robert should face the death penalty. If extenuating circumstances regarding his 'moral blame-worthiness' were agreed by the judge and the assessors, a life sentence could be imposed instead. Throughout the past two months, David Gordon had been desperately trying to get one of the injured victims of the Parade Hotel car bomb to stand up and testify in mitigation for his client. But no one who had been in either the Why Not Bar or Magoo's on the night of the explosion was prepared to come forward.

There followed three days of legal argument and debate over Robert's fate. David Gordon made a moving and emotional appeal for extenuation. He said, 'This case is a South African tragedy.' He pleaded Robert's youth, his political commitment, the violent community in which he had grown up, and the injustice against which he was fighting. He evoked the memory of Major John MacBride, executed after the Easter 1916 uprising in Ireland 'because of his role in the Boer War which was still held against him'. David Gordon compared this with the treatment of defeated Boer leaders at the end of the Boer War who were forgiven (and in one prominent case, reprieved from execution) in the name of reconciliation. David Gordon pleaded for mercy and understanding.

The law was clear. In South Africa the death sentence was mandatory for murder, unless extenuating circumstances were found to lessen 'moral blame-worthiness'. That would be decided by a three-way vote between Judge Shearer and his two assessors. Professor John Milton was opposed to the death penalty on principle; he also felt that the political nature of the case provided substantial grounds for mitigating factors. As the trial drew to its conclusion, however, he realized that Douglas Shearer himself had come to the opposite conclusion. This left Brian Leslie. Milton had no idea which way he was thinking.

Judge Shearer insisted that the decision should be made as soon as possible because he did not want the agony of the prisoner to be drawn out longer than was necessary. When the court went into recess at the end of that week, after the culmination of two-and-a-half months of detailed legal argument, David Gordon felt that there was a very good chance his client would not be sentenced to death. The judgement was due to be delivered on Monday morning. In his chambers, Judge Shearer told his two assessors that they must ponder dispassionately over the weekend what their verdicts were going to be. Before they drove off that evening, Professor Milton tried hard to convince his colleague Brian Leslie that there were sufficient extenuating circumstances to permit a life sentence instead.

He put forward five principal reasons: McBride's lack of maturity, the influence of his father's obsessive hatred of whites, the anger caused by the declaration of the State of Emergency, that the initial target had aimed to destroy property not lives, and finally that the Marine Parade decision had been made on impulse after a suggestion from Mr C. Yet Milton was unable to gauge Leslie's reaction. He appeared to concede the points without being enthusiastic.

Milton rang him on Friday and reiterated his arguments. He thought he might be able to persuade him; if he could, it would be two to one against Shearer and the death penalty. 'If you feel you need to talk about it more,' offered Milton, 'Come over to my house any time during the weekend.'

On Monday morning, April 13, Professor Milton parked his car outside the Supreme Court. He saw Brian Leslie on the other side of the parking lot; he knew immediately what he had decided.

Leslie came straight over to him. He was very tense. 'I can't find any extenuating circumstances,' he said.

Even though Greta did not risk such severe penalties, Mrs Margaret Apelgren could not face attending the court that Monday. Instead, she stayed at home and prayed.

Doris McBride felt she was close to the edge of a breakdown. That morning she was accompanied by her daughter Bronwyn and her sister Girly. 'If they pass the death sentence, just don't cry,' Doris told them fiercely. 'They are waiting to see us break down.'

The court was so crowded that there were people queuing in the corridor. The security police, fearful of a riot, were out in force. The court was also full of police. The atmosphere was volatile.

As Robert was being brought up from the cells below the court, a policeman dangled a rope in front of his face. Robert lunged at him and there was a scuffle. The police immediately announced that they intended to clear the court; McBride was in an aggressive mood, they said, and could cause mayhem.

David Gordon hastened to see Judge Shearer in his chambers. He would take personal responsibility for controlling the public gallery, he said. The lawyer, still hoping his client would not be sentenced to death, went out into the open court and begged for calm. 'I appeal to everyone,' he said. 'Whatever happens, we all must maintain the dignity of the court, as much as the accused has respected the dignity of the court.' David Gordon handed Robert a tie and thought: a rope could be going round his neck.

Then Judge Douglas Shearer entered Court A, followed by Professor Milton and Brian Leslie. There was absolute silence as he read out the sentences. Greta Apelgren was a good person, he said, and it grieved him to have to sentence her, but a substantial portion of her sentence would be suspended. Greta was effectively sentenced to one year and nine months in prison.

The ritual took only fifteen minutes.

Douglas Shearer turned to Robert McBride. 'It is with great sadness that the Court is forced to conclude that there are no circumstances which extenuate his guilt on counts 14, 15 and 16,' pronounced the Judge. 'On count 14, I am obliged by law to sentence accused Number One to death. On Count 15, I am likewise obliged to sentence him to death, and on Count 16, I am obliged to sentence him to death, which I do.'

Professor John Milton did not know where to look; he looked at McBride. The condemned man was staring fixedly ahead, betraying no emotion. Milton noticed that Greta put her hand lightly on Robert's hip. Judge Shearer rose and, followed by his two uncomfortable assessors, filed out of Court A.

Doris McBride was staring at her son's back. The court was still hushed, uncertain. Robert appeared to be very still. Then he turned and addressed the public gallery. 'I have taken you quite a distance along the road,' he said. 'Freedom is just around the corner. I am leaving you at the corner – and you must take that corner to find freedom on the other side.'

As the policemen moved in to take him away, McBride raised his fist and shouted, 'The struggle continues till Babylon falls!'

Part Five

Darkness as a Bride

32

In 1783, in the notebooks he kept for jotting down *pensées* and aphorisms, a hunchbacked Professor of Gottingen, the mathematician, physicist and experimenter Georg Christoph Lichtenberg, observed mildly, 'The American who first discovered Columbus made a bad mistake.'

In 1488, Batholomeu Dias was the first European to round the Cape; he eventually made landfall from his two caravels, the *Sao Cristovão* and the *São Pantaleão*, and it may modestly be remarked that the first South African who discovered this Portuguese explorer also made an unlucky error.

As the Portuguese put ashore near the present town of Mossel Bay they encountered a group of Khoikhoi, a small, yellow-skinned cattle-herding people. Both parties watched each other nervously and when the white men moved towards a nearby stream one of the Hottentots, as they were later to be known to the Europeans, threw a stone. The result, a professor of anthropology and psychiatry at the University of California, Robert B. Edgerton, explained in 1988, was that, 'Dias promptly put an arrow from his cross-bow through one of them.'

Professor Edgerton was outlining in his book, *Like Lions They Fought*, the colonial record in South Africa which led up to the British campaign to destroy the Zulu empire in 1879. This was a war which the British provoked in order to demolish the last black empire in Southern Africa. The Governor of the Cape Colony, Sir Henry Bartle Frere, manoeuvered the Zulus into an untenable position, while conducting a propaganda war playing on settler fears concerning black people, a strange brew of warlike nightmares and sexual phobia. Professor Edgerton recorded, 'Frere increased his campaign to justify war against the Zulus by disseminating atrocity stories about Cetshwayo, whom he depicted as a despotic savage who was planning to send his maniacally bloodthirsty soldiers – Frere called them "celibate manslaying gladiators" – to slaughter the helpless residents of Natal.'

A similar mix of projected dread is recorded in Professor Edgerton's subsequent history, *Mau Mau*, concerning the rebellion against British Colonial rule in Kenya in the 1950s. At the time, the rebellion was portrayed throughout the western world as a vicious and bestial tribal terror directed against innocent white settlers. The British authorities proclaimed that Mau Mau was a crime wave, and not a 'Land and Freedom Army'. They depicted the rebels, summarised Professor Edgerton, as 'bestial "gangsters" who, crazed by unspeakable, primitive ceremonies involving cannibalism, the drinking of menstrual blood and sexual orgies, indiscriminately terrorized white settlers, especially women and children.' While many atrocities were committed, the white phobia and propaganda bore no relation to the facts: outrages were committed on both sides, with the British forces often being the more ruthless.

After the State of Emergency, declared in 1952, over fifty thousand British-led troops and police were committed to suppress this movement, which was so badly armed that some resorted to bows and arrows. Over a million Kikuyu and Embu were forced into 'designated villages' under strict security guard, while between eighty and ninety thousand others were placed in concentration camps where many died. Over eleven thousand rebels were killed, of whom more than a thousand were hanged as criminals. On the other side, an estimated seventeen hundred Kikuyu 'loyalists' were killed, and in the ranks of the colonial forces some six hundred died in the fighting, sixty-three of them whites. Of white civilians killed by Mau Mau there were thirty-two.

This was not the bloodbath of colonial fantasy. That was a figment of their overwrought anxieties, conjured from ignorance of the indigenous people. Nor did Jomo Kenyatta, the Kikuyu nationalist leader, turn out to be the demon of their nightmares. Arrested as the 'evil genius' behind Mau Mau on the first day of the State of Emergency, the British Government had finally to allow him to return to politics in 1961, and in 1963 he became the first Head of State in newly independent Kenya.

'But the men and women of Mau Mau were not rewarded with land, or even medals, and they were not given positions in Kenyatta's government,' pointed out Professor Edgerton. 'Instead, wealthy Africans who had been loyal to the colonial government retained their land, bought other land vacated by whites, and dominated Kenya's business world. Known as 'Black Europeans', they moved into large, walled estates in formerly all-white neighbourhoods of Nairobi, where guards, dogs, and barbed wire defended their wealth against poor Africans like those who fought for Mau Mau and died in concentration camps. In their wake came newly wealthy African entrepreneurs and European investors.'

In 1943 Sir Ralph Furse, the Director of Recruitment at the Colonial Office, wrote a memorandum on the post-war training for the colonial service. In this he pointed out that after the fall of Singapore the British Empire would never be the same again. He suggested that 'as the educated native moved to the centre of the stage', more sensitivity would be required by British colonial administrators – more interest would have to be shown in the artistic and spiritual life of colonial peoples, more of the ancient Greek spirit, suggested Sir Ralph, instead of the Roman preoccupation with Pax Britannica.

One of this new breed was Peter Leyden who was posted to Kenya in 1956, by which time the Mau Mau rebellion had been largely contained. He travelled there with his new wife, Annette, who had never left Britain before, to take up his appointment as a District Commissioner. The following year when they were stationed in Kisumu, on Lake Victoria, they had a daughter, Karen; and then on July 25, 1958 in the small town of Nyeri, a second child, Paula, was born.

Paula's parents were both from North Wales: Peter had attended a Jesuit college, then Oxford University, while Annette came from the local manor at Penmaenmawr near Conway in County Clwyd, and had played hockey for North Wales. They had met at the local tennis club. In her youth, she had looked very much like Paula, slim and fair, with sharp, striking features, while Peter was tall, athletic and conventionally handsome with blue eyes, curly brown hair, a straight nose and a strong, square jaw offset by a quizzical, shielding smile.

As a District Commissioner, Peter Leyden travelled constantly from village to village, mostly by Land Rover, but often on foot. It was a life of early rising, the smell of woodsmoke, red dust, and the aromatic scent from the bush. To Paula, the distinction between what was remembered and what later told to her was uncertain, a blurred contour, like a faded black and white photograph.

There were the ants; her mother spreading hot ashes around the hearth at night as a barrier against the army ants which would otherwise march in and invade the house. There were also the ant-lions, insects living in tiny cylindrical holes in the sand, which the children would spend hours tickling with strands of grass in order to flush them out of their lair. Everywhere there was dust. The two girls wore only underpants to play outside, and the only hiding Paula can remember was for rolling around in mud puddles in a frock specially put on for Christmas Day. They were taught to look out for snakes and to stand totally still if they met one. She remembers her hair, fair and curly, being stroked a lot, as a curiosity. Paula and her sister Karen grew up speaking Swahili; her father spoke it fluently.

'He loved Kenya,' said Paula. 'He was outside the whole time, travelling a lot, and often walking great distances through the bush. We used to call him Bongbird. We grew up on Bongbird stories. It was a character he invented and he used to tell us stories about his life in Kenya and incidents that happened to him, so they were true, but he used to tell them to us as "The Bongbird stories", and they could be quite terrifying, about witches and witch doctors and magic.'

In 1962, as Kenya approached independence, Peter Leyden left the Colonial Service and returned to Britain; but the family soon returned to Africa, aboard a majestic Union Castle liner to Cape Town. There were deck games and tombolas and dances, and fancy dress parties for the children. Paula remembers one little boy causing a sensation by appearing as a cigarette, but then he wet his pants and there was public humiliation as the cigarette went soggy. From Cape Town, the family drove up to Johannesburg in an old blue Peugeot. Her sister Julia was born there, but within nine months the Leyden family moved on once more, this time to Zambia. Peter Leyden had joined the gargantuan South African conglomerate, Anglo American, and was posted to the small, neat copperbelt town of Kitwe.

It was 1964, and the colony of Northern Rhodesia was gaining its independence from Britain, becoming Zambia. Kitwe remains indistinct in Paula's consciousness, apart from the birth of her brother John, and the photograph of memory does not become focused until the family moved to the Zambian capital of Lusaka the following year, when she was seven. Here she felt at home. She and her sisters Karen and Julia attended the Dominican Convent, where the Dominican sisters taught with a proselytising zeal, one of them informing Julia that if she ever got tapeworm all she needed to do was not eat for a few days and then hold a saucer of milk in front of her mouth to lure the tapeworm out. There was Sister Leonisa who changed her name because the children used to tease her about being a lion, and Paula's friend Winifred Konkola, who shared a double desk with her, but had to leave school for an arranged tribal marriage with an elderly man.

Because of the heat, school would begin and finish early. For European adults, the Lusaka Golf Club was a focal meeting point and her parents played hockey and tennis at the Middlewater Club. Peter and Annette Leyden were not typical colonial ex-pats by any means and they looked beyond the insular white community for their social life, having many Zambian friends. They expected their children to do likewise and instilled in them a deep love of the country, an unusual independence and originality, as well as an utterly non-racial outlook.

'In many ways it was an idyllic childhood,' said Paula. 'There was lots of space, and it was hot, with no TV, so we played outside and swam. For holidays we would drive to Kenya to the beach, or go to the National Parks. It was wonderful. We also spent a lot of time on a farm twenty miles out of Lusaka, helping to dip the cattle and riding horses. It was exciting. I learnt to drive a car.

They had an old mini with the top cut off and a motorbike. It was very carefree.

'I remember the first time there were escalators in a store in Lusaka. It was at the Mwasini Stores, and it was a big event. It was the first big double-storey shop and these moving stairs were an important event. You'd go into town just to go up and down on the escalator.'

Another important event was the arrival of Haile Selassie of Ethiopia. All the school children gathered outside State House or lined Independence Avenue, waving the Zambian flag as his cavalcade passed by. The Emperor wore a lofty military hat to make him look taller.

Then, at the age of eleven, Paula was sent away to school in Britain. Our Lady of Sion Convent was an old, cold building with long, dank corridors. The nuns of Our Lady of Sion seemed particularly forbidding to the eleven-year-old girl who was used to running around barefoot, and she deeply resented this closed, constricted new life. The convent was situated on the borders of Shropshire, not far from where both her parents had been born, and the enveloping hills were startlingly green and misty and alien.

The uniform was grey; to Paula, everything seemed grey. 'My feeling was one of overwhelming resentment,' she said. 'I was incredibly homesick. I missed my family, I missed Zambia. I used to cry at night and it didn't get any better. It was like a big, crumbling castle. We slept in these little cubicles and you had a bowl to fetch your water to wash in, and then one of the nuns would come and inspect that you had washed properly – they would especially check your toes, to make sure you had washed in between them, and behind your ears.

'It was the kind of place that makes you rebel. You had to eat everything that was on your plate, even if it made you completely nauseated. On one occasion it was liver, and I said I can't eat it because I will be sick, and they said I had to eat it, so I sat there from lunchtime throughout the whole afternoon, through supper, with someone standing behind me, until about ten o'clock at night. Eventually they gave up and said I didn't have to eat liver anymore. A small victory; it was that kind of school.'

Paula began to sleepwalk and furniture was placed across the top of the stairway to stop her falling down. For being caught talking in the dormitory at night, she was made to stand with her face to the wall alone in a dark room for two hours. Her sister Karen reacted more favourably to the regime of the British boarding school, but even so she was known by the nuns as 'Vague' and Paula as 'Vaguer'. Paula was delighted to leave Our Lady of Sion when the two Leyden girls transferred to New Hall near Chelmsford in Essex, which was run by the Community of the Holy Sepulchre. It was another venerable building, with high ceilings, wood panelling and a magnificent chapel, which boasted of connections with King Henry VIII and Anne Boleyn. The prospectus promised, 'Pastoral care and religious and moral education are of primary concern.'

Their brother John went to a co-educational school in Lusaka, *Nkhwazi*, the Fish Eagle, also attended by Kenneth Kaunda's daughter, and he recalls their mother crying when her two daughters returned to Britain for a new school term after a holiday in Zambia. At New Hall they wore a uniform of a maroon skirt and a white airtex long-sleeved shirt, a maroon tie and grey jersey. As an alternative they would have a pinafore with a white nylon polo neck for Sundays. Paula found her uniform stifling and the attitude censorious: 'The first day I arrived at that school I got called in and they said, "Well, we have been told about you . . . so don't think you can try that here," and so I was even worse there because I thought, "Right – I'll show you," and I was stubborn from the start.

'My attitude towards authority there was totally different than it was towards my parents, which is why, when they sent a letter saying that I was stubborn, rude, unco-operative and a thousand other things, they did not get angry. It was as if the nuns were talking about another person completely. Each term these reports would arrive – Paula refuses to co-operate, Paula has bunked classes, she is stubborn, she is wasting her potential . . .'

There were constant prayers: in the morning, at meals, and at chapel in the evening. Once, in order to duck out of chapel Paula dived out of the crocodile line of girls and hid in a laundry basket. But a search by the nuns eventually concentrated on the laundry, and one of them came down the line of baskets, opening each one of them until she discovered Paula squatting among a pile of sheets. On this occasion she was given detention and made to write lines, 'I must not . . . I must not . . .', although at other times such naive sedition was dismissed with an airy, 'Oh those are just Zambians . . .'

During a school outing to Hampton Court, as the girls wandered in the maze, Paula cut her leg on a rose bush and started bleeding, but the nuns were aghast when she proceeded to remove her stockings and she was sent back to the school bus in disgrace. She was censured the following day in front of the class. 'In a public place,' protested Sister Mary Dismus, shocked. 'I suppose that's how they behave in Zambia.'

Once, Paula set off the fire alarm in order to avoid class. 'We used to have these double physics lessons which I really dreaded,' she said. 'The physics teacher was really fierce and I just couldn't face those lessons. Well, there were fire alarms protected by glass, saying "Do Not Break", so I took off my shoe and bashed the fire alarm and the whole school had to assemble on the front lawn while the fire engines were called.

'The fire engines came there and everyone was queueing up, and I suddenly started to feel really bad, so when the headmistress, who was called Sister Mary Francis, came and stood at the front and demanded, "Does anyone know about this?" I said yes, I was the culprit. They said, why did you do it, and I said because I didn't want to go to double physics.'

Not long after, Paula was expelled. She was summoned from her dormitory to the headmistress' study, where she was informed that she would be leaving the school immediately. She would not even be permitted to return to the dormitory to pack or say goodbye to friends. A car was waiting outside. The headmistress explained that she could not expect her staff to put up with Paula any longer.

It was 1973, the year her father was transferred from Lusaka to the Anglo-American headquarters in Johannesburg. Paula had mixed feelings: 'I had read for years of South Africa The Racist Regime, and dreaded arriving. We'd been there, but I'd been very young and didn't remember anything, so the only thing I knew was what I read. I thought, now I'm going to South Africa The Racist Regime.'

Paula, fifteen years old, was enrolled as a day girl in the fashionable St Mary's School For Girls. Situated in the leafy white suburb of Waverley, its entrance was a gracious white porch with a large plaque emblazoned with the school emblem and motto, *Candida Rectaque* (literally, White and Upright; more loosely, Purity and Rectitude). The school uniform was a blue check dress, blue frock and a straw boater with a blue ribbon; the jacket was grey. As in so much of English-speaking South Africa, the model was British but the colonial variant was more easy going. The buildings were spacious and well-equipped, while at the back there were tennis courts and well-watered hockey pitches. Paula played tennis, hockey and netball and became best friends with the headmistress' daughter, Bridget. 'We used to spend a lot of time discussing the meaning of the world,' said Paula, 'I think we thought we were quite significant.'

In many ways she found white life in South Africa bewildering. It was more like Europe than Africa. In Lusaka there had been no traffic jams and only one cinema; in Johannesburg everything was bigger, more industrial, more westernised. Suburban white attitudes she also found disconcerting.

'I was asked questions at school which didn't make sense to me like, did I go to a multi-racial school in Zambia?' said Paula. 'I'd never known what it was to be called multi-racial. It introduced me to a whole new vocabulary. I remember being confused at some of the questions asked by fellow pupils. What were *they* like? The questions being asked almost morbidly – you know, when people ask questions in whispered tones, with slightly greedy expressions on their faces?

'In Britain I had been asked about wild animals roaming the streets, and what kind of houses did we live in, and did we sleep outside, or were there thatched little round houses? And strangely enough I even got some questions like that here. It was as if Zambia was perceived as some sort of large game park, with a few houses scattered about. I didn't expect such questions from South Africans. They should have been part of Africa – and it seemed as though they weren't.'

33

'I was not expecting Robert to be sentenced to death,' said Doris McBride. 'It was a terrible, terrible time. The very next day I had to go to Derrick's trial. I think I had actually reached the end of my line by then.

'But I had to stay to see Derrick's trial through. Robert's finished on April 13 and Derrick's on May 13. We just had to keep going to court every day. Derrick's trial carried on . . . right after Robert's sentence. The morning after that, when Derrick and Antonio awoke in the morning to go the showers, Derrick said, "Well, where is Robert? Is he still asleep? Wake him up, it's time for a shower!" So they said, "No, he's gone." They took him about three o'clock in the morning while the others slept. They had taken him out and gone to Pretoria.

'Derrick didn't say too much about Robert's sentence, but I could sense he was shocked and worried about it. He had to be careful about reaction, because we did not want to give much away to the people who were the cause of the whole thing. We were always aware that they were watching us. They were just waiting for us to crack up, they were trying to push us through a wall.'

A fortnight after Robert was sentenced to death, Doris McBride received a letter at 59a Hardy Place from Pretoria Central prison.

Prisoner No. 3737
Maximum Security Prison
Private Bag X45
PRETORIA 0001

23 March, 1987

Comrade Mummy,

I've been here just over a week now. I'm OK, fit and healthy.
I am allowed as many letters as possible – to receive and to
send. I am also allowed visits throughout the week. Times for
visits are between 9 and 11, and between 2 and 3.

I saw Roshan today. It was good to see somebody from home
after what seems like a long time. There are so many people
here on Death Row. There are . . . There are so many it's
unbelievable. This thing of Capital punishment must end as
soon as possible.

A government that has to hang so many people to maintain
'law and order' should be ashamed of itself. The fact that there
are so many people here is an indictment on the social and
political structure of the South African society.

This alone is evidence of there being something drastically
wrong with South African society. I think we must be one of the
countries with the highest no. of annual executions.

The time of my trial was not in vain – regardless of the
outcome. I have come to understand the oppressor very well. I
have had sufficient time to study him and think about him.
Strangely, I don't think the oppressor knows himself; or
understands himself.

He creates a system where we have 4 distinct societies. Each
society develops its own social and moral norms. These sets of
moral values differ from society to society. But here is the
problem: All 4 societies are judged in a court of law which
aspires to and judges on a system based on White moral values
of a privileged minority. What an indictment on a judicial
system! How dare they judge us Black people! The White
judge lives in his White powder-puff, lily-white, privileged
society. How can he ever imagine the social and psychological

make-up of a person like myself – a product of the ghetto. I am a product of the ghetto, but not because of choice – because of the colour of my skin! Can he even appreciate this fact? All these things play a part in how a person behaves or will behave. It is the same system that the judge upholds that is responsible for me developing differently from him (the white judge)! But does he take these things into account when he sentences me? My sentence is not what all of South Africa wants or expects, it is what the White, minority, privileged South Africa wants. But does White S.A. live in a ghetto, is White S.A. discriminated against (by law) because of the colour of their skins, is White S.A. voteless, oppressed . . ., . . . ????

Regardless of the outcome of this tribulation, there must be no tears. Tears lead to fears, especially for the mothers of other prospective guerrillas. There is no time to fear. There is a Battle to be won. Male, Female, Young & Old all are needed on all fronts, political activists and armed combatants. It is a time of sacrifice.

Nevertheless, I am confident that Robert-Derrick's generation will be free. Their generation will not tread the road of oppression. Their generation will be free! This thing is crumbling. This Babylonian apartheid monster is giving its last kicks. But we must be careful: a wounded animal is desperate and most dangerous. But now we have to deliver the final blow to the philosophy of Racialism and Racial Supremacy. Uneasy is the head that wears the crown of white supremacy.

Your loving son

Three weeks later Derrick McBride and Antonio du Preez were sentenced by the Supreme Court in Pietermaritzburg. Derrick was jailed for twelve years, Antonio for fifteen. Both were sent to Robben Island.

In Lusaka at the ANC headquarters, Gordon Webster at last got the go-ahead for the audacious plan he had been battling to have accepted: to return to South Africa and free Robert McBride.

Although his wife Anne was pregnant they were both determined to press ahead. With the backing of Chris Hani, the

Deputy Commander of *Umkhonto we Sizwe*, the operation had
finally been given official backing. The plan was to take an
important hostage, possibly a senior Special Branch officer, and
hold him in return for McBride. The favoured target was the trial
judge, Douglas Shearer.

Gordon Webster was authorised to recruit another guerrilla to
aid him in his project. He returned to the isolated ANC base,
Pango Camp in central Angola, where two years previously under
the *nom de guerre* 'Joe Peterson' he had received his own military
training. Here the instructors recommended a twenty-nine-year-
old African from Durban, whose MK name was 'Siphiwe
Mkhonto'. He was known to the other trainees as 'Rifle', because
during his first week at the camp he had been nervous of
scorpions at night and had insisted on sleeping with his AK47.
But the nickname that had stuck was 'Casanova'.

He was called in to the small administrative office and introduced to 'Joe Peterson'. Casanova was asked if he knew the
Durban-Pietermaritzburg-Ladysmith area well and he was able
to say yes. It emerged during their conversation that Casanova
was a movie addict. Finally, Joe Peterson inquired in Zulu if he
had heard of the escape from Edendale Hospital of a wounded
ANC man.

Casanova said he had even seen the news of this breakout on
TV, and added, 'It was just like a bioscope.'

Afterwards, Casanova was put on a special crash course. He
was then flown to Lusaka where he was lodged in an ANC safe
house. Two days later Joe came to see him and said that his name
was in fact, Gordon Webster, and that it was he who had been
taken from the hospital by Robert McBride, who had subsequently been captured himself. Webster explained that he
wished now to free McBride and was looking for help. Casanova
agreed.

34

A decade earlier Paula had decided that after school in Johannesburg she wanted a change of scene. She elected to go to the University of Natal in Durban. 'I hadn't been to Durban and I thought it might be nice,' she said. 'I could go to the sea and it was hot. For the first year I stayed in the Mabel Palmer women's residence, but in the second year there was no room left in the women's residence so I went to a men's residence. I was the only woman there.

'I got involved with forming a women's movement organisation to address the issue of sexism on the campus. It was a way of getting people involved with issues that particularly affected them. When I first arrived, you had to go through this ridiculous initiation. You were humiliated, having to sing stupid songs and going back to your room at night to find all your possessions had been thrown all over the place. It was childish and I hated it.'

First-year women students were required to put on shorts, and march past a male selection committee to be chosen as 'drummies', drum majorettes. Paula refused and even succeeded in a campaign to have this undergraduate ritual abolished. To conventional white South African males, such contention was especially provoking from a slender young woman with long blonde hair and grey-blue eyes. A local newspaper article appeared, with a photo of Paula looking like an archetypal Californian surfer girl, saying she was pretty enough to be nominated for the University Rag Queen.

Her younger brother, John, remembers her hitch-hiking back from Durban during vacations, and all his school friends having crushes on his independent-minded sister. 'She used to dress in a semi-bohemian way, with Indian prints, bell-bottom jeans, and a slight contrivance of not caring,' said John. 'I remember her sitting around cross-legged on the lawn with her friends, who all seemed to be involved in communal living and healthy food. She used to give me stickers, things like: TOO MANY LAWS, TOO LITTLE JUSTICE.'

In Durban, Paula was studying English and Economic History. 'It was a very intense time,' she said. 'It was exciting on one level: reading 'radical' literature, discussions late into the night. But I always felt it was an apology for doing something real.'

During her second year at university she was elected to the Students' Representative Council and began attending seminars and national student congresses. In her third year, Paula shared a house in Moore Road with other students and a grey parrot with a yellow plume called Henry. She also spray-painted slogans at night. In September 1978, on the second anniversary of Steve Biko's death in police detention, Paula and her friends did a synchronised leaflet drop from a number of prominent buildings in central Durban.

As a student leader, Paula organised a project for university students to go and help teach junior classes in the nearby Coloured district of Wentworth. It was here, briefly, she met the fifteen-year-old Robert McBride, a student at Fairvale High. The overcrowding in schools in Wentworth was so chronic that there had to be a double shift system for pupils. The young, inexperienced university students who would travel to Wentworth in the afternoon in a small van were faced by rowdy, unruly, bored and frustrated children, up to forty of them in a class. 'It was the most practical thing we could do,' said Paula. 'Student politics was usually hot air and theory, and I felt that this project was not *playing* as much as in other areas.'

Paula decided to become a teacher. On graduating, she returned to Johannesburg and for six months worked at a recreation centre for white children; then, with friends, she hitch-hiked the seven hundred and fifty miles to Cape Town, which she so liked that on impulse she decided to stay.

During the early 1980s Paula taught at Coloured schools in and around Cape Town. She acquired a speckled brown cat called Arnold and rode to work on a motorbike, graduating from a

49cc scooter to a 400cc Honda. At the first school, only for boys, she was something of a novelty because she was female. Her subject was history. 'I remember being almost awed by the seriousness of some of those students; their seriousness about life,' said Paula. 'They were interesting and they were interested. I learnt a lot from them. They had a sense of the importance of history because of their lives. They did not see it as just a series of facts. They saw it as something that happened to people.'

By 1987, the time of Robert McBride's trial, Paula had returned to Johannesburg.

'To me, she seemed to be surrounded by people who were less committed than she was,' said her brother John. 'Actually, she is also quite domesticated. She had a good relationship with Ma and Pa, though she'd sometimes fall out with Pa over politics and there would be battles.'

Paula's parents lived in Bryanston, one of Johannesburg's most luxurious suburbs, where the wide grass verges were well tended and lined with pin oak and pine trees. The only sound to disturb the peace was the lulling coo of doves and the cool hiss of lawn sprinklers. Many of the large houses, whose curious styles ranged from mock hacienda to Hollywood baroque, had their own swimming pools and tennis courts.

The street names had a pungent British flavour. There was Highland, Sterling and Glen; Sloane, Hunt and Westminster, as well as Queen Anne and Waterloo. The Bryanston Country Club was bounded by Cumberland, Grosvenor and Curzon. This was a mannerly suburb for affluent English-speaking professionals.

Here they were singularly security conscious, with electronic gates, floodlights and closed circuit TV monitors. Bored guard dogs raced up to the gates to snarl at innocent passers-by and black delivery 'boys'.

When His Majesty King Leka the First of the Albanians went for a walk, he strapped on a 9mm pistol and five boxer dogs accompanied him on his royal progress through Bryanston. Leka was only a monarch in his own mind, of course, for in 1939 his father King Zog had been deposed from the Albanian throne by a shambolic Italian invasion. Their ex-Majesties had wandered restlessly from Britain to Egypt, France, Spain and Rhodesia, until Leka the First finally planted the Albanian royal standard 5,700 feet above sea level in Johannesburg. Like many others in Bryanston, he did not think of Africa as home. Most of his well-heeled neighbours, however, looked towards London rather than day-dreaming of returning to the Balkans in triumph.

Perhaps the lawn-girt, water-sprinkled suburb fostered such nostalgic longings. On the harsh, dry, red soiled high veld, the manicured gardens were lush, green and displaced. Red and yellow cannas, blue and white agapanthus, the purple effusions of wisteria, roses in spring: these were gardens of more temperate dreams. It was a reverie of elsewhere, only seven miles from the frantic centre of Johannesburg: a mirage in Africa.

35

Death Row is on a gentle rise overlooking Pretoria Central Prison. It is quiet up there in the high-walled citadel, and the other prisoners call it Beverly Hills. It has a fine view, but those who go in through the immense black iron gates are never intended to see the outside world again. There are no windows in 'Beverly Hills'.

'At first I could never sleep,' said Robert McBride, prisoner 3737. 'The white guards used to come and stare at me – the terrorist. I shouted, "Hey, whiteboys, what are you staring at?" Then I accepted I was going to die and thought, to hell with these people.

'The first friend I had on Death Row was executed almost immediately after I got there. Edward Heynes was in for a prison murder and he was the first guy to speak to me. After I'd been there only two weeks he was given his notice of execution. Heynes had a rosary. He held it up like a rope and said, "I'm going to hang." He was cynical and accepted it. I couldn't accept it, but then the reality hit me. I'm going to die.

'For Heynes, outwardly it was a joke. He laughed. It helped him get through it. There seemed to be no fear. The first day he was in the Pot, after he got his notice, he called to me in Afrikaans, "*Ja*, McBride – I told you they were going to get me."

'The night before an execution the other prisoners used to sing. In the first year there were no stays of execution and people were more passive and fatalistic, but then they began fighting back with appeals and stays of execution. In my first year, people were relying heavily on religion. They sang a lot, mostly hymns, in Zulu – *Rock of Ages* – and southern folk or soul songs. They'd sing *Climbing Up The Mountain*: "If I don't see you, I'll meet you on Judgement Day." If it was a comrade being hanged, then they sang freedom songs. Freedom songs help build up your spirit. It would be songs about Oliver Tambo, or "What have you done?", *Senzeni na* in Xhosa.

'The night before an execution people are very sad. Then about eight o'clock in the evening the whole place stamps its feet. It makes your hair stand on end. Other prisoners sing the whole night.

'The night Edward Heynes was to go I finally fell asleep on the table, my head in my hands, and I woke early. Everyone had been singing before. Now it was very quiet . . .'

In South Africa, the hangman was a busy man. During the previous decade there had been over fifteen hundred executions in Pretoria Central. Sometimes the queue for the gallows was so long that several were dispatched at the same time. For this purpose there were seven gallows all in a row. The gallows loomed large in the thoughts of those in Beverly Hills, and the men who were awaiting its immediate attentions were kept in an isolation cell known as the 'Pot'.

Condemned men were handed their notice of execution a week before the appointed dawn. In the Pot, during this week of preparation for the noose, the prisoner was permitted to scream and shout and sing as much as he liked. Families were issued with railway tickets to Pretoria for one last visit.

The ritual for preparing a man for his death was precise and unvarying. The condemned man had his height and weight measured to determine the exact drop necessary, while his neck size was checked to tailor the noose exactly. For his last supper, the condemned man was served a whole chicken – though the bird had been carefully deboned to prevent the possibility of a last-minute suicide attempt which might rob the hangman of his dues.

Executions took place at dawn. A chaplain would visit the subject before he was led through the final, fatal double doors. In front of him would be seven gallows, one of which had been specially rigged to his own personal specifications. The condemned man had his wrists tied behind his back and a hood placed over his head. The hangman stepped forward and fitted the noose, then pulled the lever. A trap door opened: the man was dispatched.

There were so many executions that some of the relatives simply could not believe it. Death Row generated its own myths. One was that the condemned, the dawn they were led away never to be seen again, were actually transported to a bunker below a nearby hill, where they worked on dangerous chemical and radioactive weaponry. Others said that deep underground there was a mint where the government consigned them to work as slaves manufacturing money.

In fact, the body was carried out through the black iron gates in a plain black van escorted by a police car, to a cemetery where it was buried in the presence of state officials. Only later were relatives informed of the location and number of the grave. The cemetery to which the authorities allocated each corpse was ordained by colour of skin.

In May, when Derrick's trial had finished, Doris travelled up from Wentworth to visit her son. He had lost a lot of weight. 'It was terrible, that big black door,' said Doris. 'Everytime it groaned and rolled open it gave me the creeps. But when it was closing, clanging shut, it was worse. It had a terrible effect on me, that door.'

Slowly, agonisingly, Robert McBride began to reject the idea that he was going to die. He did not want to die. 'At first when I was on Death Row everyone used to sing hymns,' said Robert. 'They were relying on religion. They had no other hope.'

One of those who had turned to religion was Menzi Thafeni, a twenty-year-old youth, already on Death Row for over a year for the killing of a policeman – for which he claimed he was innocent. 'Every time they executed someone we felt it like our own day approaching,' said Menzi. 'When people were going to be hanged, I saw them pass by my cell. Sometimes they would say, in Xhosa, "We are on our way to heaven." And as they passed they greeted me saying, "It is over." There were thirty-two steps to where they hung. After a year they took my friend Konze.'

Jacobus Konze and Menzi were such close friends they were

known as twins; then Konze was given his notice and taken to the Pot. From the Pot, Menzi could hear his friend shouting that if God in the Bible could save Shadrak, Meshack and Abednego from the fire, why could He not save him. At the last minute Konze was granted a stay of execution, and returned to his cell pending a clemency appeal.

'When a person comes back from the Pot, they can never be the same person again,' said Menzi. 'It is like they have come back from Hell. They have been to visit the death.'

Konze, Menzi felt, was already dead in his heart. His appeal was turned down, and Jacobus Konze returned to the Pot for the second time: 'On 7 March they came to him and told him to pack his things. On 14 March he was taken to the gallows machine. When he was taken away that morning he was shouting for me as he was walking. He shouted, "Menzi, my time is over now, but you must not be in sorrow, you must not cry."

'Then when I heard the bang of that machine, that is the time I know it is finished. Afterwards one of the warders came to me and said, "Yes, Thafeni, your twin is gone now." This man was laughing at me.'

One of the torments of Death Row was that the lights were never extinguished. There was no retreat, no respite; the bulb burned in the solitary cells, bare and bright, forever.

'Robert greeted me and shared things with me and we became friends,' said Menzi. 'He became like an older brother to me. He taught me English because my English was not very good. We shared our fears and he gave me strength. He taught me that I must be realistic, but strong as a man, and that I must never give up hope. It was good for me because I became strong. We talked of our future – how to behave ourselves if we ever got out. We also talked about death, that we must be strong and show them that we are not afraid of death. There is no suffering in that moment: the waiting is worse.'

Robert found that the only way to cope with the prospect of being handed his own notice of execution at any moment was to try and numb his feelings – not to think too much, never to get excited, above all to avoid emotion. Gradually, however, there were glints of hope.

'There were some stays of execution, and suddenly there was less dependence on religion,' said Robert. 'Now there was real hope – not just pie in the sky. There was hope of reprieve and there were even last-minute stays of execution, at six a.m., moments before . . .

'People would be laughing, excited, everyone would be celebrating. You are alive, you are coping.

'I began fighting, I became obsessed by it. I began to think about it all the time. My motto became: *What have I done today to save my life?*'

36

In Lusaka, Gordon Webster was again experiencing delays. Once more he went to see Chris Hani to try and get the rescue operation speeded up. Shortly thereafter, Casanova was astonished to find Hani at his front door. Hani had come to pick him up and they drove to Gordon's home. When they arrived, Gordon was reading and Anne cleaning the house; Hani informed the three of them they would be leaving that day.

'They had done some cosmetic work on Gordon in order to disguise him,' said his brother, George Webster. 'They had permed his hair so it looked slick and fashionable, and had pumped silicone into his face, to give him a fuller face and a more pronounced jaw. He looked quite trendy, and his cover was that he was a university technician.'

From Botswana, Anne crossed into South Africa first. Her task was to travel to Durban and rent a flat, which they could use as a safe house once they had a hostage. Two weeks later on September 17, Gordon and Casanova followed armed with Makarov pistols and hand-grenades. They climbed over the border fence at a deserted spot in the arid bushveld.

A courier who had driven down from Johannesburg was waiting for them. He was an African with a large old saloon car and he had brought along his wife and two children as cover, so that if stopped by police it would look as if they were on a family outing. The courier informed them that the area was crawling with soldiers. Almost immediately, on the outskirts of the tiny *dorp* of Mabaalstad, they saw a road-block. The courier turned off to take another route, but they had already been spotted and within minutes they were intercepted.

'There was a Caspir in the road, right in front of them,' said George Webster. 'They must have been tipped off. "We've been waiting two weeks," one of the soldiers said, "where've you been?"'

37

That same month, September 1987, an unlikely caller came to Pretoria Central. A number of people had agreed to become visitors for Robert McBride and, following prison procedure, Prisoner No. 3737 placed them on his visitors' list. The authorities checked the names and then authorised those whose visits were deemed appropriate. One of them was Paula Leyden.

'She came in with some other people, other friends,' said Robert. 'She did not want to push herself forward. She seemed shy.'

The visiting cubicles led off from the central courtyard, right in the centre of Death Row. On one side were the white cells, on the other the black. The visiting alcoves were gaunt, dingy concrete bunkers, where family and friends spoke to the condemned men through re-enforced, barred glass partitions with the aid of a microphone. On the other side of the dense glass partition, next to the prisoner, a warder sat throughout the forty minute visit. The prison authorities always insisted Robert use the end cubicle; often his microphone crackled and echoed, so that he would joke, 'Their tapes are not working today.'

'Paula came two more times, and afterwards I thought to myself, she likes me,' said Robert. 'I liked her. At first, though, I was suspicious of why I was attracted – that is because I am here. It is easier to survive if you do not allow yourself to feel too much. The second time she came, however, I began to flirt with her slightly and even pull her leg.

'She began to visit me every weekend. Sometimes during the week she would leave school to come and visit. At first I think she was sorry for me and sympathetic. Paula says she knew straight away. I was cynical at first. But everything went easily. I was not forward. We just flowed in one direction. Actually, I did not want

305

any emotional ties. I wanted to close myself off. It was easier to survive that way, living from day to day, just ticking over: not to let the world in, not to let feelings and emotions get hold of you.

'I fought it for two months. I can remember how I started to thaw. We used to discuss philosophy in our letters, so one day I said, "It's time you wrote love letters to me." Paula was shocked. She went red. She said, "You'll regret it!"

'At that moment I thought chauvinistically, "Got you! Ah ha, got you!" But then almost immediately afterwards I began worrying if I hadn't blown it and ruined everything.'

38

Before the Boer War, when the homely President Kruger sat in his top hat on the verandah of his tin-roofed bungalow in Pretoria and contemplated Johannesburg, he was more than usually sombre: 'Do not talk to me of gold, the element which brings more dissension and unexpected plagues than benefit in its train. For I tell you that every ounce of gold taken from the bowels of our soil will yet have to be weighed up with rivers of tears.'

This rumbustious El Dorado was a roller coaster of prodigious opulence and Kruger's miseries; some of the gold-maddened magnates rode both up and down. Barney Barnato, East End boy made Randlord millionaire, went insane at the age of forty-three and mysteriously disappeared over the railings of a luxury liner. Jacques Lebaudy filled his swimming pool with champagne, imported Oriental dancers from Baghdad and dreamed of becoming 'Emperor of the Sahara'. Years later, a paranoid recluse, Lebaudy spent his days in the New York Library, refusing to say where he slept and dying finally at the hands of his 'Empress'.

Johannesburg, *eGoli* (City of Gold) to the Zulus, fostered apocalyptic visions, perhaps because of the sudden violence of its appearance on the dusty, rocky ridge. To Olive Schreiner, whose visionary genius sprang up as unexpectedly from the barren Karoo, it was 'Hell'. To the social historian Charles van Onselen, it was, 'that cauldron of class conflict where capital and labour were daily pitted against each other'. He quotes a book published in 1913, with the modestly surreal title of *The Real South Africa*, in which the author Mr Ambrose Pratt remarked, 'Ancient Nineveh and Babylon have been revived. Johannesburg is their twentieth century prototype. It is a city of unbridled squander and unfathomable squalor.'

Kruger may have believed the world was flat, but he had

foreseen a high price for *eGoli's* bonanza: the British wrested
control of those gold reefs and the defeated Boer leader died in
exile. From the first, he had warned the *volk* against the tempta-
tions of that shimmering city. The Bible, the only book Kruger
was said to read, describes 'that great city that was clothed in fine
linen and purple and scarlet and decked with gold,' against which
it thunders in capitals, 'BABYLON THE GREAT MOTHER
OF HARLOTS AND ABOMINATIONS OF THE EARTH'
(Revelations 17:5). Babylon was 'a cage of every unclean and
hateful bird', full of drunkenness and fornication, where the
merchandise included 'slaves, and the souls of men.'

Drunkenness there was in Johannesburg, and fornication too.
Less than a decade after gold was discovered, there were ninety-
seven brothels. Charles van Onselen, in his scholarly and en-
gagingly slim two-volume *Studies in the Social and Economic
History of the Witwatersrand (1886–1914)*, states, 'Many pimps
urged the women under their control to accept black clients, since
Africans, largely new to the needs of this type of service and its
strange cultural setting, seldom lingered on the premises.'

The first law to attempt to keep the races sexually separate had
been passed in the seventeenth century, within thirty-three years
of a European outpost being established at the Cape. It had
remained an obsession ever since. In July 1903 the British
administration, prompted by Whitehall and *eGoli's* increasingly
respectable white citizenry, introduced Ordinance 46. The
'Immorality Act' was primarily designed to address the most
persistent of colonial bugaboos: sex between black men and white
women.

Naturally such activity did not stop, but what is remarkable
about Ordinance 46 and all racial 'Immorality' legislation was that
a great deal of this sexual zeal occurred in the imagination of the
white burgers. Periodic 'black peril' scares swept Johannesburg,
and white vigilante groups scoured the streets for black men
intent upon ravishing European women. 'The majority of such
attacks of public hysteria,' van Onselen demonstrates, 'coincided
with periods of stress or acute tension within the political
economy of the Witwatersrand as a whole.'

The last 'black peril' scare before the First World War led to a commission in 1913 which concluded, where sex had occurred between a black male and a white female, 'the facts seem to point to sexual perversion on the part of the female'. *The Report of the Commission Appointed to Enquire into Assaults on Women* advised that white girls should not be 'exposed to the evils of close objectionable contact with orientals and natives', especially the latter whose sexual morality was 'low in the extreme from a European point of view.' The Commission adjudicated that 'violating chastity, especially when the offender is a male of inferior race, is keenly felt among white people as an irreparable wrong to the victim and her relatives and an outrage upon the white race'.

Inter-racial sex: that was the taboo. Over the succeeding fifty years more stringent prohibitions were placed upon sexual relations between the races – until all such 'unlawful carnal intercourse' or 'any immoral or indecent act' between whites and 'non-whites' became utterly outlawed. The courts dealt severely with transgressions across the colour line. Some were convicted on the basis of a kiss. Other malefactors required more rigorous detection; as ever in South Africa, there were the ubiquitous police cameras, binoculars and tape recorders. Premises could be raided without a warrant. Special Force Order 025A/69 specified the procedures for examining bedclothes: the detection of warmth between the sheets and examination of stains. Should the potential evidence be elusive to the naked eye, linen was to be removed to the laboratory for scientific analysis.

All this forensic expertise, however, was now redundant. By September 1987, the Immorality Act had been abolished for two years. Nevertheless, among many whites, relationships between black and white remained a subject of horror and repugnance. Paula and Robert were on the threshold of a perilous and uncharted realm.

When Paula blushed, and following his immediate euphoric exultation, Robert brooded that he had made a premature and indiscreet move; after all, it was difficult to make a first pass from behind bars. But it worked.

'After that,' he said, 'we started writing more intimate letters.'

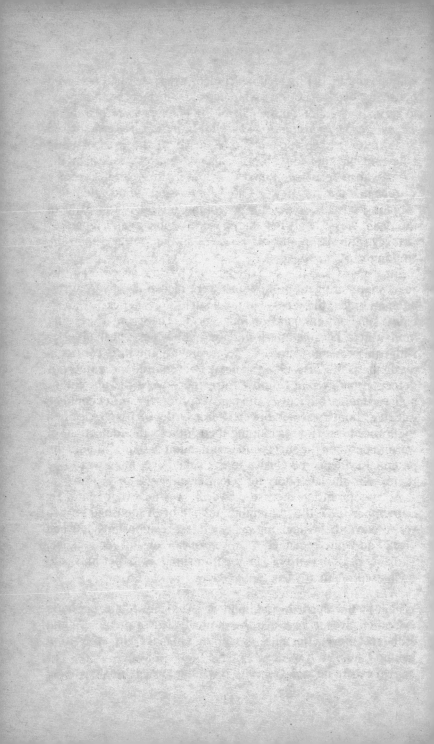

39

Robert McBride had made a formal declaration renouncing violence. He had hoped to be allowed to make such a statement the day sentence was passed on him, but that morning the court hearing was unsettlingly brief: the Judge simply announced his fate.

'Today, I feel ashamed,' said Robert. 'In a time of irrationality you can use small excuses to justify big actions. But women were killed and not enemy personnel. I think my inner self was against it. It was not against people that I was thinking I was going to detonate a car bomb; it was a military operation. You get authority from the fact that you regard yourself as a soldier. You say to yourself: this is a war. I have thought a lot about the families of the victims and there's nothing I can say. It will not help their suffering, and the suffering I have felt can never bring back their children. So to say anything – it would not be for them, it would only be for myself. Someone once said that they were also heroes, as they have contributed towards a new South Africa. I cannot agree with that. There's no way, however, I can justify their deaths.

'I could never kill a person again, so I could not participate in the armed struggle any more. Emotionally and psychologically, I could not take part. But I still feel the armed struggle was justified. No one else has waited so long to rebel. No other movement in history has waited so long or so patiently.'

When Judge Shearer had passed the death sentence, he'd also read out Professor Milton's dissenting opinion that there were extenuating circumstances; he did so in order to allow Robert's lawyers an opportunity to appeal. This was heard by the Court of Appeal in Bloemfontein in March 1988. The appeal was based solely on the majority verdict that there were no extenuating circumstances. On March 30, his appeal was dismissed.

That same month, in Pietermaritzburg, the trial of Gordon Webster began. He faced twelve counts of sabotage and terrorism, as well as being accused of attempting to murder Sergeant Roelof van der Merwe and Mr Mervyn Dunn, and of murdering Colonel Robert Wellman when he blew up the Jacobs substation. Gordon, too, risked the gallows.

This trial also lasted two and a half months, with Attorney-General Ian Slabbert again prosecuting. Gordon Webster insisted that his brother George be his attorney. 'I told him to take one of my partners, but Gordon was adamant, so I resigned from the partnership in order to devote myself to his case full-time,' said George. 'I was Gordon's attorney during the trial – and in the breaks I was his brother.'

Agnes Webster travelled to court every day from her small, isolated small-holding in the forests of New Hanover. At first, his elderly mother was baffled by Gordon's political stand. 'Did you get paid for this?' she asked. When he said no, she asked why he did it. 'By the end of the trial, she understood and completely agreed with Gordon's choice,' said George.

Agnes Webster was now seventy. All her life she had treated Gordon, *Gugwane*, as a child. 'He is a man,' she recognised at last. 'I would not have agreed before, but he has changed my mind. I am proud of him. He is a son of sons. Yes, he is a man. That is the only way to change things.'

The prospects did not look good for Gordon. Although his wife, Anne, had not been caught by the police, his accomplice Casanova had turned state witness and was going to testify against him, under the designation of Mr E.

'At first we entered a not-guilty plea,' said George Webster. 'Then we changed it, after some plea bargaining, in return for concessions from the State. We conceded almost the entire indictment, except for the charges of intent to kill and attempted murder. In return the State conceded that there was no direct intent to kill, which carried the mandatory death penalty, but *Dolus Eventualis* – that he should have foreseen the possibility, so there was a fighting chance of arguing extenuating circumstances. Right up to the last moment Gordon thought he was going to get the death penalty. The tide turned when Ismail Mahomed came in as Senior Counsel towards the end to plead extenuating circumstances. He is a difficult, very brilliant man. He lived off coke and crisps and worked on documents and law books every night till three a.m.'

On the day of sentencing, a policeman guarding Gordon dangled a rope in front of him and grinned, 'You know me – I'm the one who took Robert McBride to Pretoria. Now I've come to collect you.'

In fact, the plea of extenuation was accepted and Webster was sentenced to twenty-five years imprisonment. Like Derrick McBride and Antonio du Preez, he was banished to Robben Island, the barren, rocky penitentiary for political prisoners in the stormy bay off Cape Town.

40

Paula lived with her brother John, an impossibly tall and chaotic pop musician. He wore ragged shorts, went barefoot when possible and had a wild shock of uncombed blond hair. The house was sparsely furnished; even the fridge was seldom stocked with food. From the *Mkuhla* tree leaning over their wall and shading the tiny front garden, dangled two intricate, bee-hive nests of industrious, long-beaked weaver-birds.

When John wasn't playing gigs with his band, he was wrestling with philosophy. Pascal, Kant, Wittgenstein: the elemental questions – metaphysics, God, logic. John was finding it difficult to complete his MA thesis. He had chosen a big subject: 'Irrational Beliefs'.

A philosopher didn't need to stare into the vast African sky to go half mad contemplating infinity, logic and the irrational. It was in the newspapers: the South African Defence Force had imported a wolf from the Ural Mountains in the Soviet Union and mated it with an Alsatian to produce a wolf-dog – 'Big Red', reported the papers, hated humans, howled and had yellow eyes. It was in the 'For Sale' columns: 'Racist watchdogs', promised small print adverts, promoting a cross between bloodhounds, dobermans and rottweilers, 'especially for South African circumstances.' It was in the law: in Grahamstown, a small, sedate Cathedral city, one magistrate sentenced a banned dissident for attending a meeting in Cape Town, 580 miles distant, when it was proved that he had not been there. 'If he had been in Cape Town,' ruled the magistrate, with subtle reasoning, 'he would have attended.'

Or did any magistrate ever say this? In an atmosphere of fear and uncertainty, there was a miasma of rumour and apocryphal tales. Wild stories fuelled this fear and passed for fact. These urban legends, the subconscious manifestation of shared terrors, surfaced generation after generation in societies under stress. The South African *Weekly Mail* reported one, The Tale of the Township Decoy, which had circulated in Vichy France and again in Saigon during the Vietnam War: 'a bunch of township youths paint a potato green. As an armoured car rolls past them, with a soldier in the turret, they lob the "grenade" into the car. All the soldiers inside scramble out, sans weapons, and the youths leap in and commandeer the vehicle. The story is, naturally, hushed up by the authorities.'

Intellectuals liked to quote a passage from the Prison Notebooks of Antonio Gramsci, founding member of the Italian Communist party imprisoned by Mussolini. It was an article of faith, repeated like a Hail Mary, 'The old is dying and the new cannot be born; in this interregnum there arises a great diversity of morbid symptoms.'

In such an unpredictable cosmos, it was not for the South African government to have philosophers, as Wittgenstein demanded, 'looking into the workings of our language.' Instead, the regime invested in more technology: bugging devices, eavesdropping paraphernalia, spools upon spools of tape, secret cameras . . . a civilisation of surveillance. Even John was being spied upon. The Johannesburg City Council, ostensibly responsible for the mundane provision of services like transport, garbage removal and drains, had set aside a covert fund to investigate dissident elements. Among those under scrutiny were a novelist, trade unionists, middle-class charity ladies and the pop group Mango Groove, for whom John was bass player and song-writer.

John was an intellectual and easily distracted: if the phone rang while he was running a bath, he would allow it to overflow and flood the house. He liked watching vampire videos. Sometimes on sultry afternoons when he should have been working, he'd bask on a lilo in the mini-pool in the back garden. Much of the time, baffled by such unsettling symptoms, John was procrastinating over getting to grips with 'Irrational Beliefs'.

For some, Paula's friendship with Robert was merely another bizarre, morbid symptom of the times. Among their acquaintances, John found, there were some who were shocked, and others who were titillated. It was a hot item of gossip, and everyone indulged in speculation about Paula's motives. At first, many were cynical and said: well, they would fall in love in that environment . . . or she is just doing it for an emotional crusade. Others delved into more psychological explanations: white guilt, egotism, the masochistic pleasure of 'martyrdom', or simply a finger up against authority.

'She was very obsessive about saving him,' said John. 'When I first found out about her relationship with Robert, I was alarmed – how was she going to deal with it? All the family were worried. There seemed no hope at all for him, and our concern was what would happen to Paula. But I never doubted the depths of her feelings.'

Gradually Paula's campaign to save Robert McBride's life completely took over her own life, and eventually she gave up her job as a teacher to devote herself entirely to this quest. She worked frantically against the unknown deadline, wrote hundreds of letters to foreign presidents, prime ministers, religious leaders, anyone who might listen and appeal to the South African authorities for clemency. Incessantly she phoned embassies, academics, peace organisations. She lobbied everyone who might help and every organisation which might intercede: she rang bishops, canvassed ambassadors, wrote to world leaders and visited Robert every day. For someone so private and reserved, it was a tremendous strain.

Late one night when she was in Durban, Paula went to the home of Judge Douglas Shearer. If he had handed down the death sentence only 'with great sadness', she said, what was he now going to do to help? The judge muttered about having written to the State President, recommending that this was a case where he could exercise clemency. He was very embarrassed by her visit and pointed out that it was most irregular. Paula was not daunted by irregularities. She knew that Robert could be handed his notice of execution at any moment: for her, every day was a battle to save him from the hangman.

Paula did not talk much about her lonely campaign. She did not want to involve her family, but her brother could see the stress was beginning to tell. At home she became withdrawn, sometimes depressed. Often she would go to bed early. John wondered how Paula could make that wrenching journey to Death Row daily – when possible, twice a day – and still stay sane.

'It's a schizophrenic country,' said John. 'How do we cross over all those barriers every day? You cross over one boundary and suddenly you have to be somebody else. With white people you are one person, with a black another – you take on a white persona. You become a different person. South Africa forces that division on you and makes you play these roles. And a black with a white usually puts on a mask – he has to – so he, also, plays another person altogether. Everything's split. How does Paula cross over that divide?' John continually ran his fingers through his unruly hair. 'I don't know. The truth is, there is a Paula I know . . . and there is a Paula I don't know.'

This split was everywhere. It was on the motorway from Johannesburg to Pretoria, with the wealthy white suburb of Sandown on one side and on the other the overcrowded black ghetto of Alexandria, where the homeless even squatted in the cemetery. Most whites never dreamed of crossing that divide. They simply drove right through the middle.

'She became very obsessive in the fight to save my life,' said Robert. 'Paula is very touchy about being given instructions. I learnt that early on. I'd sit here all day, brooding and thinking about things, tactics, to further my campaign to save my life, and she'd come to visit and I'd say, "Right, now, this is what we do . . ." But I soon learnt not to give her instructions. She also tried to be bossy with me once. We had a row. So we quite quickly established we could not boss each other.

'We have a lot in common – politics and philosophy, things in general. We see eye to eye on a lot of things. We just talk very easily.

'Paula is very easy with herself. Here, in South Africa, others perceive her a "white", or "white liberal" – she hates these labels. She is natural and human, she just wants to be Paula. Even on Death Row there were two *Umkhonto we Sizwe* guys who were against our relationship. Who was this person, who was this white woman? They were suspicious. They were fearful of some kind of security breach. But between Paula and me there was always an emotional element, even before I told her I could trust her.

'The way she loves me is not passive – she fights so she can love me, not in heaven, but on earth.

'It was me who suggested we marry.'

41

'We made a pact,' said Robert, 'that if permission was granted for us to marry then we would take it as a positive sign. Neither of us believes in life after death, so we had to be optimistic.'

Others had previously applied to be allowed to marry on Death Row, but all such petitions had been refused in the past. They told the prison authorities and the social workers sent to interview them that they'd met in Durban ten years previously when Paula, as a university student, had organised the relief teaching scheme in Wentworth. Permission to marry was finally granted: the first time ever in Beverly Hills. The ceremony was set for May 10, 1989.

'My mum drove me there and waited in the car, because even though we could have family and friends, Robert and I had taken the decision not to – it was the only time we could be together,' said Paula. 'So even though we'd have to have warders, at least we could just concentrate on being with each other.

'I had to go through the usual prison procedure. Then when I went down the corridor to the right where the cells are, I saw someone cleaning the floor, and I only learnt afterwards that it was Menzi, because he had insisted he had to see me coming there to marry Robert. He wanted to be, in some way, part of the action.

'It was a bare room, and Robert was already there sitting on a bench. There were three warders in the room. The door was kept open because apparently that's Church regulations, so that people can come in and object to the wedding. It was a very simple, short ceremony. I think for both of us it passed in a sort of daze. It wasn't the words we had to say, but it was the fact we were together. We held hands, and each other's arms, throughout the ceremony. Then they said we could have forty minutes together. One of the warders stayed. But we had become accustomed to functioning in their presence, it was as if we didn't really notice them anymore. It was almost in a funny way as if we had our own little cocoon: there was me and Robert and we were together and that was that.'

'It was our first ever contact,' said Robert. 'It was more than a marriage certificate. It was the contact that was like signing a vow. We were able to touch. You cannot imagine how extraordinary something so simple could be.'

'It passed in what seemed like ten seconds,' said Paula. 'Then suddenly time was up and I had to go, and that – that felt quite desolate. We had been cut off so long by glass and bars, and I felt, now I'm close enough to hold that person, how can I let that person go? The thought of leaving him there, leaving him in the coldness of those cells, and thinking of him having to put back on the prison uniform . . . If it felt horrible for me, I know that for Robert it must have been a million times worse. Doors banged louder on that day than they had banged before.'

42

Then there began to be more stays of execution. One reason was that during the McBrides' visits, Robert would tell Paula if someone had been served with their notice and hauled off to the Pot. Paula could then alert people outside, and a desperate last week of appeals and legal manoeuvres would begin. Another reason was that gradually, painfully, South Africa itself had begun to change, and the fate of the hundreds of men on Death Row reflected the uncertain, turbulent mutations outside the prison walls.

South African society was changing, even if most of the laws attempting to regulate it had not. Even in Pretoria there were now public places where blacks could mix with whites, though it was often difficult to tell. Sometimes Paula entered a cafe with a black friend, to be told, 'We are not multi-racial here.'

'Oh but you are,' she'd reply. 'You employ blacks.'

The whites who could not accept change were very angry. Occasionally they gathered outside the prison, like a posse of the avenging Righteous, scowling at the sinful world through identical dark glasses: grim-faced men in para-military khaki uniforms, with huge pistols strapped ostentatiously at their waists. They'd stare at Paula with particular venom, especially if she was with a group of Africans. They looked as if they were longing to unholster those bombastic guns and blast her to hell.

One afternoon after visiting Robert, Paula drove into Pretoria and parked her dusty Mazda 626, stacked full of old newspapers and legal files, in a jacaranda-fringed street. As soon as she had disappeared round the corner, a woman in a nearby flat observed a young man in an army uniform slash her tyres. At first, Paula felt this hatred inside the prison from some of the warders as well. When a notice of execution was handed to the illiterate wife of a condemned man and Paula was helping her to read it, a sergeant snatched the notice out of Paula's hand and yelled, 'Don't worry, Mrs McBride – you'll be getting your own piece of paper soon enough.'

Apart from her wedding day, Paula had managed to make physical contact with her husband on only one other occasion. Knowing Robert was to see his lawyer shortly after her visit, Paula hid in one of the concrete visiting cubicles off the central courtyard. When he was being led down the corridor, she rushed up and touched him through the bars.

Of the three hundred men on Death Row, ten were white. One was a man who believed he was being consumed from the inside by a gigantic tapeworm. It was a malignant, cunning creature, lurking in his intestines and stealthily working its way through the whole system, colonising every artery until at last, like some millenial prophet on Judgement Day, the power of the insidious protozoon would be complete.

Dimitri Tsafendas had felt himself to be a helpless victim of that vast and satanic tapeworm, when in September 1966 in Parliament he stabbed to death the South African Prime Minister, Dr Hendrick Verwoerd. Believing himself possessed, Tsafendas was declared unfit to plead by reason of insanity, and was promptly locked away on Death Row. He was the only prisoner on Death Row not actually awaiting execution, but the jailers had reserved a special place for him right next to the gallows. By the time Robert discovered he was in the white section, the demented Tsafendas had been there for over twenty years, made to suffer not only the torments of his avenging tapeworm, but also reduced to hysteria every time a man was hanged. Other prisoners would hear him scream, 'You murderers, you're doing it again.'

Once when he was cleaning the corridors, Menzi Thafeni accidently saw Tsafendas, a feeble old man in his seventies, being led back to his cell by warders. During a visit, Robert told Paula that Tsafendas was being held on Death Row and the story was published in Britain by the *Guardian* newspaper; in September, two months later, the South African Prison Services announced that Tsafendas had been moved to Sonderwater Prison some miles west of Pretoria.

In late 1989, Robert's friend Menzi Thafeni was suddenly and unexpectedly released. On that Friday, after a three-hour appeal hearing, Menzi was officially cleared of having committed the murder for which he had been condemned to death. Paula McBride came to Pretoria Central to pick him up, and a disorientated, stunned young black man walked out of the walled mausoleum of Maximum Security, blinking in the strong summer sunlight, unable to really grasp what had so abruptly happened to him. He couldn't speak to anyone. 'I'm back!' was all he could shout. When he was taken to Pretoria to phone his family, Menzi could only yell into the receiver, 'I'm back! I'm back!'

But even though he was back in the world of the living, Menzi could never, ever, really believe it. He had listened to the sounds of death, he had smelt 'the death'. It was like sitting in a graveyard at night.

'You are like a tin of sardines in that place, the way you are fixed up for the death,' said Menzi. 'The way you are squashed in is like clothes packed up for the laundry, but we are not being taken to be washed; we are waiting in a bundle to be taken to the gallows machine. Waiting for the death. I know I will never be the same person again. Sometimes I feel that there is nothing outside that means anything to me anymore, there is nothing that is important.'

43

Robert felt he was in limbo. The final option was being tried: an appeal to the State President. It was his last chance. They had been waiting months for this conclusive decision. When Derrick McBride was unexpectedly transferred from Robben Island to the political section of Pretoria Central, both Paula and Doris were apprehensive. They feared the worst. Was this to allow the father a final visit to his condemned son?

Then on September 20, 1989, after a rancorous and highly public power struggle, F. W. de Klerk took over from the intractable and militaristic P. W. Botha as State President and declared that in South Africa there would be 'a new dispensation'.

Robert tried to be philosophical. 'I would have been dead long ago if it had not been for Paula, my lawyer and my mother,' he told himself, trying not to raise his hopes unrealistically. But the fluid, mutating events, so magnified and distorted when viewed from inside Death Row, were agonised over as to whether it was a step towards reprieve or a shuffle towards the gallows. One day he felt there was hope, the next he was plunged into despair.

When Robert heard the news that the government had taken the colossal stride of unbanning the ANC, the Pan African Congress and other liberation movements, he was elated. The following day, on the release of Nelson Mandela after twenty-seven years of incarceration, Robert was ecstatic. This is what they had fought for: negotiations. It was also a promising omen for his own life.

Everything was uncertain, everything was in flux. In the first week of May 1990, Paula arrived for a visit to be told by a senior prison officer that she could not see Robert. 'Why not?' she asked in panic. 'Because,' said the warder self-importantly, 'Mr McBride is in conference.'

Robert and a fellow ANC prisoner had been mysteriously summoned by the prison commander and told to select five other politicals 'for a meeting'. They were issued with jackets and driven, under guard, down to the main section of Pretoria Central, where they were ushered into a special meeting room. There, to their astonishment, sat Nelson Mandela.

The prison warders served tea while Mandela explained his mission. He had flown up from Cape Town the previous evening, after three days of negotiations with President de Klerk, and had presented himself at the gates of the prison at nine a.m. that morning. 'I have come,' he told them, 'to report back to you.'

For two hours Mandela briefed them on the progress of negotiations and answered questions from the condemned men. 'What will be our fate?' asked Robert. Mandela assured them that as far as the ANC was concerned, they were political prisoners and the ANC would be fighting for their release.

44

Suddenly Matthew Lecordier, Mr C, reappeared in Wentworth.

After the trial, although not granted immunity, Matthew had been set free. But he was obviously a marked man. 'The police suggested to me that they think it best if I leave Durban for a time,' said Matthew. 'I said, how long is "a time"? and they said, "Give it six or ten years."'

Immediately the trial finished Captain Zenardt de Beer drove Matthew down to Cape Town, a two-day journey. There, the police found him a job as an order clerk in a large store. 'But they wanted me to work for them as an informer; they wanted me to extract information from people involved in the unions,' said Matthew. 'They offered to pay me for every bit of information, but I didn't bother, and I did not hear from them again.'

By New Year 1990, Matthew was so homesick that he decided to risk returning to Wentworth. He was terrified about the welcome he might receive; he feared retribution. But Doris McBride had already let it be known that she did not want him harmed. Matthew took up his old feckless life. Nervously, through intermediaries, he approached Greta Apelgren who was back in Wentworth after her prison sentence, working as a social worker. He was fearful of how she would judge him, yet compulsively drawn to know. Instead, when they met, Matthew talked through the night, rehashing the events of the past. He had no idea what the future held for him. Matthew confided to Greta that perhaps his only prospects were to meet a rich woman.

On Robben Island the political prisoners were holding their own intense debates about the future. For Antonio du Preez, whose schooling had been sketchy, prison had been an education.

329

Associating with other political prisoners and attending their discussion groups, he said, had been his university.

Gordon Webster, during his years on the Island, had been pursuing a correspondence course in agriculture; he dreamed of a time, of a very different South Africa, when he might be farming in some remote district. In this daydream, he had written to Robert, they would work on the farm together. But as he thought about the future realistically, Gordon's main worry was Robert: whether he would ever walk out of Death Row.

Even as political prisoners were still incarcerated on Robben Island, businessmen in Cape Town began putting forward proposals to convert the rocky fortress into a tourist attraction with a luxury hotel and casino.

'Morbid symptoms' were legion. During almost the exact period Robert McBride had been in police custody, an ex-policeman had shot dead over thirty people, all black, some teenagers shot in the back. Twenty-six inquests had returned a verdict of 'justifiable homicide'. The white security guard, tall and biblically bearded, continued to patrol alone: a man with a mission. 'I'm in full production,' he announced. 'Full production.' The police public relations division in Pretoria explained that this matter had to be seen 'in its proper perspective'.

It was decidedly tricky in such a turbulent country to see things in their proper perspective. The whites were becoming increasingly jittery. Frequently it was impossible for them to distinguish between what was real and what it was they simply feared.

Thousands of blacks had been killed; no one would ever know how many. In August 1990 the Head of Public Relations for the South African Police, Major-General Herman Stadler (who as a brigadier had given evidence at Robert's trial) announced the number of white civilians killed by black freedom fighters between 1961 – the beginning of the armed struggle – and 1990 when it was suspended. It was sixty-six.

Over those years vast inventories of intelligence had been gathered. But first it was BOSS, the all-powerful Bureau of State Security, that lost touch with reality. One of its agents reported that the general in command, H. J. van den Berg, initiated recruits into the arcane lore of the spy trade with an infallible technique for identifying homosexuals – just ask a man to whistle, instructed H.J., and you will know immediately: *moffies* cannot whistle. After BOSS failed to anticipate the 1976 Soweto uprising, it was renamed DONS, which in turn was reorganised and christened NIS. This reshuffling of initials and acronyms was like a magic incantation.

Finally in 1987 a formula so secret, so incognito, was devised that not even the generals knew about it: an organisation which did not officially exist. It was so invisible that not even some of those actually working for the agency were aware they were doing so. Its job was to sniff out the enemies of the state and destroy them. Its assignment was to spy, infiltrate, disorientate, abduct, torture, poison, bomb, mutilate and eradicate. Its name was the Civil Co-operation Bureau.

Ever more formidable archives of secret intelligence were accumulated; but it was also a morbid characteristic of an *ancien régime*, this obsessive collection of data, combined with a total inability to collate it into any lucid interpretation of events. Perhaps it is the sheer volume of material that helps overwhelm *anciens régimes*. In 1783, Louis XVI's government ordered an investigation into the salt taxes in Provence: the results arrived in Paris ten years later, in documents which needed an entire mule train to carry them, on the day of the King's execution.

And now that P.W. had been replaced by F.W., was one more mutation of initials enough to bring about real change?

Derrick McBride was alternately despondent and optimistic. He was deeply fearful for his son, though confident he, himself, would soon be released. He was allowed one visit a week. A white warder would guard Derrick on one side of the thick glass partition; on the other side, a second warder sat alongside the visitor. Yet it was the jailers who seemed imprisoned and powerless as Derrick, carried away with his own exhilaration,

331

unselfconsciously discussed the need to allay white fears. 'In prison, mixing with other politicals, my anti-white attitude has been changed,' he said. 'The others pull me up over casual remarks and argue. I believe I am no longer prejudiced.' He pointed gleefully to the sullen white warders. 'You see, it's these *Boere* we'll have to educate – teach them to be more tolerant.'

On Robben Island, Gordon Webster began having a recurrent dream. He and Robert were together in Derrick McBride's Factorama workshop in Wentworth, eating a bunny chow . . . but when Gordon got thirsty, he had to ask Robert to go over to his mother's Day 'n' Nite Take-Away for a coke. Gordon was embarrassed to cross the yard as he was still in his olive-green prison uniform. Robert, also in prison fatigues, insisted that they both go. As they entered the take-away, everyone was there – Derrick, Doris, Antonio – and magically neither he nor Robert were wearing prison clothing anymore.

45

Paula McBride continues to drive to Pretoria every morning.

On the six-lane motorway out of Johannesburg the traffic moves fast and cars weave aggressively from lane to lane ignoring the warning signs: LAW ENFORCEMENT BY CAMERA. Tucked tastefully into the folds of the pigmy hillocks are neat pockets of high-tech 'business parks', glossy and futuristic. Then cresting the next rise is another sweep of mottled, parched savannah, studded with low, thorny trees. Cattle graze; a lone African walks slowly through the tall grass.

On the final curve between the tree-dotted hills, before Pretoria comes into view, from the highest knoll, Skanskop, the granite hulk of the Voortrekker monument looms over the veld. A dour Cyclopean shrine, it commemorates the Battle of Blood River when a beleaguered troop of Boers killed three thousand Zulus. There are no windows; like so much of South African history it looks in upon itself, fearful and self-righteous. The only aperture is a hole in the dome so that once a year on the Day of the Covenant, the anniversary of Blood River, a shaft of sunlight can illuminate the inscription, *Ons Vir Jou, Suid-Africa*, the last words of the national anthem, 'We for you, South Africa.'

Most days, Paula drives straight past the prison and into Pretoria. To make use of her harshly earned experience with the law and singular inside knowledge of Death Row, she had begun to work for a campaigning organisation right in the heart of the capital, Lawyers for Human Rights. Since the ANC had suspended the armed struggle and commenced negotiations with the government, Paula had also redoubled her efforts on behalf of her husband.

333

It is from work that she began to visit Robert, a five-minute drive to the outskirts of Pretoria. No longer was it possible to drive through the prison complex right up to Maximum Security. The entrance to Pretoria Central was being made more secure and all visitors to Death Row had to wait outside the wire perimeter in the shade of the jacaranda trees.

At visiting hours there is usually a small gathering of Africans, come to attend condemned relatives. Many have travelled far. The older women, in traditional dress, sit on a large stone. The men tend to wear dark, faded suits. The younger women, some with babies on their backs, wear their prettiest clothes, bold patterns and vivid colours.

Eventually the *kombi* arrives, a dun-coloured van driven by a white officer. The accompanying black warder reads off a list of numbers from a clipboard; he knows most of the visitors by name, but this is an inflexible prison ritual.

The visitors clamber aboard; some of the younger women sit on each other's knees, bumping their heads as the van lurches off. The *kombi* rattles through the small walled city: Klawer, Oasis Road, Papwater . . . to the right the dusty expanse of ground with patches of sun-scorched grass, a chain-gang of black convicts at work. The *kombi* turns uphill, past the Kommandant-General's splendid mansion, and at the top of the hill it stops outside the great black iron gates of Maximum Security. The visitors, however, file through a small side entrance, with the sign: NO FLOWERS OR BOUQUETS TO BE LEFT FOR ANY PRISONER.

It is a routine Paula followed every day.

Epilogue

'If I must die,
I will encounter darkness as a bride,
And hug it in my arms.'
Measure for Measure, Act III, Scene 1

The electric bulb burned all day and all night, light without end, in Robert McBride's cell.

Then on April 16, 1991 – two weeks before the deadline negotiated for the release of all political prisoners – the South African Minister of Justice announced Robert's death sentence had been commuted: to life imprisonment.

Robert had spent 1,463 days on Death Row.

He and Paula now prepared to battle for his unconditional release. For them, the struggle continues.

'I owe my life to Paula,' says Robert. 'I've started picturing life afterwards. You don't want to allow yourself too much hope. That's dangerous. You just have to try and face the truth, that's the only way to cope.

'But I do sometimes picture myself walking out. And then I stop there, at the gates – I don't want to be too disappointed.

'I don't think it will be a happy-ever-after. I know things will be difficult. People may even want to get even. If I do get out, I expect an unsettled life.

'We talk about having a family and how many children we'd have and so on. Sometimes it's three or four. I said twelve and Paula disagrees. But it's just talk. We don't know what's going to happen.'